Music of the World War II Era

Recent Titles in
American History through Music

Music of the Counterculture Era
James E. Perone

Music of the Civil War Era
Steven H. Cornelius

Music of the Colonial and Revolutionary Era
John Ogasapian

Music of the Great Depression
William H. Young and Nancy K. Young

Music of the Gilded Age
John Ogasapian and N. Lee Orr

Music of the Postwar Era
Don Tyler

Music of the World War II Era

William H. Young and Nancy K. Young

American History through Music

GREENWOOD PRESS
Westport, Connecticut • London

Library of Congress Cataloging-in-Publication Data

Young, William H., 1939–
Music of the World War II era / William H. Young and Nancy K. Young.
p. cm. — (American history through music)
Includes bibliographical references (p.) and index.
ISBN 978-0-313-33891-5 (alk. paper)
1. Popular music—United States—1931–1940—History and criticism 2. Popular music—United States—1941–1950—History and criticism. 3. World War, 1939–1945—Music and the war. 4. Music—Social aspects—United States. I. Young, Nancy K., 1940– II. Title.
ML3477.Y683 2008
780.973'09044—dc22 2007035359

British Library Cataloguing in Publication Data is available.

Library of Congress Catalog Card Number: 2007035359
ISBN: 978–0–313–33891–5

First published in 2008

Greenwood Press, 88 Post Road West, Westport, CT 06881
An imprint of Greenwood Publishing Group, Inc.
www.greenwood.com

Printed in the United States of America

The paper used in this book complies with the Permanent Paper Standard issued by the National Information Standards Organization (Z39.48–1984).

10 9 8 7 6 5 4 3 2 1

To Our Two Dougs—We Miss You Both
In Memory of Douglas E. Sederholm: May you still hear the music of your war
&
In Memory of Douglas J. Sederholm: You proved Mr. Wolfe wrong; you can go home again.

Contents

Acknowledgments

In any research-based undertaking, thanks must go to many individuals and institutions that provide assistance along the way. More specifically, everyone at the Lynchburg College Library has, as always, been gracious and giving of time and expertise. Director Chris Millson-Martula made all the library's research tools, traditional and electronic, available to us. Ariel Myers, the college archivist and the person to see for interlibrary loans, located materials that others thought might be lost or inaccessible. Elizabeth Henderson once again showed us how easily some of the more sophisticated computer software can supply answers about niggling questions dealing with dates and copyrights.

The nation's capital, just a few hours away for us via Amtrak, is home to another library, the Library of Congress, or LOC among the cognoscenti. We always feel welcome there, especially at the Prints and Photographs Division, our primary source for illustrations. Particular thanks go to Jan Grenci and all the other helpful experts who led us to pictorial riches we probably would not have found on our own. The library serves as one of the best uses of tax dollars anywhere in Washington, D.C.

Photofest, a commercial supplier of photographs on virtually any topic, likewise proved useful in the process of selecting illustrations. Musicologist Bryan Wright, the proud and knowledgeable owner of a vast collection of period 78-rpm recordings, allowed us to locate and photograph some representative record labels from his holdings and, in the process, shared the covers from his equally extensive sheet music collection.

As always, the people at the Greenwood Publishing Group have been most cooperative with this project from start to finish. Debby Adams, our primary editor, answered lots of questions, gave useful advice, kept us focused on finishing the book, and supplied good cheer with pictures and news of her cats.

As always, any errors of commission or omission remain ours and ours alone.

Introduction

When surveying the music of the war years, where to begin? On April 30, 1939, the New York World's Fair opened its doors. Promoters called it "The World of Tomorrow," and the exposition promised a look at scientific, technological, and consumer wonders never before seen. It had as its theme song "Dawn of a New Day," a composition based on incomplete music left by George Gershwin before his untimely death in 1937. His brother Ira, along with composer Kay Swift, finished the number, with Ira contributing the lyrics. Given "The World of Tomorrow" theme, "Dawn of a New Day" doubtless seemed at the time a fitting accompaniment and a possible way to introduce the music of the 1940s.

But then September 1, 1939, rolled around, and German troops invaded Poland, plunging the world into the most horrific conflict it had ever witnessed. England and France braced for war, and across the far Pacific, Japan had already begun its march toward Asian dominance. But peace prevailed in the United States, and the foreign news seemed remote and of little concern to most Americans. Among the popular hits for late August and early September that year were "(Hep! Hep!) The Jumpin' Jive" by Cab Calloway and his orchestra and Glenn Miller's recording of "Over the Rainbow," neither of which reflected in any way a new day nor the political realities of the time.

The Swing Era, that nostalgic period of the big bands and dance halls and jitterbugs, continued to roar along in high gear, and few foresaw the shifts in popular music that would take place as the new decade and new styles displaced the once-reigning formats of the 1930s. Most people continued to

In 1942, a soldier learns how to play chords in the recreation hall at his Virginia military camp. Library of Congress, Prints & Photographs Division.

listen and dance to Artie Shaw's "Frenesi," Jimmy Dorsey's rendition of "The Breeze and I," and Tommy Dorsey's "I'll Never Smile Again," with Frank Sinatra doing the vocal honors. They had little reason to think that much would change very soon, but they would be mistaken.

Although the United States did not become an active combatant until the attack on Pearl Harbor in December of 1941, the majority of Americans realized, with the eruption of fierce fighting on the European continent in late 1939, that the country must eventually participate in the conflict. The question became not if? but when? Popular music, seldom an accurate reflector of ongoing events, for the most part turned a blind eye to history, and only with the country's plunge into the war that fateful December did songwriters compose their responses. Once the nation assessed the enormity of the attack and recovered from the initial shock caused by it, the "phony wars" of Europe and the vast distances of the Pacific were forgotten, and a unified United States moved ahead with full-scale preparations for a war already under way.

With war, songs ridiculing the Axis powers ("We'll Knock the Japs Right into the Laps of the Nazis" [1941], "You're a Sap, Mr. Jap" [1941], "Der Fuehrer's Face" [1942], "Yankee Doodle Ain't Doodlin' Now" [1942], among many others) flooded the market, along with patriotic calls to duty ("Allegiance to the Red White and Blue" [1942], "Dig Down Deep" [1942], "For the Flag, for the Home, for the Family" [1942], and others). If the foregoing titles lack a familiar ring, it is because only a handful of war-related tunes achieved any real commercial success. By and large, the public rejected most overtly patriotic music; as far as concerned their record and radio listening, consumers much preferred romantic ballads and up-tempo swing numbers. In short, the early 1940s provided a wide selection of pop music of every description, and the war effort per se occupied but a part of those offerings.

The war nevertheless took its toll on the music business. The Selective Service and Training Act, put into effect in October of 1940, would eventually draft many younger male musicians, making it increasingly difficult to fill all the positions in a large orchestra. All-girl bands sprang up, and smaller aggregations, or combos, began to change the face of music. Vocalists and vocal groups took over the spotlight from instrumentalists, and the powerhouse big bands that characterized the later 1930s faded into memory. Newly imposed entertainment taxes as well as gasoline rationing and curfews, cut back on nightclub attendance, and both musicians and audiences found it difficult to travel and make engagements.

In addition, the American Federation of Musicians, in August of 1942, launched a crippling strike against the recording industry, accusing it of unfair practices. The issuance of new records, with the exception of V-Discs for servicemen, came to a virtual halt, a situation that would endure until the fall of 1943, when most record companies capitulated (but not until a year later for two of the biggest labels, RCA Victor and Columbia) and resolved the dispute. To compensate, numerous recordings featuring unaccompanied vocalists and choruses came out. The union allowed singers to perform, but they proved no substitute for the absent instrumentalists.

The recording ban had wide-ranging effects; in the areas of swing and jazz, ongoing forays into new musical expressions could not find a commercial outlet, and this in turn hampered developing an appreciative public. Without recording contracts, musicians often had to look for alternative employment. On the other hand, the ban gave players the freedom to pursue their experiments without pressures to market records. In the end, the resumption of recording found many instrumentalists ready to move into new artistic territory,

Vocalist Frank Sinatra started a new trend in the early 1940s: rapturous teenage fans who would swoon when he sang his latest tune. This Pittsburgh group, photographed in 1942, stood in line for hours and braved the December cold to attend his performance. Library of Congress, Prints & Photographs Division.

and the emerging worlds of bebop and modern jazz began to take shape. For most musicians, however, the relaxation of restrictions meant something more basic: a return to work, a chance to play and earn a paycheck.

Any study of popular music must rely on numerous variables when examining the commercial side of artistic expression. To be popular, to attract a large, diverse audience, a song should achieve substantial record and sheet music sales, as well enjoy repeated plays on jukeboxes and radio shows. All this has to be accomplished in a short period of time, a period usually measured in weeks. Traditionally, songs possessed a popular life that encompassed months and even years. But in an age of rapid communication because of radio, the

A display window in a Detroit department store features a special summer 1941 issue of *Life* magazine devoted to defense. Although the country remained at peace, the future looked ominous and the chances of war concerned everyone. Library of Congress, Prints & Photographs Division.

lifespan for most commercial music shrank during the 1930s and 1940s into briefer and briefer increments. If a tune had no impact, such as initially high sales and extensive airplay within days of its release, it more than likely disappeared into a musical limbo. Only a few exceptions enjoyed late discovery by consumers, and fewer still came back years later in new adaptations. The window of opportunity in popular music remained open at best for a fleeting moment.

Within the pages of *Music of the World War II Era,* readers will find a broad-ranging survey of American music during these crucial years. The opening chapter, "Music about World War II," discusses the government-sanctioned search for war-related songs that would stir the public. But just a handful of tunes, such as "Comin' in on a Wing and a Prayer" (1942) and "Praise the Lord and Pass the Ammunition" (1942), attracted much attention; by and large, the government's quest proved fruitless. Instead, as the chapter makes clear, the old stand-by subjects of love and romance swamped any musical reminders of the conflict.

Consequently, chapter 2, "Popular Hits and Standards," looks at an array of songs that did succeed in capturing the public's imagination. Because of the sheer volume of newly published music during the 1939–1945 era, those tunes that did particularly well commercially receive the most attention. At times, however, a composition came out that did not immediately rise to the top of the hit charts. For example, Rodgers and Hart's "I Didn't Know What Time It Was" (1939), today an American standard, went relatively unnoticed when originally released. Thus some of the songs surveyed in chapter 2 cannot be thought big hits at the time, but they have established themselves as standards years after their original release and thus deserve mention.

"Swing, Jazz, and Rhythm 'n' Blues," the third chapter in *Music of the World War II Era,* considers how these three genres fared amid all the changes occurring in American popular music at the time. Swing went into a long, slow decline but nevertheless continued to attract a wide array of enthusiasts; it refused to become an anachronism. Jazz, on the other hand, for so long overshadowed by swing, began to assert itself once more, exploring new artistic fields and thereby appealing to a youthful audience eager for change. Finally, rhythm 'n' blues, in many ways a child of both swing and jazz, was poised to burst on the scene after a long gestation out of view of the mainstream

A uniformed soldier inspects a pair of "zoot suits" during a June 1942 performance by the Woody Herman Orchestra in Washington, D.C. Despite the war, fashions for the young carried their own identity, often to the chagrin of their elders. Library of Congress, Prints & Photographs Division.

audience. Not yet fully recognized by the mid-1940s, this primarily black area of music would shortly become a raucous addition to the growing divisions within American popular culture.

Commercial success in music, as in any artistic endeavor that demands a financial return, ultimately gets measured in dollars, units sold, attendance figures, and the like. For much of American music, recordings serve as the lifeblood for many entertainers. Chapter 4, "Recordings and the Music Business," therefore studies the constantly evolving business realities of the industry. Without hit songs (recorded performances that sell well), bands, groups, and singers soon find themselves in difficulty. But the 1940s proved boom years for many musical artists. Demand for recorded music, pent up since the Great Depression, and despite boycotts and bans, caused the industry to prosper in the midst of war.

Chapter 5, "Music on Radio," illustrates how so much music at this time involved the ubiquitous radio—a device found in virtually every American home by the early 1940s. Although rationing, blackouts, labor disagreements, and a myriad of other problems faced performers, listeners had merely to turn a dial to find an endless variety of programming on their receivers. Popular recording stars, such as Bing Crosby, Frank Sinatra, Kate Smith, and Dinah Shore, hosted their own top-ranked shows, as did singing cowboys like Gene Autry and Roy Rogers. Those musicians and vocalists not so fortunate could still make the rounds of countless variety programs as guests. Without some radio recognition, musical artists faced obscurity in their chosen field of entertainment. It all added up to hours and hours of live and recorded broadcasting on America's radio stations, plus *Your Hit Parade* kept everyone abreast of the latest hits.

Success on radio often meant a jump to stage or screen, just as a hit play or film almost certainly guaranteed a spot on radio. All three—radio, stage, and screen—enjoyed a certain interdependence, especially radio and movies. Chapter 6, "Music on Stage and Screen," looks at how popularity in one medium often gets translated into popularity in another. Hollywood, in particular, turned out an endless succession of musicals during the war years, some of them patriotic flag-wavers, but most just typical escapism. Even Broadway, especially with the rise of Rodgers and Hammerstein through the productions of *Oklahoma!* (1943) and *Carousel* (1945), enlivened the field of music. A stage musical might not draw an audience anywhere close to that attending its Hollywood counterpart, but recordings leveled the discrepancies and allowed millions to become familiar with the scores (or individual songs) from countless productions.

A relative newcomer to national musical attention in the 1940s, country music receives discussion in chapter 7. By the end of World War II, many people had become familiar with the music featured on *The National Barn*

Sailors on leave enjoy a Saturday dance at the United Nations Service Center Canteen in Washington, D.C. By 1943, canteens and other recreational services across the country catered to service personnel. Library of Congress, Prints & Photographs Division.

Dance and *Grand Ole Opry,* two long-running and popular radio variety shows that broadened the nation's tastes. Individual artists, such as Red Foley, Patsy Montana, Bob Wills and His Texas Playboys, Roy Acuff, and Ernest Tubb, among many others, all enjoyed fame and hits under the country banner. They proved so popular that noncountry performers, for example, Bing Crosby and the Andrews Sisters, could record tunes like "Pistol Packin' Mama" (1943) and "Don't Fence Me In" (1944) and have every expectation they would rise on the charts and become hits that appealed to all. By the end of the period in question, country music occupied its own niche, and *Billboard* magazine tracked it on a separate national chart.

Hardly as dominant as the many forms of popular music, classical performances nonetheless occupied a part of the larger American musical spectrum and serve as the subject for the book's eighth and final chapter. Many radio stations put aside portions of their programming schedules to accommodate classical artists. The networks supplied these broadcasts to their affiliates on a national scale, and sponsors equated classical shows with a certain prestige lacking in other musical offerings. During this period, composer Aaron

Copland would premiere three of his best-known works, *Billy the Kid* (1940), *Rodeo* (1942), and *Appalachian Spring* (1944), and emerge as the best-known classical composer in American music. But others, such as Virgil Thomson, Roy Harris, and William Grant Still, also contributed to this genre.

Collectively, these eight chapters provide a wide-ranging overview of trends and events that formed the musical landscape during the years 1939–1945. In addition to a survey of the music popular during 1939–1945, *Music of the World War II Era* offers the following special features:

- Each chapter contains sidebars that further explain particular terms that occur within the text.
- Throughout the book, readers will find captioned illustrations relevant to the text at hand.
- At the conclusion to the regular textual matter, a musical timeline highlights some significant musical events occurring between 1939 and 1945.
- Following the timeline, two appendices should prove helpful to readers:

  Appendix A lists virtually all the Broadway musicals produced during the war years as well as a good sampling of the movie musicals released at that same time. Space precludes listing every film in that category, but 284 separate titles do receive mention. Crossovers between Broadway and Hollywood are also noted.

  Appendix B lists many of the songs written and recorded during 1939–1945. In addition, the release dates and the composers and lyricists also appear in parentheses following the titles. In all, 715 tunes are alphabetically listed by title.

- After the appendices, a chapter-by-chapter tabulation of citations gives appropriate credit to sources.
- A selected bibliography of print and audio sources, along with Web sites should provide ample opportunity for follow-up reading or listening.
- A detailed index completes *Music of the World War II Era.*

1

Music about World War II

BACKGROUND

No war has ever generated such enthusiasm among Americans as did World War II. Despite terrible casualties (292,000 American troops killed, 672,000 wounded) and mind-boggling costs in money (some $845 billion in direct expenditures—equivalent to over $9 trillion in current dollars, when adjusted for inflation) and materials, this four-year conflict has come down to the present as "the Good War," one that few Americans challenged in any way. Very possibly the most unified period in the nation's history, citizens immediately took up the cause, especially in the days following Pearl Harbor, eager to do their part in effecting a speedy victory. People from all walks of life planted victory gardens; collected tons of scrap metals, rubber, and other materials to be converted into guns, planes, ships, and tanks; bought government-backed war bonds and stamps to help finance the war; and endured the inconveniences imposed by shortages and the rationing of many varied items.

With the war so widely accepted in the public mind, it should surprise no one that American popular culture rallied in support of the nation's involvement in every way imaginable. Commercial music proved no exception when it came to showing patriotic fervor, although few flag-waving compositions stirred sustained interest. The old reliables—love and romance, boy and girl—sustained most American songwriting throughout the war years.

1939–1941

The Selective Training and Service Act of 1940 took effect in the fall of that year. A law that authorized the drafting of qualified male citizens, it immediately began inducting men into the military, while headlines from Europe and Asia spoke grimly of the Axis powers (Germany, Italy, and Japan) and their seemingly endless victories on many fronts. The military draft provided inspiration for a handful of tunes, most of them long since forgotten: as more and more males were called up, the Prairie Ramblers of *The National Barn Dance* recorded a song in January 1941 about a soon-to-be service member who promises to do his best each day for his country so the girl he's leaving behind will continue to love him. Optimistically called "I'll Be Back in a Year, Little Darlin'" (1941; words and music by Ben Shelhamer Jr., Claude Heritier, and Russ Hull), it sparked an immediate response in a recording called "I'll Be Waiting for You, Darlin'" (1941; words and music by Russ Hull). Performed by Louise Massey and the Westerners, as well as Patsy Montana, it has sweetheart, wife, or mother vowing to be brave and true while waiting for the soldier's return. It soon became apparent, however, that American participation abroad would more than likely extend for some time, and the content of draft-related tunes shifted to a more pessimistic tone with numbers like "I Won't Be Back in a Year, Little Darling" (1941; words and music by Bradley Kincaid and Buck Nation).

Other pop songs about the abrupt move from civilian to soldier include "C for Conscription" (1941; words and music by Millard Lampell and Pete Seeger), "Gone with the Draft" (1940; words and music by Earl Dramin, Wesley Price, and Nat King Cole), "Gone with What Draft?" (1941; music by Benny Goodman), "He's 1-A in the Army (and He's A-1 in My Heart)" (1941; words and music by Redd Evans), "I Feel the Draft Coming On" (1940; words and music by Bill Nettles), "In the Army Now" (1941; words and music by Big Bill Broonzy), and "$21 a Day—Once a Month" (1941; music by Felix Bernard, lyrics by Raymond Klages). Ephemeral songs all, none of these titles possessed any staying power, but merely reflected their immediate times.

While the United States began the arduous process of rearming, traditional allies, like Britain and France, had to face the Axis alone. Less than a year following Germany's 1939 invasion of Poland, France fell in June of 1940, an event remembered in the sadly evocative song "The Last Time I Saw Paris" (1940; music by Jerome Kern, lyrics by Oscar Hammerstein II). A melody from the 1941 film *Lady Be Good,* it won an Academy Award for Best Song. France's surrender completed the Nazi sweep of continental Europe, and although American sympathies might lie with England, the United States could do little other than watch helplessly while offering Lend-Lease and moral support. Aware of the doughty nation's plight, songwriters from both countries answered with a number of songs that celebrated courage and looked to a more peaceful future; their efforts produced some enduring melodies about steadfastness and loyalty, capturing many a listener's heart in the process.

A trio of English tunes, "There'll Always Be an England" (1939; words and music by Ross Parker and Hughie Charles), "We Must All Stick Together" (1939; words and music by Ralph Butler and Raymond Wallace), and "He Wears a Pair of Silver Wings" (1941; music by Michael Carr, lyrics by Eric Maschwitz), reached American shores and quickly received airplay and reasonably strong record sales. The title of the first song says it all—England will prevail, no matter how desperate the odds. The second composition, of course, urges the English and their American allies to stand united. Finally, "He Wears a Pair of Silver Wings" speaks admiringly of those who serve their country. The silver wings refer specifically to the RAF (Royal Air Force) pilots then fighting in the skies over England, but American audiences could also interpret it as referring to U.S. Army Air Corps pilots who would soon be heading overseas to join in battle.

The one song of this type that achieved the biggest hit status, however, originated not in England, but in New York's Tin Pan Alley, that famous section where so many composers, lyricists, and publishers congregated. "(There'll Be Blue Birds Over) The White Cliffs of Dover" (1941) had Americans Walter Kent penning the music and Nat Burton writing the lyrics. Its subject matter, especially the reference to Dover, had people thinking it was an import. Plus, Vera Lynn, an immensely popular English vocalist, recorded what many consider to be the definitive version, although a host of other interpreters, including Bing Crosby, Kate Smith, Glenn Miller, Guy Lombardo, and Kay Kyser (who introduced it first in the United States), cut their own sides. With its images of birds flying freely above the landscape, and its message of eventual peace, "The White Cliffs of Dover" touched a collective nerve. For the remainder of the war, it played on radios and jukeboxes, as well as selling countless copies in sheet music and recordings. For many years thereafter, people associated this lovely song, especially the Vera Lynn rendition, with World War II.

Pro-English sentiments aside, few doubted that the United States would soon be dragged into the growing conflict, but isolationism continued to run deep, and a number of organizations, particularly a group calling itself America First, campaigned vociferously against any foreign engagements. Folk musicians led the way, especially the Almanac Singers, a quartet made up of Woody Guthrie, Lee Hays, Millard Lampell, and Pete Seeger. Active participants in the peace movement opposing U.S. intervention in the looming war, they recorded an album for the American Peace Mobilization organization titled *Songs for John Doe* (1941). It included titles like "Ballad of October 16" (words and music by Millard Lampell), "Billy Boy" (words and music by Lee Hays and Pete Seeger), and "Plow Under" (words and music by Lee Hays and Pete Seeger). "Ballad of October 16" condemns the 1940 date that American men first had to register and thus place themselves on the eligibility rolls for the draft, while "Billy Boy" explains a young man's reluctance to fight. "Plow Under" presents an analogy between war and the New Deal's Depression-era Agriculture Adjustment Act that authorized the reduction or "plowing under" of crops, just as a world war would plow under countless young soldiers. Musically, however, only a few overtly antiwar songs received even the scantest public notice.

1942–1943

On December 7, 1941, any lingering doubts about American neutrality were put to rest amid the explosions and destruction at Pearl Harbor. Several days later, Germany and Italy followed suit by declaring war on the United States, and the global conflict no one really wanted, but that few doubted the country could avoid, became a reality. Following these formal declarations of hostilities, and in a manner akin to putting grain into a hopper, composers, both professional and amateur, wrote thousands of songs dealing with the war in one way or another. As these new tunes were shaken and strained, publishers picked out hundreds and released them as sheet music. The record companies likewise stood in line and selected their share, ever hopeful of a hit with unpredictable consumers. What therefore emerged, at the bottom of this metaphorical hopper, served as but a sampling of the war-oriented songs that represented the nation's musical response to World War II. Most would-be songwriters labored in anonymity, and their efforts no doubt also spoke of a nation enraged by events, but lacking copyrights and seldom printed or distributed, they remain lost to posterity.

Following the attack on Pearl Harbor, the Almanac Singers ceased any antiwar campaigning and began to write in a more interventionist vein. In February 1942, they recorded a new album of six songs, but this time the music supported the American role in the conflict. The group labeled its work *Dear Mr. President,* and the title song, written by Pete Seeger, offers an apology to President Franklin D. Roosevelt for *Songs of John Doe.* For his part, Woody Guthrie saw the war as a way to give his support to a stand against fascism, penning a propaganda song called "Round and Round Hitler's Grave" (1941; music adapted by Woody Guthrie from the traditional song "Old Joe Clark," words by Woody Guthrie, Millard Lampell, and Pete Seeger). As proof of his newfound advocacy, Guthrie volunteered for the Merchant Marine in 1942. Upon his discharge in 1945, he found himself drafted for the Army, but with the war over, he returned to civilian life shortly thereafter. While in the Merchant Marine, Guthrie composed the words and music for "Seamen Three"

(c. 1942). This tune tells of Guthrie and two friends shipping out to beat the fascists and "workin' and a-fightin' for peace across my lands and seas."[1]

For some songwriters at the onset of World War II, the horrors of World War I remained fresh in their minds, and they approached the new conflict gingerly, if at all. The majority, however, tried to express an air of bravado about the country's new role as a combatant. Compositions like "The Sun Will Soon Be Setting on the Land of the Rising Sun" (1941; words and music by Sam Lerner), "Good-Bye, Mama (I'm Off to Yokohoma)" (1942; words and music by J. Fred Coots), "It's Taps for the Japs" (1942; words and music by James Cox), "(We'll Be Singing Hallelujah) Marching through Berlin" (1942; words and music by Bob Reed and Harry Miller), "(We're Gonna Make Sure) There'll Never Be Another War!" (1942; words and music by Nelson Cogane, Ira Schuster, and Joseph Meyer), "They Started Somethin' (but We're Gonna End It!)" (1942; words and music by Robert Sour, Don McCray, and Ernest Gold), "We Did It Before and We Can Do It Again" (1941; words and music by Cliff Friend and Charles Tobias), "We've Got to Do a Job on the Japs, Baby" (1942; words and music by Edgar Leslie, Abel Baer, and George W. Meyer), and "Yankee Doodle Ain't Doodlin' Now" (1942; words and music by Pearl Fein) proclaimed that, forced into war, the United States would again be victorious, and in relatively short order.[2]

And yet, despite the unceasing flow of new sheet music and records, despite jukeboxes, disc jockeys, radio shows, movies, and musicals, the nation could never agree on a single song that would become the most memorable, the most played, the most listened-to tune about the war. New songs came and went, a few made the charts and lingered a while, but most received little notice. Who recalls "Allegiance to the Red White and Blue" (1942; words and music by Ethel Lee Buxton), "(There's a) Big Parade in the Sky" (1942; words and music by Cecil Taylor), "I've Changed My Penthouse for a Pup Tent" (1942; words and music by Bob Crawford), or "Since He Traded His Zoot Suit for a Uniform" (1942; words and music by Carmen Lombardo and Pat Innisfree)? Yet these four selections, now forgotten and all from 1942, just months following Pearl Harbor, represent the tip of the proverbial iceberg—a slew of recordings and sheet music, most with hackneyed lyrics, that attempted to reflect the country's zeal to get into the war and achieve a quick, resounding victory.

One of the most immediate responses to Japan's December attack on Pearl Harbor came from country songwriter Fred Rose; his "Cowards over Pearl Harbor" was recorded for Decca Records on December 22, 1941, by singer Denver Darling. It expresses the shock and anger felt by Americans at their sudden and undesired entry into the war. During the next year or so, Darling continued to record for the company, and he included some war songs at each session.

SONGS ABOUT THE WAR IN THE PACIFIC

Topical World War II songs often combined entertainment with social and cultural asides. A truly global conflict, the war had two theaters of operation: the European and the Pacific. The music that addressed the European conflict tended to focus primarily on Hitler and the Nazis, not the German people. The songs about the war in the Pacific, however, often displayed a darker side, one that utilized racism of the worst kind.

Following the sneak attack on Pearl Harbor, the war with Japan immediately commenced. On the music front, composers and performers offered horrified Americans songs full of anger and revenge. RCA's Bluebird label quickly released a disc containing two novelty songs performed by Carson Robison, a successful cowboy and hillbilly artist. Side A contained "Remember Pearl Harbor," a 1941 tune written by Frank Luther (not to be confused with a 1942 composition bearing the same title by Sammy Kaye and Don Reid) that manages to call Japanese "rats," "vultures," and "yellow scum" and asks Americans to "wipe the Jap from the map."

Side B held another anti-Japanese tirade titled "We're Gonna Have to Slap the Dirty Little Jap (and Uncle Sam's the Guy Who Can Do It)," written by Bob Miller. As in "Remember Pearl Harbor," the song refers to the Japanese as "yellow," and the sheet music version even employs garish yellow paper in its printing. Other similarly retaliatory numbers of the day include "Cowards over Pearl Harbor" (1941), "Get Your Gun and Come Along (We're Fixin' to Kill a Skunk)" (1942), "It's Taps for the Japs" (1942), "We'll Knock the Japs Right into the Laps of the Nazis" (1941), "We've Got to Do a Job on the Japs, Baby" (1942), and "You're a Sap, Mr. Jap" (1941).

Whatever the intention—harmless banter, scornful commentary, tasteless stereotypes, or blatant racism—this musical war against Japan help Americans vent their outrage, but not in a healthy or useful way. Fortunately, the more vicious anti-Japanese diatribes did not become popular or lasting songs about World War II.

It momentarily appeared that Darling would be the first country singer to base his career on war-related music, but many of his selections, such as "Care of Uncle Sam" (1942; words and music by Denver Darling, Vaughn Horton, and Harry Duncan) and "We're Gonna Have to Slap the Dirty Little Jap (and Uncle Sam's the Guy Who Can Do It)" (1942; words and music by Bob Miller), gained him but a modicum of success. Although the recordings clearly attack and debase America's enemies, they could not sustain Darling; even with his own repertoire of traditional cowboy songs, he disappeared from public view after 1945.

On the other hand, Carson Robison, a country songwriter who had been active in the 1920s, returned to performing and recording with the outbreak of hostilities. When he released a number of his own compositions, he quickly gained more celebrity in the war-related genre than most of his counterparts. Robison produced his first real wartime country music hit with a rewrite of a traditional standard, "Turkey in the Straw." His rendition, called "1942 Turkey in the Straw" (1942; words and music by Carson Robison), offers a violent parody about a monkey and a baboon, the latter representing the Axis powers. He followed that with four more tunes in 1942 alone: "Get Your Gun and Come Along (We're Fixin' to Kill a Skunk)," "The Story of Jitterbug Joe," "Plain Talk," and "It's Just a Matter of Time" (all words and music by Carson Robison). In each, he shows a clever mix of humor and anger.

In a series of musical letters between Germany's Hitler and, first, Italy's Mussolini, and then Japan's Emperor Hirohito, Robison created some of his most memorable work. The initial correspondence, "Mussolini's Letter to Hitler" and "Hitler's Reply to Mussolini" (both 1942; words and music by Carson Robison) assumes Hitler's disdain for the pompous Italian dictator. Three years later, and with the war going badly for the remaining Axis, Germany and Japan, Robison paints a distraught pair of fallen leaders in "Hirohito's Letter to Hitler" and "Hitler's Last Letter to Hirohito" (both 1945; words and music by Carson Robison). A skillful blend of satire and political awareness, the letters display a level of urbane humor unusual for most country music of the time.

In the first days of World War II, the phrase "Remember Pearl Harbor" came readily to many lips, and it took little time for two songs bearing those words to be released. Carson Robison had the first, with lyrics and music by Frank Luther, in the closing days of 1941. Sammy Kaye and his band likewise recorded "Remember Pearl Harbor" in early 1942, a different version that featured music by Kaye, with assistance from lyricist Don Reid. Both numbers attracted country and mainstream listeners, and the two, especially Kaye's rendition, briefly established themselves as favorites for radio stations, plus family, community, and religious gatherings used them for group singing. Even with this initial popularity, neither version of "Remember Pearl Harbor" became the nation's war song, and both faded from the public's attention as the initial fury about the Japanese attack waned.

"There's a Star Spangled Banner Waving Somewhere" (1942; words and music by Paul Roberts and Shelby Darnell [pseudonym of Bob Miller]) served as another early contribution by country artists to the musical war effort. Although it never emerged as the top song associated with World War II, its widespread acceptance revealed a growing interest in the genre's quick response to events. Outwardly, "There's a Star Spangled Banner Waving Somewhere" tells the story of a crippled mountain boy who cannot actively join the fighting but yearns to be a hero and get recognition. A careful reading of the lyrics would, however, show that the speaker displays more interest in self-aggrandizement than patriotism, but it nonetheless sold 1.5 million records

With the outbreak of World War II on December 7, 1941, publishers issued a number of songs commemorating the event. None attained any enduring status, and "Remember Pearl Harbor" (1942), although earnest in its sentiments, soon got lost among a host of similar tunes. Picture by William H. Young.

and nearly the same in sheet music, high figures for any musical genre, but especially so for a country song at that time. Singer Elton Britt's recorded version earned him the honor of being the first country musician to be awarded a gold record.

Even with these patriotic songs, both country and mainstream, on the far-flung battlefields the nation did not do well in 1942 and 1943. As the United States went from peace to war, from plenty to rationing, from optimism to serious doubts about victory, officials fretted about sagging public morale. In the face of military setbacks, many in government felt the country needed, if not demanded, stirring martial music for the nation to be victorious. They wanted a rousing, patriotic melody everyone could agree on. Surely, out of the hundreds of compositions being written, there must be such a tune. But as 1942, a bad year militarily, dragged on, no such number appeared, nothing that would inspire both the troops abroad and the folks back home. The songs kept coming, but not the right one.

With defeat following defeat and only an occasional victory brightening people's outlook, two tunes surfaced that urged listeners to keep their spirits up. Things might be tough, but they were bound to get better. The first, "Praise the Lord and Pass the Ammunition" (words and music by Frank Loesser), was released in 1942. Based on a reportedly true event that occurred at Pearl Harbor during the Japanese attack, a Navy chaplain, or "sky pilot" in the song, helped his shipboard comrades pass shells to the gunners on deck. Sources differ, but either Captain William A. Maguire or Captain Howell M. Forgy uttered the phrase, but fact quickly evolved into myth, with some solemn historians eventually stating that a brave chaplain took over a machine gun from a wounded gunner and single-handedly manned it from the ship's altar while pleading for more ammunition from his comrades.

Frank Loesser, a Broadway songsmith, adapted the incident, already memorialized in newspapers and magazines, and made it a rallying cry in the dark days of 1942. Whatever the facts in the case, "Praise the Lord and Pass the Ammunition" turned out to be one of the first real mainstream hits about the war. Over time, it sold several million records and probably almost as many copies of sheet music. Kay Kyser and his band boasted the biggest seller, making it to #1 in early 1943, although lesser-known groups like the Merry Macs and the Southern Sons Quartet (performing it as a gospel number) also recorded the song. In a time of war, such stories—even with added layers of exaggeration—serve as morale boosters, and critics can argue about the details at a later time. Loesser himself told the unlikely story of the gunner in the opening verse, but most listeners doubtless recall the chorus that says, in effect, as a nation, people must act in unison and "pass the ammunition" (i.e., keep the troops supplied) so that "we'll all stay free."

The following year, American forces notched a few victories, but the war's outcome had by no means been decided. Some citizens even urged a negotiated peace with Germany (but not with Japan—no one could forgive the Pearl Harbor attack), so that precious resources would not be stretched so thin. As if in response, a tune released late in 1942 carried the title "Comin' in on a Wing and a Prayer" (music by Jimmy McHugh, lyrics by Harold Adamson), and it quickly received considerable popular acclaim. The lyrics, elegant in their simplicity, describe a bomber crew, their plane shot up during a mission, attempting to make it home on nothing much more than will alone. This McHugh-Adamson collaboration, coupled with Frank Loesser's "Praise the

Lord and Pass the Ammunition" just a few months earlier, gave a weary nation the kind of tonic it needed. "Comin' in on a Wing and a Prayer" likewise climbed the charts and became a major hit during that crucial period.

Adamson's words spin an allegorical story for the nation: the bomber (the United States) has "really hit our target" (the Axis), but the effort exacted an expensive toll. Nevertheless, the country must continue to attack its enemies and pay whatever price might be involved. As long as American forces persevere and bring pressure on the enemy, victory will eventually come, even if it means limping home "on a wing and a prayer." Citizens on the home front should do no less.

Because the song came out during the AFM recording ban (see chapter 4, "Recordings and the Music Business," for more on this event), several versions of the song received a cappella performances. Groups like the Song Spinners, who claimed the #1 version of the tune, the Four Vagabonds, and the Golden Gate Quartet relied on voices to imitate instruments. The Song Spinners also recorded "Johnny Zero" (1943; music by Vee Lawnhurst, lyrics by Mack David) on the flip side of their Decca recording. It quickly assumed a successful life of its own, and although it never achieved the popular success of "Comin' in on a Wing and a Prayer" (aside from being piggybacked on that million-seller), this tale of a young fighter pilot did well both with records and sheet music.

Neither "Praise the Lord and Pass the Ammunition" nor "Comin' in on a Wing and a Prayer," however, ever emerged as the iconic war song that everyone—troops and civilians alike—claimed to want. They both sold well and enjoyed considerable success for a number of months, but then they faded, as does most popular music, replaced by newer tunes and different artists. And this lack of an overriding favorite bothered a number of people, some of whom determined to do something about it.

The NWMC and the MWC

The federal government, in an effort to maintain public morale and control the flow of information about the war, had, in June of 1942, formed the Office of War Information (OWI). Elmer Davis, a respected newsman from the studios of the Columbia Broadcasting System (CBS radio), took on the job of directing the OWI, a bureaucracy destined to grow and carry considerable heft in official wartime Washington, D.C. It immediately assumed the duties previously undertaken by a number of smaller agencies and then began growing on its own accord. The OWI hired artists to create propaganda posters on subjects as varied as rationing and saboteurs, put together several hundred newsreels about both the war and the home front to show in theaters, hired photographers to document ongoing events related to the conflict, and utilized radio by producing numerous broadcast series that heightened public awareness about current events.

The OWI also addressed the issue of popular music and the war effort. In November of 1942, Davis's group established the National Wartime Music Committee (NWMC), a group that functioned to evaluate the suitability of certain songs over others. The committee sought to find that particular song capable of boosting morale and maintaining it throughout a lengthy, costly war. The NWMC extended the heavy hand of government into the music business, acting as a quasi-clearing house for new compositions as NWMC members assumed the unaccustomed role of national music arbiters. Because it lacked any real power other than that of suggestion, the agency, from its inception, faced an impossible task and almost immediately encountered opposition or indifference from both those in the music business and the public. No matter how sincere or patriotic the intentions of the people in the NWMC, their efforts produced little if anything of substance. The mass market seemed in no mood to endorse war-oriented songs, and music publishers and recording companies stayed much more attuned to the wishes of citizens, their primary constituency. No one, it appeared, really wanted the advice and counsel of the NWMC. In April 1943, just six months after it had been created, the NWMC voted itself out of existence.[3]

In its place came the similarly named Music War Committee (MWC), another ill-guided attempt to find a collectively agreed-upon war song, something that would pump up the troops on the battlefield and raise civilian spirits. The committee, created by the American Theatre Wing, a Broadway service organization formed in late 1939, assisted in national mobilization. The new group chose as its leader Oscar Hammerstein II, one of the most prominent individuals in musical theater at that time. Even with the esteemed Hammerstein at its helm, the MWC, like its predecessor, the NWMC, faced a hopeless task. Not that tunes relating to the war did not keep coming—"Don't Worry, Mom" (1943; words and music by Harry Duncan and Paul William), "Let's Put the Axe to the Axis" (1942; words and music by Paul Mann and Stephan Weiss), and "Sing and Fight for America!" (1943; music by Henry Kane, lyrics by Mark Minkus) made their unheralded appearances and then went to that limbo of forgotten melodies. Despite the earnest efforts by Hammerstein and the MWC, persuading Tin Pan Alley or any other songwriters to compose war songs on demand never produced any conspicuous successes.

But the problem went beyond the music industry. During the countless bond drives that were held across the nation and on radio to raise funds for the war, the sponsoring groups played it safe as far as selecting music. To encourage the sale of bonds, a number of composers attempted to create suitable tunes, such as "Dig Down Deep" (1942; words and music by Walter

Hirsch, Sano Marco, and Gerald Marks), "The Road to Victory" (1943; words and music by Frank Loesser), and the insistent "Buy a Bond" (1945; music by Jimmy McHugh, lyrics by Harold Adamson), but they seldom achieved any lasting hit status. Probably the best, or at least most memorable, song in this area would be Irving Berlin's "Any Bonds Today?" (1941).

Despite this plethora of bond tunes, when Bing Crosby, Dinah Shore, Kate Smith, the Andrews Sisters, or any of a multitude of popular entertainers took the stage or microphone to encourage everyone to "dig down deep," it meant they would perform their latest hits—the real crowd-pleasers—to accompany their pleas for money. Audiences at rallies turned away from marches and service songs, or any other overtly martial choices, and radio listeners likewise tuned out when this kind of music came over the airwaves. Even the most enthusiastic bond songs had but limited appeal, but not so mainstream popular music, as promoters quickly learned.

Sentimental, or Slush, Songs

What the proponents of rousing war songs could never seem to grasp was that a tune's success or failure rested in the hands of stateside civilians and military personnel stationed abroad. As their nickels in jukeboxes and record and sheet music purchases made abundantly clear, the homefront population preferred more traditional popular tunes. Troops in both the European and Pacific theaters seconded that decision and overwhelmingly demanded songs about those things they left behind (and for which they fought): wives, girlfriends, home, and family. This category of sentimental composition—or what the MWC disparagingly called "slush"—consistently won out every year of the conflict.

Among the many slush songs that achieved popularity from late 1941 to early 1943, the following compositions refer to the conflict, but often only in the oblique terms of romance, loyalty to a loved one, saying good-bye, and the loneliness caused by separation:

"Better Not Roll Those Blue, Blue Eyes (at Somebody Else)" (1942; music by Al Goodhart, lyrics by Kay Twomey)

"A Boy in Khaki—A Girl in Lace" (1942; music by Allie Wrubel, lyrics by Charles Newman)

"Don't Sit Under the Apple Tree (With Anyone Else But Me)" (1942 [popular revival of a 1939 song]; music by Sam H. Stept, lyrics by Lew Brown and Charlie Tobias)

"He's My Guy" (1942; music by Gene DePaul, lyrics by Don Raye)

"I Don't Want to Walk without You" (1942; music by Jule Styne, lyrics by Frank Loesser)

"I Left My Heart at the Stage Door Canteen" (1942; words and music by Irving Berlin)
"I'll Be True While You're Gone" (1941; words and music by Gene Autry and Fred Rose)
"I'll Be with You (in Apple Blossom Time)" (1941 [popular revival of a 1920 song]; music by Albert Von Tilzer, lyrics by Neville Fleeson)
"I'll Keep the Love Light Burning" (1942; words and music by Harry Tobias, Nick Kenny, and Harold Leavey)
"I'm Dreaming Tonight of My Blue Eyes" (1943; words and music by Don Marcotte and A. P. Carter) [Also called "I'm Thinking Tonight of My Blue Eyes"]
"I've Got a Gal in Kalamazoo" (1942; music by Harry Warren, lyrics by Mack Gordon)
"Johnny Doughboy Found a Rose in Ireland" (1942; music by Al Goodhart, lyrics by Kay Twomey)
"Just As Though You Were Here" (1942; music by John Brooks, lyrics by Eddie DeLange)
"Rose Ann of Charing Cross" (1942; music by Mabel Wayne, lyrics by Kermit Goell)
"Silver Wings in the Moonlight" (1943; words and music by Hughie Charles, Leo Towers, and Sonny Miller)
"Somebody Else Is Taking My Place" (1942 [popular revival of a 1937 song]; words and music by Russ Morgan, Dick Howard, and Bob Ellsworth)
"Somebody's Thinking of You Tonight" (1942; music by Teddy Powell and Ira Schuster, lyrics by Marty Symes)
"Something to Remember You By" (1942 [popular revival of a 1930 song]; music by Howard Schwartz, lyrics by Howard Dietz)
"Somewhere, Sometime (I'll Come Back to You)" (1942; music by George Dunning, lyrics by Bill Hampton)
"Sunday, Monday, or Always" (1943; music by Jimmy Van Heusen, lyrics by Johnny Burke)
"That Soldier of Mine" (1942; music by Matt Dennis, lyrics by Paul Herrick)
"There Will Never Be Another You" (1942; music by Harry Warren, lyrics by Mack Gordon)
"There Won't Be a Shortage of Love" (1941; words and music by Carmen Lombardo and John Jacob Loeb)
"We'll Meet Again" (1942 [popular revival of a 1939 song]; music by Ross Parker, lyrics by Hughie Charles)
"White Christmas" (1942; words and music by Irving Berlin)[4]
"Wonder When My Baby's Coming Home" (1942; music by Arthur Kent, lyrics by Kermit Goell)

The preceding list should not be thought exhaustive; dozens of other songs not mentioned above also touched on the war and its effect on personal relationships. In addition, literally hundreds more compositions from this period never addressed the conflict at all, but fall instead into the much broader category of straight popular music.

As 1943 progressed, slowly and bloodily, a gradual shift occurred, both in the Allied fortunes of battle and in domestic attitudes toward the conflict. With American forces increasingly taking the offensive against the Axis powers, a few songwriters reflected this turn of events in their music such as "The Road to Victory" (1943; words and music by Frank Loesser); "So Long 'Til Victory" (1943; words and music by Sam W. Braverman, Audrey Bradshaw, Loreen Bradshaw, and Sammy Watkins); and an upbeat tribute to the Russians for stopping Hitler cold on the Eastern Front, "Stalin Wasn't Stallin' (a Modern Spiritual)" (1943; words and music by Willie Johnson). These tunes constituted a minority, however, and the tried-and-true themes of romance and home remained dominant.

Soldiers and civilians, defying the assumptions of the MWC, continued to reject most tunes that celebrated anything military and demanded instead the latest hits. Most military personnel, when pressed, said they had experienced enough fighting and all the associated horrors of war; they needed no musical reminders. Plus, in modern, mechanized combat, troops did not pour out of trenches or storm across open fields singing heroic lyrics about the glory of their cause accompanied by a marching band in full regalia.

Stateside, the same thoughts held true. Civilians did not want musical descriptions of fierce battles or words denouncing the terrible enemy; they wanted the same pop songs the troops wanted. And so when records about war and duty appeared in stores, they usually sold slowly, at best. Radio stations reported minimal demand for that kind of music, and jukebox operators refused to stock such records for their machines because people would not put their nickels in for "Be a Hero, My Boy" (1943; music by Henry Kane, lyrics by Mark Minkus), "Dear God, Watch Over Joe" (1944; words and music by Jenny Lou Carson), or "Last Page of *Mein Kampf*" (1945; words and music by Jack B. Johnstone and Will Livernash).

By the same token, songs bearing lugubrious messages, as in, for example, "There's a Gold Star Hanging in the Window (Where a Blue Star Used to Be)" (1943; words and music by Floyd Wilkins, Ray Marcell, and Russ Hall) and the similarly titled "There's a Gold Star in Her Window" (1944; words and music by Tex Ritter and Frank Harford), found few listeners. Conversely, if a tune possessed a good, danceable rhythm, then it might stand a better chance. "Bell Bottom Trousers" (1945 [possibly taken from a traditional sea chantey]; contemporary words and music by Moe Jaffe), "(There'll Be a) Hot Time in the Town of Berlin (When the Yanks Go Marching In)" (1943; words and music by Joe Bushkin and John De Vries), "Saturday Night Is the Loneliest Night of the Week" (1944; music by Jule Styne, lyrics by Sammy Cahn), "Shoo-Shoo, Baby" (1943; words and music by Phil Moore), and "Vict'ry Polka" (1943;

There may have been a war, but people still liked to dance. This enlisted men's event occurred in Brownsville, Texas, early in 1942. Library of Congress, Prints & Photographs Division.

music by Jule Styne, lyrics by Sammy Cahn) fit this category admirably and collected their fair share of nickels.

A swinging beat propelled one song in particular to true hit status. In the days immediately before Pearl Harbor, and with more and more men clearly in uniform, "The Boogie Woogie Bugle Boy (of Company B)" (1941; music by Hughie Prince, lyrics by Don Raye), an up-tempo delight, came along and quickly climbed the charts. It may have reminded some about the draft, but its lighthearted attitude probably dispelled most thoughts about the possibility of a war. The extraordinary success of the recorded version performed by the Andrews Sisters (Patty, Maxene, and Laverne) helped make the trio one of the leading singing groups of the 1940s. Its rolling boogie-woogie beat reflected a jazz style that had become all the rage at the time and challenged jitterbugs everywhere, and its tongue-twisting lyrics provided great fun for listeners. The war becomes secondary to the music in such cheerful songs, and the lyrics carry no hints of suffering or sadness. Instead, they stand first and foremost as good dance tunes.

On the country music side of things, however, a significant number of war-related tunes take on a more somber note, as is characteristic of the genre. With messages of a personal nature, they describe the anxieties and sadness of the soldiers' loved ones back home. Examples include "Silver Dew on the Bluegrass Tonight" (1943; words and music by Ed Burt) and "Did You See Daddy over There?" (1943; music by Bill Shownet, lyrics by Eddie Arnold). "Soldier's Last Letter" (1944; words and music by Ernest Tubb and Redd Steward), a song calculated to bring tears to the listener's eyes, tells of a mother's sorrow on receiving word of her son's death. "Searching for a Soldier's Grave" (1945; words and music by Jim Anglin and Roy Acuff) recounts a trip made abroad in an attempt to find the final resting place of a loved one. Another category of songs contained expressions of the worries experienced by servicemen, such as "Have I Stayed Away Too Long?" (1943; words and music by Frank Loesser), or the lights out time in the barracks that leads to introspection, as in "Each Night at Nine" (1944; words and music by Floyd Tillman).

Women and the War

With the United States emerging as "The Arsenal of Democracy" and facing the daunting task of producing most of the weapons and supplies for the Allies throughout the war, more women than ever before joined the workforce. The Office of War Information soon launched a campaign urging women to "Do the Job He Left Behind," a reference to the increasing numbers of soldiers shipping out for foreign shores and the need for wives, mothers, sisters, and sweethearts to take on the men's work. No task proved too difficult, and this new resource received celebration in a number of wartime tunes. "On the Swing Shift" (music by Harold Arlen, lyrics by Johnny Mercer), which premiered in the 1942 movie *Star Spangled Rhythm,* served as one of the first songs to acknowledge this change in the nation's traditional labor patterns. Composer Harold Rome contributed "On That Old Production Line" in 1943 for the *Lunch Time Follies,* a traveling musical theater group that entertained war workers. With "Milkman, Keep Those Bottles Quiet" (1944; words and music by Don Raye and Gene DePaul), those poor souls who worked the graveyard shift and needed sleep at odd hours had a melody they could call their own.

The working American woman, however, received her most lasting symbol with Rosie the Riveter, a fictional creation first seen in posters and other illustrative materials. A 1942 poster, created for the Westinghouse Corporation by artist J. Howard Miller, shows a woman rolling up her sleeve and saying, "We Can Do It!" The following year, Norman Rockwell painted another famous interpretation, this time of a muscular woman welder with one foot firmly planted on *Mein Kampf,* for a *Saturday Evening Post* cover. Finally, in 1944,

THE ARMED FORCES BANDS

Musical accompaniment, at least drums and flutes, has long been a part of military drills, marches, and ceremonies. Recognizing the importance of music in the armed forces, the U.S. Congress in 1911 authorized funding for a school to train Army bandleaders. During World War I, the institution flourished, and with the onset of World War II, the demands for musical support again grew, with the result that approximately 500 bands marched with the troops.

The United States Army Band, the U.S. Military Academy Band, and the U.S. Army Air Corps Band comprised a special music division that performed at concerts, parades, and recruiting drives. In 1943, the Army Band embarked on a two-week wartime tour which ended up lasting two years; it gave performances at countless USO dances as well as playing at concerts for civilians.

Glenn Miller, leader of one of the most popular commercial orchestras, enlisted in 1942 and served as director of Army bands. Then, with a transfer to the U.S. Army Air Force in 1943, he and a 45-piece aggregation aired a weekly half-hour radio program called *I Sustain the Wings,* a network show that played good dance music, recruited men into the service, and sold war bonds.

The United States Navy Band, organized in 1925, likewise played at official ceremonies and memorial services and assisted in national recruiting efforts and war bond drives. This group benefited from the 1943 enlistment of Artie Shaw and his entire band; it served in the Pacific theater and played as many as four concerts a day in battle zones. Another naval band unit achieved a wide audience when it formed a small jazz ensemble called The Jive Bombers; they performed weekly at bond rallies and participated in parades and various Navy functions.

A third service branch, the U.S. Coast Guard, also boasted a celebrity. Singer Rudy Vallee joined in 1941 and led a 40-piece orchestra with great success. In 1944, they appeared in a 10-minute movie short titled *Rudy Vallee and His Coast Guard Band.*

The many military bands also could be heard on network radio. The Army, the Navy, and the Marines all boasted shows at one time or another. Servicewomen, not as visible as their male counterparts, but active nonetheless, also became involved in the musical side of the war. The Women's Army Auxiliary Corps, or WAACs, formed five all-female bands in 1943. At the close of World War II, however, the Army deactivated all women's bands, except one.

---

popular music did its part with "Rosie the Riveter" (words and music by Redd Evans and John Jacob Loeb). A minor hit, it nonetheless recognizes what had become an icon for the homefront war effort.

As more and more males entered the military, either by enlisting or thanks to the draft, women everywhere encountered a real shortage of men. "Girls, Don't Refuse to Kiss a Soldier" (1943; words and music by K. Davis), despite a double entendre in the lyrics, urges women to show affection for men in uniform; almost macabre, the words also suggest—given high casualties and long tours of duty—that it might be the only opportunity for a woman to make such overtures to military personnel, and a kiss would serve as a morale booster. "No Love, No Nothin'" (1943; music by Harry Warren, lyrics by Leo Robin) addresses this problem in a much more lighthearted way; a proper woman would remain faithful to her man in service, and no advances by any man—civilian or otherwise—should be countenanced. The tune enjoyed a hit recording by vocalist Ella Mae Morse. "No Love, No Nothin'" also received performances in three separate motion pictures: *Home in Indiana* (1943), *The Gang's All Here* (1943), and *Sweet and Low-Down* (1944).

In a similar way, "Nothing Can Replace a Man" (1944; words and music by Jerry Seelen and Lester Lee) expresses the obvious, and the humorous "They're Either Too Young or Too Old" (1943; music by Arthur Schwartz, lyrics by Frank Loesser) acknowledges the wartime scarcity of eligible males. The latter tune receives an unexpected rendition by Bette Davis, a star generally acclaimed for her dramatic abilities, not her vocal ones, in Hollywood's patriotic anthology *Thank Your Lucky Stars* (1943).

For the most part, however, the music industry responded to this issue of need with songs about loneliness. The dearth of men on the home front only heightened the awareness that millions of males served overseas, and countless tunes underscored this fact with romantic lyrics about couples separated by the war and the difficulties of sustaining a relationship under these circumstances. Typical titles include "I Wish That I Could Hide Inside This Letter" (1943; music by Nat Simon, lyrics by Charlie Tobias), "No Letter Today" (1943; words and music by Frankie Brown), "Tomorrow (When You Are Gone)" (1943; words and music by Margaret Kennedy and Erich Wolfgang Korngold), and "Wait for Me, Mary" (1943; music by Nat Simon and Charles Tobias, lyrics by Harry Tobias). In short, the songwriters continued to turn out the very slush the WMC wanted them to avoid.

Popular Music and Humor

Of course, not everything musical revolved around romance. The need for wartime secrecy even received some attention, albeit in a lighthearted vein. The popular Glenn Miller Orchestra featured a pleasant swing tune with "Shhh! It's a Military Secret" (1942; words and music by Alan Courtney, Earl Allvine, and Walter Bishop), although the "secret" turns out to be a profession of love. Playing on many of the slogans abounding about spies and saboteurs ("Careless Talk Kills," "Button Your Lip," "Don't Be a Blabber," etc.), the Duke Ellington aggregation added "A Slip of the Lip (Can Sink a Ship)" (1942;

words and music by Luther Henderson and Mercer Ellington) to its extensive repertoire. Few dancers would worry much about divulging vital information while jitterbugging to either number, but behind the up-tempo arrangements, there rests a serious message, especially at a time when German submarines continued to take a heavy toll of Allied shipping. Hardly big hits for these top-ranked bands, but they reflected, as did much music of the era, an awareness of current events. Plus, given the fact that both the Miller and Ellington aggregations recorded them, they generated some interest among swing fans.

In the early 1940s, a bandleader came along who injected a welcome dose of humor into his performances. He went by the name Spike Jones (but was born as Lindley Armstrong Jones in 1911), and he called his group the City Slickers, a play on the hillbilly music then receiving increased exposure, a format that often employed gags and costumes for effect, such as in the performances by the popular Hoosier Hot Shots. (See chapter 7, "Country Music," for more on this pioneering group.) Spike Jones and his City Slickers, usually attired in suits with outlandish patterns and colors, first achieved fame—or notoriety—for comic renditions of both original materials and old favorites.

It started with a 1942 cartoon from the Walt Disney studios titled *Donald Duck in Nutzi Land*. Before the film's release, a number from the animated feature, "Der Fuehrer's Face" (1942; words and music by Oliver Wallace), had already been heard on commercial recordings and radio, especially in a version arranged for Spike Jones. This satire on German dictator Adolf Hitler elicited an immediate—and favorable—response from the American public, and the Disney organization promptly renamed the cartoon, using the song's title.

The success of "Der Fuehrer's Face" cast Jones and his musicians as hot properties in the music business. Their unique instrumentation, such as so-called birdophones, klaxons, cowbells, pots and pans, washboards, and squeeze bulbs, delighted listeners, as did the band's unique skill in creating Bronx cheers, raspberries, and other impolite sounds. Red Ingle usually did the vocals during the early 1940s, and he possessed many voices.

Songs like "Little Bo-Peep Has Lost Her Jeep" (1942; words and music by Spike Jones and band members), "Siam" (1942; words and music by Del Porter), and "Hotcha Cornia" (1943; parody adaptation of a traditional 1800 Russian folk melody called "Otshi Tshornye" ["Dark Eyes"]) soon followed "Der Fuehrer's Face." "Hotcha Cornia" was featured in the aforementioned big-budget Hollywood musical *Thank Your Lucky Stars* (1943). Shortly thereafter, the group claimed two successful hits with "Cocktails for Two" (1944 [parody adaptation of a 1934 tune]; music by Sam Coslow, lyrics by Arthur Johnston) and "Chloe" (1945 [parody adaptation of a 1927 tune]; music by Gus Kahn, lyrics by Charles N. Daniels). Spike Jones and His City Slickers continued their shenanigans for years following World War II, and their absolute disregard for musical niceties kept them in the limelight and audiences laughing. In actuality, the Jones band was capable of playing straight music in a pleasing manner. His musicians possessed considerable versatility; to play an instrument humorously, the performer has to know how to play it well and correctly.

Johnny Mercer, one of the great American songwriters and lyricists, also brought occasional humor to composing. Throughout the war years and long thereafter, he created a remarkable body of work, and the majority of his accomplishments from the period 1939–1945 receive discussion in chapter 2, "Popular Hits and Standards." Only a few of Mercer's many sets of lyrics address the ongoing conflict directly, and when they do so, it is usually with humorous intent. At his best, he wrote the kind of music a majority of the public wanted and enjoyed.

Thus, when "The G.I. Jive" (1944; words and music by Johnny Mercer) came along, it only dealt with G.I.s and World War II in the most superficial way. A hip treatise on language patterns, or *jive,* by a master of easygoing lyrics, this 1944 entry amused much more than it informed. Mercer, then riding a crest of popularity for tunes that always pleased the ear and occasionally touched the heart, voiced the age-old complaints of servicemen everywhere. Not that he ignored the war. He occasionally referenced it, but usually in a humorous, slyly suggestive way, as in "He Loved Me Till the All-Clear Came" (1942; music by Harold Arlen, lyrics by Johnny Mercer). Innuendo, a trait his many fans clearly enjoyed, also plays a role in "I'm Doing It for Defense" (1942; music by Harold Arlen, lyrics by Johnny Mercer).

"Ac-Cen-Tchu-Ate the Positive" (1944; music by Harold Arlen, lyrics by Johnny Mercer), one of his big hits of the 1940s, boasts lyrics that urge people to keep up their spirits, that the dark days will pass. He even refers, humorously, to familiar stories from the Bible—Jonah in the whale, Noah in the ark—to boost his argument for optimism. A good businessman in addition to his considerable musical talents, in 1942, Mercer and two partners founded Capitol Records, a label that rocketed to popularity and soon became, along with Columbia, Decca, and RCA Victor, one of the major providers of popular music to an eager public during the war years and thereafter.[5] (More on Johnny Mercer can be found in chapter 2, "Popular Hits and Standards.")

Music with a touch of humor obviously held little appeal to government agencies that still dreamed of the ideal wartime song. The U.S. Army tried to lend a hand in making musical choices for its own active-duty personnel. Despite its honorable intentions, the Army's program fared little better than anything proposed by the Music War Committee. Beginning in March 1943, the Special Services branch of the Army put together what it called "Hit Kits," pocket-sized songbooks of music deemed appropriate for American soldiers to carry into battle. Sort of a printed military version of the popular *Your Hit Parade* radio show, along with a sampling of music from other genres and eras, these pamphlets of sheet music and lyrics, mailed out monthly a million at a time, stirred little enthusiasm among recipients.

The authorized sheet music usually consisted of some patriotic melodies that had already fizzled back home, an old favorite from the past, and some pedestrian pop numbers preapproved by committee. This last grouping might have engendered a tepid cheer or two, except the Hit Kits arrived so late at the front lines that their so called new songs were usually out of date. Plus, most soldiers could hear all the latest tunes on Armed Forces Radio, and shortwave broadcasts could deliver *Your Hit Parade* live. Discouraged, the Army cancelled the Hit Kits program in the summer of 1944, just over a year after it had initiated it.[6]

One bright spot in the military's effort to get music to servicemen and women around the world centered on the V-Disc program. Further details about this successful effort to distribute the latest hits without the problems of committees or censorship can be found in chapter 4, "Recordings and the Music Business."

1944–1945

With the dawn of 1944 and the sure scent of victory in the air, songwriters shifted their point of view somewhat. The loneliness remained, in songs like "Goodnight, Wherever You Are" (1944; words and music by Dick Robertson, Al Hoffman, and Frank Weldon), "I'll Walk Alone" (1944; music by Jule Styne, lyrics by Sammy Cahn), and "Since You Went Away" (1944; music by Ted Grouya and Lou Forbes, lyrics by Kermit Goell), but the thought of a loved one coming home reasonably soon also emerged as a theme, especially after the June 1944 invasion of Europe and the continuing success with the campaign of island hopping in the Pacific. By 1945, Americans everywhere anxiously awaited the eventual surrender of the Axis forces, although occasional setbacks still proved costly and delayed that momentous event.

"Counting the Days" (1945; words and music by Alex Kramer and Hy Zaret) summed up the hopes of the country, and "Waitin' for the Train to Come In" (1945; words and music by Sunny Skylar and Martin Block), along with "I'll Be Walkin' with My Honey (Soon, Soon, Soon)" (1945; music by Sam Medoff, lyrics by Buddy Kaye), voiced the impatience of most separated couples. "I Was Here When You Left Me (I'll Be Here When You Get Back)" (1945; words and music by Sam H. Stept), along with "I'm Coming Home" (1945; music by Lyn Murray, lyrics by Sylvia Golden), "Welcome Home" (1944; words and music by Tommie Tucker, Paul Cunningham, and Leonard Whitcup), "I'm Glad I Waited for You" (1945; music by Jule Styne, lyrics by Sammy Cahn), and "I'm Gonna Love That Guy [Gal] (Like He's [She's] Never Been Loved Before)"

(1945; words and music by Frances Ash), reflect the relief felt by everyone that the terrible war was inexorably drawing to a close. Even the irrepressible Spike Jones and his zanies had a song for the anticipated return of the troops: "Leave the Dishes in the Sink, Ma" (1945; words and music by Spike Jones, Milton Berle, and Gene Doyle).

The formal end to hostilities took time, however; Germany capitulated in early May of 1945, but Japan hung on for another three costly months, finally surrendering in August after a pair of atomic bombs demolished the cites of Hiroshima and Nagasaki. The Japanese resistance included two of the most ferocious actions of the entire war, the 1945 battles for the possession of the islands of Iwo Jima (February and March) and Okinawa (April and May). Both encounters received musical memorials: "Stars and Stripes on Iwo Jima Isle" (1945; words and music by Bob Wills and Clifton "Cactus Jack" Johnson) and "There's a New Flag On Iwo Jima" (1945; music by Jimmy McHugh, lyrics by Harold Adamson), plus "White Cross On Okinawa (1945; words and music by Bob Wills, Clifton "Cactus Jack" Johnson, and Cliff Sundin).

Within the folk music arena, Burl Ives popularized "Rodger Young" (1945; words and music by Frank Loesser), a story of a brave fighting man. Although few associate Tin Pan Alley composer Loesser with country or folk music, he demonstrated his versatility with this ballad. It recounts the life of a soldier who died heroically in 1943 on the island of New Georgia in the Solomon Islands; he posthumously received a Congressional Medal of Honor. Although the song did not advance to any hit charts at its release in March of 1945, *Life* magazine shortly thereafter devoted seven pages to a photo spread about the real Rodger Young, writer Loesser, and the song itself. At the same time, the Army organized the Combat Infantry Band to play this number specifically. All these ongoing events gave "Rodger Young" a much-needed boost and briefly made it a widely played composition among the crop of war-related songs.

Even the sheer destruction rained on the country's enemies (Japan, in this particular case) had its brief moment in "Dig You Later (A Hubba-Hubba-Hubba)" (1945; music by Jimmy McHugh, lyrics by Harold Adamson), when the lyrics mention the smoking ruins of Tokyo. Despite its humorous title rendered in contemporary slang, or *jive talk,* the tune would most likely be thought in poor or questionable taste today, but when seen in the context of the 1940s and a world at war, most Americans probably found such reminders entirely appropriate. None of these songs achieved any real hit status, but the mere fact they got recorded so late in the war and so close to victory suggests the publicity and national concern shown toward such intense fighting.

With the eventual surrender of Japan, American military actions came to an end after four grueling years. The musical reaction to peace ranged from the elation of "My Guy's Come Back" (1945; music by Mel Powell, lyrics by Ray McKinley) to the intimacy of "It's Been So Long, Darling" (1945; words and music by Ernest Tubb). The reunion of loved ones found delightful expression in "It's Been a Long, Long Time" (1945; music by Jule Styne, lyrics by Sammy Cahn). Adjustments to peacetime also challenged songwriters, with tunes like "When You Put on That Old Blue Suit Again" (1944; words and music by Robert Sour, Floria West, and Gordon Andrews), "Just a Blue Serge Suit" (1945; words and music by Irving Berlin), and "Reconversion Blues" (1945; words and music by Steve Graham and Fleecie Moore).

One final wartime song merits discussion. During World War I, a German soldier and poet named Hans Liep in 1915 composed some lines about a young sentry who sees a woman outside the gates of his garrison. The poem remained unnoticed until 1937, when another German, composer Norbert Schultze, set Liep's words, somewhat altered, to music. Schultze's song carried the title "Lili Marleen." Few people paid attention to the song, despite several recorded versions, and it languished until 1942, when German radio stations began broadcasting it with some regularity to troops in southern Europe and North Africa. Since radio recognizes few physical boundaries, Allied soldiers also heard the haunting melody on their receivers.

In short order, British soldiers took a liking to the tune and requested English lyrics for it. Unwittingly, the Nazis complied through propaganda broadcasts aimed at Allied forces. Their radio translation, sung by German vocalist Lale Andersen, contained a straight rendering of the Liep/Schultze lyrics, and the song took on a life of its own among British troops. An English songwriter, Tommie Connor, was recruited to create a commercially viable version of "Lili Marleen." In 1943, Connor's "Lili Marlene" came out on recording and proved especially popular in an interpretation by Vera Lynn, at that time the reigning wartime vocalist in England.

The popular American documentary film series, *The March of Time,* had in the meantime given the song its U.S. premiere in the spring of 1943. *Time* magazine (the sponsoring organization for *The March of Time*) also published an article about the work, and by 1944, American versions had begun to be heard on radio and records. It took, however, the talent and husky voice of entertainer Marlene Dietrich, herself German-born but a naturalized American citizen, to put the song over for U.S. audiences. Tirelessly performing it on USO (United Service Organizations) tours, personal appearances, and on radio broadcasts, Dietrich almost single-handedly established "Lili Marlene" as a popular wartime favorite. Lyricist Mack David receives credit for the American version, although a fictional "Phil Park" also occasionally gets mentioned as a co-songwriter/lyricist. Park, probably created by publishers for copyright reasons, given Connor's competing British music and the tune's German roots, later disappeared entirely from the credits.

Many world-famous entertainers appeared at wartime USO (United Service Organizations) events. Marlene Dietrich was no exception; here she poses in her USO uniform, wrapped in various national currencies. Courtesy of Photofest.

Its twisted history aside, "Lili Marlene" emerged as unique in the annals of wartime music. A favorite of friend and foe, its story of Lili, patiently awaiting—a glimpse? a conversation? a tryst?—with her soldier, touched lonely troops everywhere. Although it never topped the charts, it sold steadily as both sheet music and recordings. People worldwide knew the melody, a fact that made "Lili Marlene" possibly the most popular song directly related to World War II, and certainly, with its huge German-British-American military following, one of the few common denominators to be found in the conflict.[7]

CONCLUSION

Despite the attempts of well-meaning government officials, no one piece of martial music ever emerged as *the song* associated with World War II. A few earnest efforts were doubtless made by tunesmiths, but neither the civilian public nor the troops fighting the war ever responded to their labors in a positive way. Most war-related music slumped; a song might attract momentary attention, but it usually proved fleeting. Romance in all its forms, the slush so derided by those in authority, remained the people's choice, and the most successful compositions in this area seldom referred to the conflict at all. Much memorable music came out during the 1939–1945 era, and to succeed, it stuck to well-established traditions that seldom included topicality.

2

Popular Hits and Standards

BACKGROUND

For most Tin Pan Alley songsmiths, war or no war, business continued as usual. The public wanted traditional pop tunes about love in all its varieties, and record manufacturers and sheet music publishers, radio stations, and jukebox distributors wanted whatever the public bought. Federal bureaucrats might bemoan the absence of an all-purpose war song, but they made up a tiny minority and lacked much influence. So, with a few best-selling exceptions like the mainstream "Praise the Lord and Pass the Ammunition" (1942; words and music by Frank Loesser), "Comin' in on a Wing and a Prayer" (1942; music by Jimmy McHugh, lyrics by Harold Adamson), and the country song "There's a Star Spangled Banner Waving Somewhere" (1942; words and music by Paul Roberts and Shelby Darnell [pseudonym of Bob Miller]), few war-related numbers ever attracted much more than passing attention and mediocre sales.

Despite the paucity of stirring, patriotic music, the late 1930s and the World War II years witnessed a remarkable flow of enduring popular tunes. Many went on to become standards, those melodies and lyrics that transcend time and have left their imprint on the pages of the "Great American Songbook," a term that has gained considerable usage in the present. Latter-day crooners continue to perform "Over the Rainbow" (1939; music by Harold Arlen, lyrics by E. Y. Harburg) and "Bewitched (Bothered and Bewildered)" (1941; music by

Richard Rodgers, lyrics by Lorenz Hart); many a shower singer has lathered up while giving a rendition of "Oh, What a Beautiful Mornin'" (1943; music by Richard Rodgers, lyrics by Oscar Hammerstein II); and at the sight of the first winter flake, somebody somewhere will burst out with "Let It Snow! Let It Snow! Let It Snow!" (1945; music by Jule Styne, lyrics by Sammy Cahn).

How many twenty-first-century music lovers realize that these songs all date from the war years? Certainly, nothing in the lyrics gives any hint of the ongoing conflict, and melodically they fit the pattern of a typical pop composition. In other words, they have become standards.[1] A brief chronological survey of some, but hardly all, of the major popular songs from 1939–1945 follows.

After entertaining troops in a USO show, screen and recording star Judy Garland accepts a bouquet of flowers while accompanied by a smiling sergeant. Courtesy of Photofest.

1939

The honors for #1 song for the year fell to a bouncy novelty number, "Beer Barrel Polka" (1939; music by Jaramir Vejvoda, lyrics by Lew Brown and Wladimir A. Timm). This cheerful, up-tempo piece seemed to appeal to everyone, even those who had never danced a polka. Will Glahe's Musette Orchestra, which specialized in ethnic music, first made the charts with a Victor recording of the tune; most people probably became, in time, more familiar with the version cut by the then up-and-coming Andrews Sisters.[2]

The year also saw the movie release of MGM's classic *The Wizard of Oz* (1939). A perennial favorite ever since, many of the songs in the score, composed by Harold Arlen, with lyrics by E. Y. Harburg, became hits, such as "We're Off to See the Wizard," "If I Only Had a Brain," "Ding Dong, the Witch Is Dead," and "Follow the Yellow Brick Road." Topping them all, however, was "Over the Rainbow," the #2 song for the year. In the film, Judy Garland, playing Dorothy, cemented her fame for all time with her poignant soundtrack rendition of the tune. The movie came out in August, but the enormously popular Glenn Miller Orchestra, with Ray Eberle as the vocalist, jumped the gun by releasing a pressing of "Over the Rainbow" before the motion picture went into theaters and thus briefly had the one and only version. Since record buyers tended to purchase almost all of Miller's output, he took the #2 slot for the latter part of the year, and Judy Garland's interpretation did not gain its place on the charts until later. In the meantime, Bob Crosby's band, with singer Teddy Grace, also briefly came in ahead of Garland. Only with the passage of time did Garland's rendition become the definitive one, ultimately eclipsing any and all musical competition.[3]

THE *BILLBOARD* CHARTS

Launched in 1894 as *Billboard Advertising,* a monthly journal dedicated to the bill posting trade, the weekly magazine known today as *Billboard* gradually shifted its focus from outdoor advertising to the broader subjects of show business and amusements. In 1897, it became *The Billboard,* a name it would carry until 1961, when it went to its present one-word title. Celebrity gossip filled most of its pages, until the rise of phonograph recordings and radio broadcasting caused it to shift direction and emphasize popular music. The advertising support of the growing jukebox industry got it through the Great Depression. In 1936, the now-weekly periodical introduced its "Chart Line," a feature that listed the most played songs on the major radio networks.

Four years later, in its July 27, 1940, issue, the magazine ran its first "Best Selling Retail Records" chart, the forerunner of the many different song-tracking listings found in various media today. "I'll Never Smile Again," as performed by Tommy Dorsey with a vocal by Frank Sinatra, occupied the #1 position. *Billboard*'s new chart, along with radio's ongoing *Your Hit Parade,* thus gave fans and those in the music industry an easy, weekly means of following trends and best sellers on a nationwide basis.

During the 1940s, *Billboard* premiered several additional tracking features: in 1942, it introduced the first chart of black music, "Harlem Hit Parade"; it also had "Disks with Most Radio Plugs," a chart that shifted to "Records Most Played on the Air" in 1945. "Most-Played in Juke Boxes" came along in 1944, as did its "Folk Records" category, the latter in recognition of the rising popularity of country music. This chart changed to "Hillbilly" in 1947 and finally evolved into the more inclusive "Country and Western" in 1949. With its proliferation of charts tracking the fortunes of many types of music, *Billboard* became the leading source for reliable information on the industry, a position it continues to hold today.

As proof of the remarkable appeal of the Miller aggregation, in 1939, the band held down five of the top-10 slots in the *Billboard* charts: #2, "Over the Rainbow"; #6, "Moon Love" (1939 [adapted from a theme in Tchaikovsky's *Fifth Symphony*]; music by Andre Kostelanetz, lyrics by Mack Davis and Mack David); #7, "Wishing (Will Make It So)" (1939; words and music by Buddy Desylva); #8, "Stairway to the Stars" (1935, 1939; music by Matty Malneck and Frank Signorelli, lyrics by Mitchell Parish); and #9, "The Man with the Mandolin" (1939; music by Frank Weldon, lyrics by James Cavanaugh and John Redmond). No other band came close to their popularity at the time, although contemporary charts of hits can prove misleading. That same year, Miller's orchestra also recorded "Moonlight Serenade" (1939; music by Glenn Miller, lyrics by Mitchell Parish), a tune widely associated with the group, but one that failed to make the national rankings. "Wishing (Will Make It So)," however, a lesser effort and virtually forgotten today, climbed to seventh place on the strength of the bandleader's name.

If Judy Garland owns "Over the Rainbow," then jazz vocalist Billie Holiday certainly does likewise with "Strange Fruit" (1939; words and music by Lewis Allan [pseudonym of Abel Meeropol]). Only a minor hit in 1939 on a small, independent label, it has taken on a life of its own as a social commentary. Abel Meeropol, a New York schoolteacher who hated the barbaric practice of lynching, first wrote "Strange Fruit" (the title refers to a body hanging from a tree) as a poem. Based on a photograph he saw of two victims, the poet eventually set his words to music.

Meeropol showed the lyrics to a dubious Holiday, who tried it out at several nightclubs. The enthusiastic crowd responses led her to attempt a recording. Columbia, her parent label, wanted nothing to do with such a controversial topic; the company did, however, give Holiday permission to record the song for Milt Gabler's pioneering Commodore Records. Musical artists, just like movie stars in those days, often labored under binding contracts. Because he had longtime connections with the Communist Party and might be seen as a rabble-rouser in some eyes, Meeropol gets listed as "Lewis Allan" in the credits, a move aimed at defusing criticism of the composition because of the author's politics. Over the years, the furor over "Strange Fruit" has died down, and a number of other musicians have attempted it, notably Nina Simone in 1972. In its original 1939 format, however, the song remains a Billie Holiday classic.

Among the many other tunes that premiered during the year, "Dawn of a New Day" (1939; music by George Gershwin, lyrics by Ira Gershwin and Kay Swift) merits brief mention. Hardly the greatest tune of 1939, it represents the last work by renowned composer George Gershwin. Although he had died in 1937, he left enough information and notation in his papers that this composition could be pieced together. His brother Ira and Kay Swift did the adaptation and supplied the lyrics. The result became the official song of the 1939–1940 New York World's Fair, ensuring that hundreds of thousands of people eventually heard it.

From the theatrical side of things, the famous writing team of (Richard) Rodgers (music) and (Lorenz) Hart (lyrics) continued their winning ways with "I Didn't Know What Time It Was," a romantic ballad from their Broadway show *Too Many Girls.* Widely recorded over time, and considered a prime example of the duo's work, it made no real dent in the charts during its initial release, a fate not uncommon to standards when initially released. Like fine wines, many of them improve with age and find the public they possibly lacked when they initially appeared. (See Appendix B, "The Songs, Composers, and Lyricists of World War II, 1939–1945," for a more complete listing of the popular songs written during these years.)

1940

An eerie mood of unreality descended on the nation in 1940. Following the invasion of Poland in September of 1939, the German army appeared unbeatable. The European continent collapsed before the combined onslaughts of the *Wehrmacht* and the *Luftwaffe,* and only England held out. In the United States, however, the America First organization, dedicated to keeping the country out of war, gained significant support, and people escaped the headlines with radio shows and movies, along with a rich menu of music that focused on romance, not defense.

"In the Mood" (1939; music by Joe Garland, lyrics by Andy Razaf), a dancer's delight, led the pack. It actually came out in late 1939 and, as performed by the Glenn Miller Orchestra, remained on the *Billboard* charts for 28 weeks in 1940, including 13 weeks at the vaunted #1 position. The clouds of war might be gathering, but America's musical preferences gave no indication of the fact.

Although Glenn Miller dominated the big-band scene, he did not lack for rivals. Clarinetist Artie Shaw, whose best-selling recording of "Begin the Beguine" (1935; words and music by Cole Porter) first came out in 1938, found that his version of the song continued to sell well throughout the war years. Not content to rest on his laurels, Shaw won the #2 position with another danceable number, "Frenesi" (1940; music by Alberto Dominguez, lyrics by Sidney K. Russell and Ray Charles). As a side note, William Grant Still, the distinguished American composer, supplied Shaw with the orchestral arrangement

In February 1945, vocalist Frank Sinatra reported to his local draft board in Jersey City, New Jersey, for a preinduction physical examination (shown here). He received a 4-F classification because of a perforated ear drum. Library of Congress, Prints & Photographs Division.

for this particular composition. (See chapter 8, "Classical Music," for more on Still.)

The year 1940 also marked the popular emergence of Johnny Mercer, a multitalented singer, songwriter, and, most importantly, lyricist. Although he had done considerable work of distinction throughout the 1930s—"I'm Building Up to an Awful Let-Down" (1935), "I'm an Old Cowhand" (1936), "Bob White" (1937), "Hooray for Hollywood" (1938), among many others—the opening of the new decade marked his rise to the top tier of American popular music. During 1940, he supplied the lyrics for "Fools Rush In (Where Angels Fear to Tread)" (music by Rube Bloom), "I'd Know You Anywhere" (music by Jimmy McHugh), "Mister Meadowlark" (music by Walter Donaldson), and the totally forgotten "On Behalf of the Visiting Firemen" (music by Walter Donaldson). This last tune Mercer recorded in a 1940 duet with his friend Bing Crosby, and the two give the lyrics a humorous reading.

No other major lyricist equaled Mercer's prodigious output during the war years. One memorable song after another flowed from his pen, and his fame and influence allowed him, in 1942, to create, along with two other individuals, Capitol Records, a major new record label. This move guaranteed him a venue for his own music, plus that of hundreds of other artists.[4]

Of course, Johnny Mercer cannot be thought the only significant figure in American popular music. Singing cowboys, who constituted almost a subgenre of movie Westerns, began to make inroads on mainstream tastes and preferences. Gene Autry emerged as one of the most popular of the many cowboy performers, and in late 1939, he starred in *Rovin' Tumbleweeds,* one of countless low-budget Westerns that Republic Pictures put out in the 1930s and 1940s. In the film, Autry gets to sing "Back in the Saddle Again" (1940; words and music by Gene Autry and Ray Whitley), a tune destined to become his virtual theme song, one that enjoyed respectable sales throughout the nation. Although it did not make the top-40 lists, its relative success demonstrated the growing influence and popularity of country-style music. (See chapter 7, "Country Music," for more on the growth of this genre.)

"I'll Never Smile Again" (1940; words and music by Ruth Lowe) marked the ascendancy of another entertainer who would loom large for much of the remainder of the twentieth century: Frank Sinatra. The youthful crooner had already elicited headlines because of his personal appearances as a vocalist with the Tommy Dorsey band. Teenagers, or *bobby soxers,* as many called them, made him their new musical rage, and their screams and swoons when he came on stage presaged the later reactions of adolescents toward celebrities like Elvis Presley and the Beatles.

Sinatra had sung briefly with Harry James and his orchestra in 1939, leaving the group at the end of the year for a more lucrative contract with Dorsey. His first hit with his new employer was this romantic tune, and it took third place in the 1940 charts. A lush ballad, it suited Sinatra's baritone well and furthered his rising fame. His skill at intonation gave any ballad an intimate quality, a talent that would make him a rival to Bing Crosby, at the time the leading crooner in popular music. Many more hits would come from Sinatra, but "I'll Never Smile Again" signaled the real beginning of his lengthy career.

Finally, Walt Disney and his associates released a new cartoon feature in 1940 called *Pinocchio*. Based on the classic 1883 children's story by Carlo Collodi, it proved an immediate box office success. In addition to the splendid artwork by then associated with the studio, the movie also claims an exceptional score, created by the team of composer Leigh Harline and lyricist Ned Washington. One tune in particular, "When You Wish Upon a Star" (1940), captured the fancy of everyone, young and old. Sung on-screen by the diminutive Jiminy Cricket (actually the voice of Cliff Edwards, better known as Ukulele Ike, a popular entertainer of the era), it climbed the Billboard charts, and Glenn Miller's orchestra also made a successful recording of the tune. It went on to win an Academy Award for Best Song in 1940. The movie also boasted "Hi-Diddle-Dee-Dee," "Give a Little Whistle" (1940; both by Harline and Washington), and other favorites.

1941

The false peace of 1940 carried over into 1941. Men were drafted into the growing military forces, American industry turned increasingly to armaments, and Lend-Lease doled out desperately needed supplies to beleaguered Britain, but the United States continued in its attempts to stay neutral and out of the deepening crisis engulfing much of the world. Not until the end of the year, the seventh of December, to be exact, did everything change. With the attack on Pearl Harbor, the country threw off its last pretensions to neutrality and prepared to wage full-scale war in both the Atlantic and Pacific theaters. But a glance at the popular musical choices of the American public would suggest that nothing out of the ordinary had happened. It should be remembered, however, that the Japanese attack did not occur until December, and so most of the year's music predates the nation's actual entry into the conflict.

On the musical front, people hummed the strains of "Amapola (Pretty Little Poppy)" (1941; music by Joseph M. Lacalle, lyrics by Albert Gamse). The successful revival of a tune first popularized in 1924, Jimmy Dorsey, the saxophone-playing brother to trombonist Tommy, claimed the hit version of the song and with it the #1 spot for the year. Dorsey's band vocalists, Bob Eberly and Helen O'Connell, sang the lyrics. The widespread acceptance of this number clearly intimated that listeners wanted no reminders of the increasingly gloomy world situation.

Close behind "Amapola" came Glenn Miller's rendition of "Chattanooga Choo Choo" (1941; music by Harry Warren, lyrics by Mack Gordon), another completely nontopical tune. In Miller's hands, it became a million-seller for Bluebird Records, the parent label for the band. The recording industry deemed this achievement significant enough that in early 1942, it awarded Miller a gold record for breaking the million sales mark, the first instance that

Novelty songs have always been a part of American popular music; the nonsense lyrics of "The Hut-Sut Song" made it a big hit for a brief time in 1941. Freddie Martin (shown here) was one of many bandleaders performing and recording this "Swedish Serenade." Picture by William H. Young.

this ritual, since then often repeated, occurred. At the time of the ceremony, the United States had thrust itself into the conflict, battles raged abroad, and yet music executives felt comfortable calling time-out for their celebration, a brief public morale booster of sorts.

Audiences had first heard "Chattanooga Choo Choo" on the soundtrack of *Sun Valley Serenade* (1941), a 20th Century Fox musical extravaganza that features skater Sonja Henie, the dancing Nicholas Brothers, a sparkling score by composer Harry Warren and lyricist Mack Gordon, and, of course, the full Miller orchestra. Shot on location at the relatively new—it opened in 1936—skiing resort in Sun Valley, Idaho, the cheerful picture substitutes music for plotting. In addition to "Chattanooga Choo Choo," the band performs such Miller hits as "Moonlight Serenade" (1939; music by Glenn Miller, lyrics by Mitchell Parish), "In the Mood" (1940; music by Joe Garland, lyrics by Andy Razaf), "At Last" (1942; music by Harry Warren, lyrics by Mack Gordon), plus a number of other favorites. During the 1930s and 1940s, a good original movie score often translated into substantial airplay and availability as a jukebox selection, which then produced strong record and sheet music sales.

In the meantime, the unanticipated popularity of "Amapola" sent publishers scurrying for other Latin tunes, especially in light of the ASCAP (American Society of Composers, Authors, and Producers) versus BMI (Broadcast Music Incorporated) feud then ongoing. Songs written in South America usually did not bear the ASCAP stamp and could therefore be played on radio. Jimmy Dorsey capitalized on this loophole and soon recorded additional Latin hits like "Green Eyes" ("Aquellos Ojos Verdes," 1941; music by Nilo Menendez, lyrics by Adolfo Utrera, E. Rivera, and Eddie Woods), "Maria Elena" (1941 [popular revival of a 1933 tune]; words and music by S. K. Russell, Lorenzo Barcalata, and William H. Heagney), and "Yours" ("Quiereme Mucho," 1941 [popular revival of a 1931 song]; music by Gonzalo Roig, lyrics by Augustin Rodriguez, English adaptation by Jack Sherr). Thus, during much of 1941, the airwaves often carried the sounds of the country's southern neighbors. (See chapter 4, "Recordings and the Music Business," for details on this dispute.)

Capitalizing on Latin themes, the team of Harry Warren and Mack Gordon (neither of whom had any discernable South American roots) made a 1941 return with another 20th Century Fox musical called *That Night in Rio*. Carmen Miranda, an exuberant Brazilian performer, steals the show whenever she comes in range of a camera. Noted for her outlandish costumes, especially "tutti-frutti" hats, usually piled high with colorful and exotic edibles, Miranda sings and dances to some quasi-Latin Warren-Gordon numbers, including "I Yi Yi Yi Yi (I Like You Very Much)" (1941) and "Chica Chica Boom Chic" (1941). Between 1940 and 1944, she starred in nine American feature films, creating, in the process, an inimitable character beloved by a generation of movie fans.

If the music of South America can produce hits, why not that of Scandinavia? With that kind of thinking, "The Hut-Sut Song (A Swedish Serenade)" (1941 [popular revival of a 1939 song]; words and music by the decidedly un-Scandinavian team of Jack Owens, Leo V. Killion, and Ted McMichael) made a second appearance, since it had done little in its 1939 debut. A nonsense composition, not an authentic folk song, it commences with the words "Hut Sut Rawlson on the Rillerah" and goes from there. It existed as a fun tune and one that many groups wanted to record, perhaps just to see if they could do it. Well-known bands, such as those led by Freddy Martin, Sammy Kaye, and Horace Heidt, cut versions, as did comedian Eddie Cantor, and vocal groups like the King Sisters, the King's Men, and the Merry Macs, a popular close harmony quartet. Freddy Martin's and Horace Heidt's interpretations even made the charts during the early summer, but like most novelties, the bubble burst, and today "The Hut-Sut Song" survives primarily as a curiosity from the early 1940s, although many people can still recall the tongue-twisting lyrics.

In contrast, "My Ship" (1941; music by Kurt Weill, lyrics by Ira Gershwin) can easily claim to be one of the loveliest songs of the war years. A standard today, "My Ship" brought together the gifted German composer Kurt Weill and the astute lyric sense of Ira Gershwin. Composed as part of the score for the 1941 Broadway production of *Lady in the Dark,* the song matched the talents of star Gertrude Lawrence. When the play made a transfer to the movies in 1944, Ginger Rogers also did the number justice. On records, countless singers have since performed "My Ship," giving it a life far beyond the confines of stage or screen.

Johnny Mercer continued his winning ways with lyrics for "Blues in the Night" (1941) and "This Time the Dream's on Me" (1941; both with music by Harold Arlen). These two classics first attracted attention in the 1941 film *Blues in the Night* but quickly outgrew their cinematic beginnings, becoming hits in their own right. He also penned both the words and music for the humorous "The Waiter and the Porter and the Upstairs Maid" (1941). Bing Crosby and Mary Martin performed it in *The Birth of the Blues,* a 1941 musical from Paramount Pictures. But these efforts all seemed mere rehearsals when compared to what he would produce the following year.

At the same time, Frank Sinatra demonstrated that he could go beyond just crooning romantic ballads. With Tommy Dorsey behind him, he created a moderately up-tempo rendition of "Oh! Look at Me Now" (1941; music by Joe Bushkin, lyrics by John DeVries). It did well on the charts, and he also recorded a popular version of "Dolores" (1941; music by Louis Alter, lyrics by Frank Loesser). With "This Love of Mine" (1941; music by Sol Parker and Harry Sanicola, lyrics by Frank Sinatra), the vocalist both contributed the lyrics and sang them, suggesting his talents exceeded merely standing in front of a microphone.

Crooner Bing Crosby (with pipe) and dancer Fred Astaire (in helmet) ham it up during a 1944 USO show in France. Entertainers were frequently close behind the troops throughout the war. Library of Congress, Prints & Photographs Division.

1942

A continuing string of Axis victories heightened the earnestness of the American war effort as the country realized, perhaps for the first time, just how serious the conflict would be. Citizens buckled down to the enormous task ahead—nothing less than total victory—and songwriters assuaged their worries with a menu filled with cheerful love songs and assorted other melodies that usually ignore any references to the war. The music industry also offered a number of patriotic flag-wavers, but they usually fell short in sales, suggesting that people did not relish reminders of the battles being waged overseas. (See chapter 1, "Music about World War II," for more information about the songs that directly addressed the conflict.)

Irving Berlin, as versatile a songwriter as any Tin Pan Alley has ever produced, had previously pumped up the country's spirits with his rousing "God Bless America" in 1938, a remarkable revival of a tune he originally penned in 1917. In many ways, especially airplay and record sales, this song served as the national anthem for the duration of the war. In the dark days of 1942, he put together an upbeat Broadway show called *This Is the Army,* a stage production that quickly went to celluloid in 1943. (See chapter 6, "Music on Stage and Screen," for further discussion about both versions.)

In addition to these obviously war-related efforts, Berlin, who probably touched more patriotic nerves than any other songwriter of the era, in 1942, composed the words and music for a lighthearted motion picture called *Holiday Inn.* A tale about an implausible lodge that opens only for specific holidays, it stars Fred Astaire and Bing Crosby, then two of the biggest male names in movies. The score includes "Be Careful! It's My Heart" (1942), "You're Easy to Dance With" (1942), plus some earlier chestnuts Berlin managed to interpolate into the story. But during the course of the plot, Crosby gets to croon a new Berlin offering, "White Christmas." Hardly a war song, in the context of the film, its wistful lyrics have the singer dreaming of a white Christmas, one that he probably will not experience firsthand. Given the war, however, the song turned out to be the perfect vehicle for summarizing the feelings of troops far from home as well as the hopes of their loved ones back in the States, although Berlin more than likely did not intend for that reaction. In point of fact, he composed the tune in 1940, well before Pearl Harbor and the country's entry into the conflict.

Crosby had introduced "White Christmas" on his *Kraft Music Hall* radio show on December 25, 1941, but it elicited little attention and failed to be recorded at the time. Months later, the movie had its U.S. premiere in the late summer of 1942, followed by a Decca recording taken from the soundtrack. The picture enjoyed immediate box office success and became a Christmas favorite, even though it hit theaters long before the start of the holiday season. The studio had not marketed *Holiday Inn* as a Christmas movie since the picture recognized a number of other traditional holidays in the course of its story. But by October, Crosby's recording had rocketed up the charts, quickly establishing itself as the #1 song for 1942, and its good fortune did not end with the start of a new year.

In 1943 and 1944, Berlin's composition continued to sell at a remarkable clip, and in 1945, three years later, it still showed up at #13; in 1946, it continued its winning ways with a respectable #20 on the *Billboard* charts. Because of unprecedented demand, Decca wore out the master, and in 1947, Crosby had to re-record this perennial favorite, note for note, to create a fresh copy. Over a period of 58 years, "White Christmas" established itself as the best-selling single of the twentieth century, with some 100 million copies sold both in the United States and abroad. It remains a seasonal favorite even today.[5]

For 1942, "Moonlight Cocktail" (music by Lucky Roberts, lyrics by Kim Gannon) took second-place honors. Not surprisingly, the ever-popular Glenn Miller and his orchestra, with a vocal by Ray Eberle, boasted the hit version.

His band also held down #4 with "(I've Got a Gal in) Kalamazoo" (1942; music by Harry Warren, lyrics by Mack Gordon) and #7 with "A String of Pearls" (1941; music by Jerry Gray, lyrics by Eddie De Lange). Although all three tunes have long sustained their popularity with swing fans, none of them at the time approached "White Christmas" in sales or emotional impact with the general public.

In the fall of 1942, a little-heralded film titled *The Forest Rangers* went into general theatrical release. In the course of the movie, an action picture about forest fires and the men who fight them, a chorus sings "(I've Got Spurs That) Jingle Jangle Jingle" (1942; music by Joseph J. Lilley, lyrics by Frank Loesser). A number of artists subsequently recorded it for 1943, and several had hits with its catchy Western themes. Kay Kyser's band, one seldom associated with anything remotely Western, came away with the #3 song for the year. It featured a vocal shared by Harry Babbitt and Julie Conway. The Merry Macs also did well with the number, further suggesting that Western tunes enjoyed a large audience, larger than most people in the music business suspected.

Johnny Mercer enjoyed an almost miraculous streak of successes in 1942. Below is a listing of 16 notable songs (he wrote others) that bore his signature that year. Primarily romantic or lightly humorous tunes, along with a smattering of war-related efforts, they suggest the range of his skills as a songwriter. Alphabetically, his partial 1942 output includes the following:

"Arthur Murray Taught Me Dancing in a Hurry" (1942; music by Victor Schertzinger, lyrics by Johnny Mercer); performed by Betty Hutton in the film *The Fleet's In* (1942)

"Dearly Beloved" (1942; music by Jerome Kern, lyrics by Johnny Mercer); performed by Fred Astaire in the film *You Were Never Lovelier* (1942)

"He Loved Me Till the All-Clear Came" (1942; music by Harold Arlen, lyrics by Johnny Mercer); performed by Betty Hutton in the film *Star Spangled Rhythm* (1942)

"Hit the Road to Dreamland" (1942; music by Harold Arlen, lyrics by Johnny Mercer); performed by Mary Martin and Dick Powell in the film *Star Spangled Rhythm* (1942)

"I Remember You" (1942; music by Victor Schertzinger, lyrics by Johnny Mercer); performed by Dorothy Lamour and others in the film *The Fleet's In* (1942)

"I'm Doing It for Defense" (1942; music by Harold Arlen, lyrics by Johnny Mercer); performed by Betty Hutton in the film *Star Spangled Rhythm* (1942)

"I'm Old Fashioned" (1942; music by Jerome Kern, lyrics by Johnny Mercer); performed by Rita Hayworth and Fred Astaire in the film *You Were Never Lovelier* (1942)

"Mandy Is Two" (1942; music by Fulton McGrath, lyrics by Johnny Mercer)

"Old Glory" (1942; music by Harold Arlen, lyrics by Johnny Mercer); performed by Bing Crosby in the film *Star Spangled Rhythm* (1942)

"On the Swing Shift" (1942; music by Harold Arlen, lyrics by Johnny Mercer); performed by Dona Drake in the film *Star Spangled Rhythm* (1942)
"Sharp As a Tack" (1942; music by Harold Arlen, lyrics by Johnny Mercer); performed by a chorus in the film *Star Spangled Rhythm* (1942)
"Skylark" (1942; music by Hoagy Carmichael, lyrics by Johnny Mercer)
"The Strip Polka" (1942; words and music by Johnny Mercer)
"Tangerine" (1942; music by Victor Schertzinger, lyrics by Johnny Mercer); performed by Bob Eberly and Helen O'Connell in the film *The Fleet's In* (1942)
"That Old Black Magic" (1942; music by Harold Arlen, lyrics by Johnny Mercer); performed by Johnny Johnston in the film *Star Spangled Rhythm* (1942)
"You Were Never Lovelier" (1942; music by Jerome Kern, lyrics by Johnny Mercer); performed by Fred Astaire in the 1942 film of the same name

Most of the above-listed songs have come down to the present as standards. Certainly "Hit the Road to Dreamland," "I'm Old Fashioned," "Skylark," and "That Old Black Magic" continue to draw enthusiastic fans, and Mercer himself worked with the best composers of the day, collaborating with the likes of Jerome Kern, Hoagy Carmichael, Harold Arlen, and others. Since he did most of his writing on the West Coast, Mercer developed contacts within the movie industry; thus the disproportionate number of songs in the above listing that come from motion pictures. Given his many successes, little wonder also that he has come down to the present as the dean of lyricists for the 1940s.

Many other popular songs and artists likewise had their moments in 1942—vocalist Dick Haymes, along with the Benny Goodman band, doing "Idaho" (1942; words and music by Jesse Stone); Frank Sinatra, with Tommy Dorsey, crooning "Lamplighter's Serenade" (1942; music by Hoagy Carmichael, lyrics by Paul Francis Webster); "Lover Man (Oh, Where Can You Be?)" (1942; words and music by Jimmy Davis, Ram Ramirez, and Jimmy Sherman) as interpreted by Billie Holiday; actor-dancer Ray Bolger singing "Nobody's Heart" (1942; music by Richard Rodgers, lyrics by Lorenz Hart), from the musical *By Jupiter;* Glenn Miller again, with Ray Eberle on the vocal, playing "Serenade in Blue" (1942; music by Harry Warren, lyrics by Mack Gordon); and Harry James, his trumpet and his band, performing on both "Sleepy Lagoon" (1942 [popular revival of a 1930 song]; music by Eric Coates, lyrics by Jack Lawrence) and "Mister Five by Five" (1942; music by Gene DePaul, lyrics by Don Raye). All in all, despite the gloomy headlines, a music-filled year.

1943

In January of 1943, the tide of war showed an almost imperceptible shift. The Allies increasingly changed from defensive to offensive operations, but on the home front, the government nevertheless extended the ages for Selective

Service eligibility, factories were ordered to operate a minimum of 48 hours a week, and the casualty lists kept growing. The road to victory might hold some promise, but getting there would be grim.

Such a mix of gloom and faint hope influenced musical tastes little; the #1 hit for 1943 turned out to be "I've Heard That Song Before" (1943; music by Jule Styne, lyrics by Sammy Cahn), a cheerful composition by a songwriting team that would have many more successes. Harry James, riding high after a rousing 1942 season, recorded it, with Helen Forrest doing the vocal honors. The tune had actually been performed some months earlier in a 1942 movie musical called *You on Parade;* Margaret Whiting's voice can be heard on the soundtrack singing the lyrics.

Right behind "I've Heard That Song Before," in the #2 slot, stood a popular revival of a 1915 composition, "Paper Doll" (1943 [originally 1915]; words and music by Johnny S. Black). The Mills Brothers—John, Herbert, Harry, Donald—a vocal quartet that had been around since the 1920s, capitalized on the restrictions on instruments imposed during the 1942–1943 recording ban. If one listens carefully to their version of "Paper Doll," he or she will be struck that, other than a few chords strummed on a guitar, no horns, no pianos, and no drums can be discerned. Furthermore, the absence of instrumentation takes nothing away from their performance; casual listeners will not even be aware of it. (See chapter 4, "Recordings and the Music Business," for more details on the recording ban.)

Most recorded performances, however, still utilized bands or combos, since the companies knew the ban was coming and stockpiled music of all descriptions. As their backlog of prerecorded material ran thin, they turned to reissues of older recordings or, as with the Mills Brothers, a cappella performances from their stables of vocal performers.

Benny Goodman, the "King of Swing" and a powerful force in American dance music during the later 1930s, returned to the charts in January with "Why Don't You Do Right?" (1943 [popular revival of a 1939 song]; words and music by Joe McCoy). Aside from being a hit, Goodman's rendition served to acquaint the public with a young singer destined to have a long and successful career: Peggy Lee. At home with pop tunes and jazz, Lee soon thereafter left the Goodman band and became an important performing and recording artist under her own name.

With the approach of the 1943 holiday season, the success of Irving Berlin's "White Christmas" in 1942 led producers to search for similar numbers that might also appeal to the public. No one held out false hopes that a rival to Berlin's masterpiece would come along, but "I'll Be Home for Christmas" (1943; music by Walter Kent, lyrics by Kim Gannon and Buck Ram) made a respectable showing for the year, topping the charts at #23. For many holiday seasons thereafter, this nostalgic offering attracted substantial sales, and it continues to show up in various Christmas anthologies. "I'll Be Home for Christmas" enjoyed the added bonus of having Bing Crosby—who had also sung "White Christmas"—as the number's vocalist. Reflecting the sadness felt by many Americans, both those with loved ones in service and those far away longing to be home, the title effectively summarizes the dilemma faced by millions during wartime.

Placing a respectable #20 on the 1943 charts, "As Time Goes By" (1943 [popular revival of a 1931 song]; words and music by Herman Hupfield) again demonstrated the effect a successful movie could have on record purchases. *Casablanca* (1943), a Humphrey Bogart/Ingrid Bergman vehicle, turned out to be an unexpected hit. Since then, it has attained cult status and lives on in late-night television and VHS and DVD rentals and sales. "As Time Goes By," a tune that supplies a major thematic element in the story, has become inseparable from the motion picture. It stands as one of those love songs that speaks to romantics everywhere. When someone says (in a slightly inaccurate quotation from the movie), "Play it again, Sam," it is assumed that the listener knows that *it* refers to "As Time Goes By."

Originally written by Herman Hupfield in 1931 as part of the score for a minor Broadway show called *Everybody's Welcome,* "As Time Goes By" had little impact at the time of the theatrical production. Bandleader and singer Rudy Vallee, who enjoyed great popularity in the 1930s, recorded it, as did several other artists, but the song eventually sank from sight. Not until Warner Bros. decided to produce *Casablanca* did director Michael Curtiz decide to use some older popular tunes for background music to accompany the story. Audiences get to hear "It Had to Be You" (1931; music by Isham Jones, lyrics by Gus Kahn), "Shine" (1910; music by Ford Dabney, lyrics by Lew Brown and Cecil Mack), "The Very Thought of You" (1934; words and music by Ray Noble), and several other well-known melodies, but all anyone remembers from the film is "As Time Goes By." Since *Casablanca*'s release, the song has been recorded countless times, and Rudy Vallee's 1931 effort, reissued in conjunction with the movie's success, enjoyed a far better second life in 1943. "As Time Goes By" will doubtless continue to be a staple in any collections featuring romantic themes.

The year 1943 also saw the first theatrical production by the new writing team of Richard Rodgers and Oscar Hammerstein II. Rodgers' previous partner, Lorenz Hart, died that year, thus ending the fruitful pairing long known as Rodgers and Hart, a collaboration that dated back to the time of World War I. *Oklahoma!* served as the initial Broadway offering by Rodgers and Hammerstein, and it wowed everyone, critics and audiences alike.

A show that made theatrical history, it ran for an unprecedented 2,212 performances, or five years and nine months. Out of it came five hits, with "People Will Say We're in Love" (1943; music by Richard Rodgers, lyrics by

Oscar Hammerstein II) leading the pack. Both Bing Crosby and Frank Sinatra appeared on the *Billboard* charts with this number. But "Oh, What a Beautiful Mornin'" (1943), "The Surrey with the Fringe on Top" (1943), the title song "Oklahoma!" (1943), and "I Cain't Say No" (1943; all the foregoing with music by Richard Rodgers, lyrics by Oscar Hammerstein II) also performed well. Although no one might blink an eye at a musical having a song or two in the listings of current hits, to have five at one time was highly unusual and a testament to the skills of the songwriting duo. They would not disappoint; they would do eight more shows after *Oklahoma!* and all would be hits and contain memorable music. For the 1943–1945 period, their next Broadway success would be *Carousel* in 1945. (See chapter 6, "Music on Stage and Screen," for more on both *Casablanca* and the rise of Rodgers and Hammerstein.)

In late 1943, *Billboard* magazine, witnessing the success of several Western-oriented tunes, decided to create a new chart to broaden its coverage when tracking the rise and fall of popular songs. Calling the addition "Folk Music," the journal designed it to illustrate the commercial fortunes of folk and country tunes; in addition, its 1944 introduction reflected the growing interest in and viability of music within these genres. "Pistol Packin' Mama" (1943; words and music by Al Dexter), an up-tempo, humorous narrative, received the honor of being the first #1 hit in this new category. To have a title that better fit changing tastes, *Billboard,* in 1949, renamed its "Folk" entry "Country and Western."

And what was Johnny Mercer doing in 1943? Although he did not, and probably could not, repeat his banner year of 1942, he nonetheless contributed the lyrics for "My Shining Hour" (music by Harold Arlen), "One for My Baby (and One More for the Road)" (music by Harold Arlen), "The Old Music Master" (music by Hoagy Carmichael), and "Trav'lin' Light" (music by Jimmy Mundy and Trummy Young). Standards all, the two pieces he created with composer Harold Arlen appear in *The Sky's the Limit* (1943), an RKO musical.

The Sky's the Limit stars Fred Astaire, and during the course of the movie, he introduces the Arlen-Mercer classic, "One for My Baby (and One More for the Road)." But Astaire's rendition has, over the years, been overshadowed by Frank Sinatra's subsequent identification with the number. Yet Sinatra did not initially record "One for My Baby (and One More for the Road)" until four years later. He would later cut better-known versions of the tune, but not until the 1950s and after. What merits attention for Astaire in *The Sky's the Limit* involves both singing and dancing. He not only does a fine job with Mercer's lyrics, but he simultaneously dances atop a bar while smashing cocktail glasses in time with his steps and words. Astaire or Sinatra, "One for My Baby (and One More for the Road)" has transcended time, emerging as possibly the ultimate saloon song and one of Mercer's most memorable efforts, yet another 1940s song that has absolutely nothing to do with World War II.

1944

In the war zones, the pendulum finally began to swing in the Allies' favor. Bloody island by bloody island, U.S. Marines leapfrogged across the Pacific, and June witnessed the massive invasion of Normandy, France. The curtain of defeat was being rung down on the Axis, but at horrific cost and not immediately. Perhaps the realization that final victory could be in reach explains the continuation of cheerful songs that dominated the ratings for the year.

"Swinging on a Star" (1944; music by Jimmy Van Heusen, lyrics by Johnny Burke) laid claim to the year's #1 spot. Taken from the popular film *Going My Way,* it also won an Academy Award for Best Song. Johnny Burke's relentlessly upbeat lyrics urge listeners to be all they can be, or else they could end up as mules (or pigs, or fish). Bing Crosby, playing a priest, stars in the motion picture and sings the tune on record, but the success of "Swinging on a Star" marked only a part of a remarkable year for Crosby. He also performed another song from the film, "Too-ra-loo-ra-loo-ral, That's an Irish Lullaby" (1944 [popular revival of a 1914 song]; words and music by James Royce Shannon), a sentimental favorite that likewise did well.

Cole Porter, the talented composer and lyricist, contributed an unlikely #2 song for 1944, "Don't Fence Me In" (1944 [popular revival of a 1934 tune]; words and music by Cole Porter [with Robert Fletcher]). He had originally written it for a movie that never went into production and actually professed disdain for the song. And so the number languished, until Warner Bros. released *Hollywood Canteen,* a celebrity-filled musical. The "King of the Cowboys" himself, Roy Rogers, appears in a cameo as one of the guest stars, and he reprises "Don't Fence Me In," while his horse, Trigger, does a dance. But earlier that year, Bing Crosby had gone into a recording studio with his favorite trio, the Andrews Sisters, where they cut the hit version of the Porter song. No other rendering came close in popularity. Undeterred, a year later, Rogers filmed a routine Western called *Don't Fence Me In* (1945), and as the title would suggest, he performs the song once more, and it again went unnoticed.

But the Crosby story for 1944 does not end there; in addition to "Swinging on a Star" and "Don't Fence Me In," he also boasted hits with "(There'll Be a) Hot Time in the Town of Berlin (When the Yanks Go Marching In)" (1943; words and music by Joe Bushkin and John De Vries), which ranked #6; "San Fernando Valley" (1944; words and music by Gordon Jenkins), #8; "I Love You" (1944; words and music by Cole Porter), another Porter entry, charting at #10; "I'll Be Seeing You" (1944 [popular revival of a 1938 song]; music by Sammy Fain, lyrics by Irving Kahal), at #13; and "Amor" (1944; music by Gabriel Ruiz, English lyrics by Sunny Skylar), coming in at #20. Thus he recorded the major hit interpretations of 7 out of the top 20 songs for the year, or roughly one-third of them. And those numbers do not count the many other records he cut in 1944 that did not make it to the top, but nonetheless claimed substantial sales.

Then, as now, each Christmas season saw a new crop of holiday music. Most ended up forgotten, but an occasional tune captured the public fancy and did well. Nineteen forty-four proved no exception, especially since memories of the overwhelming 1942 success of "White Christmas" remained fresh in producers' minds. "Have Yourself a Merry Little Christmas" (1944; music by Hugh Martin, lyrics by Ralph Blane) served as an ideal seasonal song while the nation celebrated its fourth consecutive Christmas locked in worldwide conflict. Judy Garland sings its poignant lyrics in *Meet Me in St. Louis* (1944), a nostalgic film about the United States in 1903 and the proposition that families should not be uprooted or separated. With millions of American troops overseas, Christmas morning would be a sad occasion, a "little Christmas," until everyone could be reunited.

Garland, by 1944 an adult star, although she could still pass on-screen as a teenager, also gets to perform "The Boy Next Door" (1944) and her classic "The Trolley Song" (1944; both also feature music by Hugh Martin and lyrics by Ralph Blane) in this tuneful movie. "The Trolley Song" lost out to the aforementioned "Swinging on a Star" at the Academy Awards, but it has remained inextricably connected to Garland. For its part, "The Boy Next Door" has emerged a romantic standard; in 1953, Frank Sinatra changed the lyrics a bit, singing about "The Girl Next Door" in a hit recording of his own and thereby broadened the range of singers able to perform it.

With all the foregoing competition, Johnny Mercer still managed to make his influence felt: he wrote four of 1944's bigger hits. Released late in the year, Paramount Pictures' *Here Come the Waves* (1944) brought Mercer and composer Harold Arlen together again. The movie stars none other than Bing Crosby, and he gets to perform, among several other numbers, "Ac-Cen-Tchu-Ate the Positive" (1944), which urges war-weary folks to be optimistic, hold out a while longer, and things will look up. Additionally, "Let's Take the Long Way Home" (1944), a lighthearted look at courtship, and the classic "That Old Black Magic" (1944; all songs with music by Harold Arlen, lyrics by Johnny Mercer), which details the thrills of falling in love, can be found on the soundtrack. "Ac-Cen-Tchu-Ate the Positive" (1944) went to #11 in early 1945, and the recording features Mercer himself doing the vocal. In contrast, Crosby, singing with the Andrews Sisters, only managed to climb to #22 with the song. Mercer also teamed up with Hoagy Carmichael for "How Little We Know" (1944), yet another standard.

Spike Jones and His City Slickers, a wacky aggregation that delighted in parodying—some would say wrecking or destroying—music of any and all kinds, had two hits in 1944: "Cocktails for Two" (1944 [parody adaptation of a 1934 tune]; music by Sam Coslow, lyrics by Arthur Johnston) and "You Always

One of the most popular vocal groups of the 1940s, the Andrews Sisters enjoyed countless hits. Above, from the left: Maxene, Patti, and LaVerne. Library of Congress, Prints & Photographs Division.

Hurt the One You Love" (1944 [parody adaptation]; words and music by Alan Roberts and Doris Fisher). Just as his impudent "Der Fuehrer's Face" had amused millions in 1942, these two take-offs on more serious music had them laughing again. A straight version of "You Always Hurt the One You Love" by the Mills Brothers had made the charts in the fall; Jones and his band took it on soon thereafter and probably made it impossible for anyone to listen to the song in its original format without thinking of the shambles the City Slickers made of it.

Finally, another novelty tune for the year carried the unusual title "Mairzy Doats" (1944; words and music by Jerry Livingston, Milton Drake, and Al Hoffman). To read the sheet music lyrics, the words look like nonsense—"Mairzy Doats"? But to hear the recording, and by listening carefully, it sounds like "mares eat oats" and so on, including (on paper) "Liddle Lamzy Divey," or aurally, "little lambs eat ivy." Based loosely on some old English nursery rhymes, "Mairzy Doats" gave the Merry Macs, the group with the most popular version (#11 for the year), a surprise success and spurred others to record it.

1945

Despite some costly last-ditch enemy encounters, such as the Battle of the Bulge, Iwo Jima, and Okinawa, American and Allied forces emerged victorious

Before she rose to stardom, Doris Day was known as a capable big-band singer. For a time, she received billing as "featured with Les Brown and his Orchestra," but with "Sentimental Journey" (1944) she came into her own. Library of Congress, Prints & Photographs Division.

in 1945. Germany capitulated in May, followed by Japan in September, although it took two atomic bombs, directed at the cities of Hiroshima and Nagasaki in August, to force Japan to the surrender table. Americans reacted with dancing in the streets, fireworks, relief, and euphoria; their responses may have taken many forms, but little in popular music reflected the end of the long, bloody conflict.

The Andrews Sisters, so often the bright vocal complement to Bing Crosby, hit the #1 spot on their own with "Rum and Coca-Cola" (1945 [adapted from Lionel Belasco's 1906 "L'Annee Passee"]; music by Paul Baron and Jeri Sullavan, lyrics by Morey Amsterdam), a slyly satirical description of life in Trinidad. Performed in a pseudo-Caribbean patois that clearly came from lyricist Amsterdam's imagination, it all seems happy-go-lucky on one level, but on another, when they sing about girls and their mothers "working for the Yankee dollar," it takes on darker meanings. Some radio stations expressed unhappiness about the double entendres in the lyrics and the title's use of rum, along with the clear brand reference to Coca-Cola. But popularity prevailed over station managers' fears, and the concerns disappeared as they added it to their playlists.

The effervescent trio also reunited with Crosby for a rendition of Johnny Mercer's aforementioned "Ac-Cen-Tchu-Ate the Positive," which came in at #22. They joined with Crosby once more for the #24 song "Along the Navajo Trail" (1945; words and music by Dick Charles, Eddie De Lange, and Larry Marks). Roy Rogers likewise performs this tune in his 1945 Western *Don't Fence Me In,* and he repeated it a month later in another picture called, appropriately enough, *Along the Navajo Trail.* Neither of Rogers' performances, however, received much notice.

A relative newcomer to the world of ranked hits, singer Doris Day made the big time with her interpretation of the year's #2 song, "Sentimental Journey" (1944; music by Ben Homer and Les Brown, lyrics by Bud Green). Although released late in 1944, her recording, backed by Les Brown and His Band of Renown, took off in 1945 and made her one of the most popular vocalists of the day. Thought by some to be a war song because of its message of nostalgic yearning to be back home, careful attention to the lyrics would reveal that the speaker, in Day's case, a woman, has traveled about and now desires to return to her roots. Nothing in the song alludes to the war. But with victory looming and the vision of millions of troops coming home, many stateside listeners doubtless heard it as a sentimental reference to loved ones, and it probably echoed the desire on countless soldiers' part to get out of uniform and return to normalcy. Hal McIntyre's band, with a vocal by Frankie Lester, also recorded it, as did the Merry Macs.

Riding high on their success with 1943's *Oklahoma!* Rodgers and Hammerstein brought a new show to Broadway in the spring. Called *Carousel,* its story comes from a 1921 fantasy by Ferenc Molnar, but the two songwriters transferred the locale from Hungary to New England. Tunes like "If I Loved You" (1945), "June Is Bustin' Out All Over" (1945), and "You'll Never Walk Alone" (1945; for all, music by Richard Rodgers, lyrics by Oscar Hammerstein II) captivated audiences and made the *Billboard* charts. In short order, they had created another stage classic, one that would run for almost 900 performances.

Four months later, and while *Carousel* still bedazzled Broadway, a new movie musical titled *State Fair* opened. The only film that Rodgers and Hammerstein ever attempted without a prior stage version, they demonstrated a deft Hollywood touch. With stars Jeanne Crain, Dana Andrews, and Dick Haymes anchoring the production, it too proved a hit. Three more standards came from the picture: "Isn't It Kind of Fun?" (1945), "It's a Grand Night for Singing" (1945), and "It Might As Well Be Spring" (1945; for all, music by

Composer Jule Styne (left) and lyricist Sammy Cahn collaborated on a number of big war-era hits, such as "I'll Walk Alone" (1944), "It's Been a Long, Long Time" (1945), "Let It Snow! Let It Snow! Let It Snow!" (1945), and "Guess I'll Hang My Tears Out to Dry" (1945). Library of Congress, Prints & Photographs Division.

Richard Rodgers, lyrics by Oscar Hammerstein II). The last-named composition also carried off an Academy Award for Best Song.

At the tail end of 1944, Broadway welcomed a fresh, innovative production that suggested the direction musicals would take in the postwar era. Called *On the Town,* this essentially 1945 show boasted the collective talents of composer Leonard Bernstein, writers/lyricists Betty Comden and Adolph Green, and choreographer Jerome Robbins. Their arrival announced that Rodgers and Hammerstein would not lack for competition on the musical stage. *On the Town* also reflects a bit of wartime America because its plot involves three sailors on

EIGHT SIGNIFICANT LYRICISTS

During the war years, eight lyricists rose to particular prominence in American popular music: Irving Berlin, Johnny Burke, Sammy Cahn, Mack Gordon, Oscar Hammerstein II, E. Y. "Yip" Harburg, Frank Loesser, and Johnny Mercer.

Appendix B, "The Songs, Composers, and Lyricists of World War II, 1939–1945," catalogs 715 songs by a wide variety of writers. A close reading of this listing will reveal that the eight most-mentioned lyricists contributed a disproportionate number of titles. Although far more than 715 songs were written and published during the years in question, space alone would preclude listing every one of them. Even these lyricists contributed more than can be found in Appendix B, but their identified work, coupled with the output of others, provides a statistically suggestive thesis, as follows:

Between 1939 and 1945, Johnny Mercer wrote the lyrics for 40 individual songs, or 6 percent of the total 715 listed songs (all percentages rounded to the nearest whole).

In second place, Mack Gordon contributed 20 sets of lyrics, or 3 percent of the total.

Third place goes to Irving Berlin, with 18 sets of lyrics, or 3 percent also.

Frank Loesser's 17 lyrics give him 2 percent of the total.

Johnny Burke's contribution of 15 lyrics also nets him 2 percent.

Close behind, Oscar Hammerstein's total of 14 gives him 2 percent.

Sammy Cahn, with 12 sets of lyrics (or 2 percent), comes in at seventh place.

And E. Y. Harburg closes out this distinguished grouping with 11 songs, or 2 percent.

Collectively, these eight individuals wrote 147 songs, or 21 percent of the total 715 listed compositions, a striking accomplishment during a time of intense musical production by many capable lyricists.

leave in New York City. As the sailors, and the girls they meet, dance and sing their way through a stylized Manhattan, they perform, among others, "Carried Away" (1945), "Lonely Town" (1945), and "New York, New York" (1945; for all, music by Leonard Bernstein, lyrics by Betty Comden and Adolph Green).

Only a handful of American stage musicals, aside from Irving Berlin's flag-waving *This Is the Army* (1942), even referred to the war or to the home front during that period. As a rule, Broadway preferred to ignore the conflict altogether. (See chapter 6, "Music on Stage and Screen," for more on this subject.) An important difference between *On the Town* and other contemporary musicals (primarily film productions) that employed the war revolves around the lack of obviously patriotic numbers in the scores. *On the Town* tells a typical

Lyricist Sammy Cahn, who often collaborated with composer Jule Styne, rose to be one of the leading wordsmiths of the 1940s. "Vict'ry Polka" (1943) reflected the ongoing war, but served mainly as a vehicle for energetic dancers. Picture by William H. Young.

love story: boy meets girl, pursuit, complications, and so on. The sailors' uniforms, so commonplace at the time, give the scenes a certain period authenticity and little else.

While Bernstein, Comden, and Green were making their mark as newcomers on the theatrical scene, steady, reliable Tin Pan Alley continued to produce hundreds of tunes—some good, some mediocre, some awful, and a few great ones—year in and year out. Songsmiths like Mack Gordon, Irving Berlin, Frank Loesser, Cole Porter, E. Y. Harburg, Harold Arlen, Harry Warren, and

Johnny Burke all produced dozens of new melodies and lyrics throughout the 1939–1945 era. Johnny Mercer, for sheer quantity, coupled with quality, perhaps stood alone during these years, but he had plenty of sharp competition. For example, in 1945, lyricist Sammy Cahn, collaborating with composers Paul Weston and Axel Stordahl, wrote the words for such standards as "Day by Day" (1945) and "I Should Care" (1945; from the film *Thrill of a Romance*). At about the same time, working with composer Jule Styne, Cahn's output included "Guess I'll Hang My Tears Out to Dry" (1945), "I Fall in Love Too Easily" (1945; from the film *Anchors Aweigh*), and "Let It Snow! Let It Snow! Let It Snow!" (1945). And, like Mercer, Cahn stayed busy almost constantly, writing many other tunes and becoming esteemed among his peers and anonymously popular with the public. Few people might actually know his name; lyricists then or now seldom become celebrities, leaving that honor to the singers who perform their songs.

Mercer himself contributed words and music to "Dream" (1945), a project for his newly created Capitol label. He also wrote the lyrics for "Laura" (1945; music by David Raskin), a song performed in the 1944 film of the same name. He supplied the words for "Out of This World" (1945; music by Harold Arlen), the theme from the 1945 movie also bearing that title. Last, but hardly least, "On the Atchison, Topeka, and Santa Fe" (1945; music by Harry Warren) came from his gifted pen; it can be heard in the 1946 picture *The Harvey Girls*. In this film (made in 1945, but not generally released until January of 1946, thus the confusion in dates), Judy Garland sings "On the Atchison, Topeka, and Santa Fe," while Ray Bolger dances, a winning combination. The tune went on to win an Academy Award for Best Song. Mercer's own rendition of this number ranked #4 for 1945, and Bing Crosby also recorded a popular version that year.

CONCLUSION

For the duration of World War II, the most popular songs in the United States continued to be those that described love and romance. For every composition that referred to the conflict, many more deliberately shied away from the subject. The imagined loneliness of lovers separated by circumstance might resonate with people who, in reality, the war kept apart, but the lyrics accompanying the music seldom made any overt reference to events. The best-selling, most listened-to pop songs, especially those destined to become standards, existed outside of time and place. This situation frustrated many in government looking for a stirring, chart-topping war song, but most Americans, men and women, in civvies or uniform, preferred to stay with the tried-and-true familiarity of the love song.

3

Swing, Jazz, and Rhythm 'n' Blues

SWING BACKGROUND

The roots of swing grew deep and twisted throughout the 1920s. In the later years of the decade, black musical artists, such as Cab Calloway, Duke Ellington, Louis Armstrong, Fletcher Henderson, Earl Hines, Bennie Moten, and Fats Waller, held sway as pioneers in the movement, playing arrangements that featured a propulsive, toe-tapping energy that attracted listeners. A handful of white bands, including those led by Larry Clinton, Glen Gray (and the Casa Loma Orchestra), Ben Pollack, and Paul Whiteman, early on proved receptive to the infectious rhythm in this as-then unnamed music. By the mid-1930s, all other forms and styles of American popular music increasingly took a backseat to the popularity of this particular format.

As it evolved, swing claimed a mixed jazz heritage, blending New Orleans, Chicago, Kansas City, Dixieland, and blues, that demanded melodic freedom and a percussive beat. But it also employed the practice of playing pop songs and standards in which little or no improvisation occurred, performances that relied on formal arrangements that remained faithful to the melody. This dichotomy coalesced into a wildly popular new format, one that demonstrated that even the most innocuous tune could be made to swing.

The term *swing,* as applied to music, first began appearing in the 1920s with such song titles as "Georgia Swing" (1928; music by Jelly Roll Morton) and "Saratoga Swing" (1929; music by Duke Ellington). Not until 1932, however, did the word assume its role of identifying a musical style; Duke Ellington that year released an up-tempo composition he called "It Don't Mean a Thing (If It Ain't Got That Swing)," with the result that *swing* henceforth took on its contemporary meaning of popular, rhythmic dance music. But if black musicians nurtured this blend of styles, white bandleaders came to dominate it with the approach of the war years. Orchestras led by the likes of the Dorseys (Tommy and Jimmy), Benny Goodman, Glenn Miller, Artie Shaw, and a host of others assimilated swing into their repertoires and profited mightily from it, far more so than did any of the black aggregations that had helped so much in bringing it to maturity.

The Rise of the Big Bands

More often than not, the purveyors of swing consisted of large orchestras, often 12 or more musicians, playing arrangements that blended jazz and the popular idiom in such a way that the results attracted both dance and listening audiences. With the onset of the 1940s, the bands at first continued marching on. The big powerhouse aggregations fronted by Charlie Barnet, Count Basie, the Dorsey brothers, Duke Ellington, Benny Goodman, Harry James, Glenn Miller, and Artie Shaw led the way into the new decade. But close behind came innumerable others, with veteran leaders like Bob Crosby, Xavier Cugat, Jan Garber, Shep Fields, Sammy Kaye, Kay Kyser, Guy Lombardo, Jimmie Lunceford, Freddy Martin, and Charlie Spivak—from the sweetest to the most hard-driving—keeping dancers and record buyers happy. Space does not permit mentioning them all, but a sizable library of books listing both the famous and the many relative unknowns exists for anyone anxious to find details about personnel, dates, and selected recordings from this rich era.[1]

Swing during the War Years

Change, in the form of new musical expressions and styles, may have been stirring in the winds, but at first, no one paid any real attention, and awareness of innovation and experimentation resided mainly with the artists attempting anything novel or out of the ordinary. In the days just before the entry of the United States into World War II, the big bands, the most prominent exponents of swing, could do no wrong in the eyes of the mass audience. And then came Pearl Harbor in December of 1941, and nothing would ever be the same again.

Certain inescapable economic realities influenced the destiny of swing as it had once been known. By 1942, the military draft (also called selective service and conscription) was taking more and more men, with the result that the big orchestras shrank appreciably in size. Small groups, like sextets, quintets, quartets, and trios, took on an increasingly important role in music. The larger aggregations, to compete, often had a band within the band; for example, Artie Shaw showed off his Gramercy Five, Chick Webb featured the Little Chicks, Tommy Dorsey had the Clambake Seven, Benny Goodman had both his Trio and Quartet, Bob Crosby showcased the Bobcats, Woody Herman the Woodchoppers, and Cab Calloway had the Cab Jivers. From an artistic standpoint, this period of social and economic uncertainty led to the dominance of small groups in the evolving area of modern jazz and encouraged the exploration of new musical formats. These changes, some gradual, some almost overnight, occurred at the expense of traditional big-band swing.

Vocalists

The most telling evidence of changing times for the big bands involved the role of vocalists, or, in the parlance of the day, the *boy singers* and *canaries,* that accompanied every group, large and small. Traditionally paid less than the musicians, they tended to stand off at the edges of the stage, only in the spotlight when their turns came up. Since most bands usually played a number of instrumental numbers during a set, many people, especially the leaders themselves, saw the singers as virtual part-timers and deserving of a lower paycheck. With the war, however, the status of vocalists changed. Manpower shortages reduced the size of many orchestras, and the soothing sounds of a band crooner often held greater appeal for audiences than did a wailing sax section. Record sales and bandstand requests reinforced the growing popularity of the singers. This perception also held true for vocal groups; public taste underwent a significant shift during the early 1940s.

Table 3.1 lists some of the better-known singers that performed and recorded with the leading bands in the nation. Hardly complete, it merely suggests the large number of vocalists then pursuing careers in popular music.[2]

Challenges to Swing's Dominance

The traditional mainstays for booking the many swing orchestras, such as clubs, dance halls, and restaurants, had to cut back on their hours of operation with the onset of the war. The rising popularity of band vocalists had little effect on falling attendance. Food rationing made serving dinners problematical—a patron might not be able to order what he or she wanted because of availability—and lack of personnel, from chefs to waitstaff, caused

Table 3.1
Some Representative Big Band Vocalists Active during the Period 1939–1945

Name	Primary Band Affiliation(s)	Comments
Ivie Anderson	Duke Ellington, 1931–1942	
Harry Babbitt	Kay Kyser, 1938–1944, 1948–1964	
Mildred Bailey	Red Norvo, 1936–1939	Moved to a solo career
Wee Bonnie Baker	Orrin Tucker, 1939–1941	
Tex Beneke	Glenn Miller, 1938–1942	
June Christy	Stan Kenton, 1945–1949	
Nat "King" Cole	Led a trio with Oscar Moore (guitar) and Wesley Prince (bass), 1939–1949	Moved to a solo career
Perry Como	Ted Weems, 1936–1942	Moved to a solo career
Kay Davis	Duke Ellington, 1945–1950	
Dolly Dawn	George Hall, 1935–1941	Became Dolly Dawn and Her Dawn Patrol, 1941–1942
Doris Day	Bob Crosby, 1940; Les Brown, 1940, 1943–1946	Moved to a solo career
Irene Daye	Gene Krupa, 1938–1941; Charlie Spivak, 1944–1950s	
Blossom Dearie	Woody Herman's Woodchoppers, others, 1945–1952	
Johnny Desmond	Bob Crosby, 1940–1941; Gene Krupa, 1941–1942; Glenn Miller, 1943–1945; Casa Loma Orchestra, 1945–1946	
Mike Douglas	Kay Kyser, 1945–1951	
Ray Eberle	Glenn Miller, 1938–1942; Gene Krupa, 1942–1943 (brother of Bob Eberly)	
Bob Eberly	Jimmy Dorsey, 1935–1943 (Bob changed his spelling of the family name)	
Billy Eckstine	Earl Hines 1939–1943	Moved to a solo career
Ella Fitzgerald	Chick Webb, 1935–1942 (led the Webb band after 1939)	Moved to a solo career
Helen Forrest	Artie Shaw, 1937; Benny Goodman, 1939–1941; Harry James, 1942–1943	
Kenny Gardner	Guy Lombardo, 1940–1978	
Connie Haines	Harry James, 1939–1940; Tommy Dorsey, 1940–1941	
Dick Haymes	Harry James, 1939–1942; Tommy Dorsey, 1942; Benny Goodman, 1942	Moved to a solo career

Table 3.1
(continued)

Name	Primary Band Affiliation(s)	Comments
Al Hibbler	Jay McShann, 1942; Duke Ellington, 1943–1951	
Harriet Hilliard	Ozzie Nelson, 1932–1944	
Billie Holiday	Wilson, 1935–1939 (erratic); also Count Basie, 1937; Artie Shaw, 1938	Moved to a solo career, 1940
Lena Horne	Charlie Barnet, 1940–1941	
Helen Humes	Count Basie, 1938–1942	Moved to a solo career
Marion Hutton	Glenn Miller, 1938–1942	
Herb Jeffries	Duke Ellington, 1940–1942	
Ish Kabibble [Merwyn Bogue]	Kay Kyser, 1938–1950	
Kitty Kallen	Artie Shaw, 1938–1939; Jack Teagarden, 1940; Bobby Sherwood, 1941; Jimmy Dorsey, 1942–1943; Harry James, 1944–1946	
Peggy Lee	Benny Goodman, 1941–1943	Moved to a solo career
Jack Leonard	Tommy Dorsey, 1935–1939	
Mary Ann McCall	Woody Herman, 1939; Charlie Barnet, 1939–1940	
Velma Middleton	Louis Armstrong, 1942–1947	
Vaughn Monroe	Led his own band, 1940–1953	
Ella Mae Morse	Jimmy Dorsey, 1939; Freddie Slack, 1942–1943	Moved to a solo career
Helen O'Connell	Jimmy Dorsey, 1939–1943	
Anita O'Day	Max Miller, 1939–1941; Gene Krupa, 1941–1943; Stan Kenton, 1944–1945	
Tony Pastor	Artie Shaw, 1936–1939	Formed his own band, 1939–1959
Betty Roche	Duke Ellington, 1943–1944	
Jimmy Rushing	Count Basie, 1935–1950	
Kenny Sargent	Casa Loma Orchestra, 1931–1943	
Dinah Shore	Various bands, 1939	Moved to NBC radio and *The Chamber Music Society of Lower Basin Street*, 1940–1942; innumerable radio guest spots thereafter

(continued)

Table 3.1 (continued)

Name	Primary Band Affiliation(s)	Comments
Ginny Simms	Kay Kyser, 1938–1941	
Frank Sinatra	Harry James, 1939; Tommy Dorsey, 1940–1942	Moved to a solo career
Jo Stafford	Tommy Dorsey, 1938–1942; Paul Weston, 1943–1944	Moved to a solo career
Kay Starr	Glenn Miller, 1939; Joe Venuti, 1942; Bob Crosby, 1942; Charlie Barnet, 1943–1945	
Maxine Sullivan	John Kirby, 1937–1941	
Martha Tilton	Jimmy Dorsey, 1935–1936; Benny Goodman, 1937–1939; Artie Shaw, 1940; Betty Mills Orchestra, 1941	
Sarah Vaughan	Earl Hines, 1943–1944; Billy Eckstine, 1944–1945; John Kirby, 1945–1946	
Bea Wain	Larry Clinton, 1937–1939	
Helen Ward	Benny Goodman, 1934–1936; Hal McIntyre, 1942–1943; Harry James, 1944	
Dinah Washington	Lionel Hampton, 1943–1946	Moved to a solo career
Frances Wayne	Charlie Barnet, 1942; Woody Herman, 1943–1946	
Margaret Whiting	Freddie Slack, 1943–1944; Billy Butterfield, 1945–1946	
Lee Wiley	Eddie Condon, 1939–1942; Jess Stacy, 1943–1946	
Jimmy witherspoon	Jay McShann, 1944–1948	

serving difficulties. Getting to and from a club or restaurant also created problems: gasoline rationing severely limited personal travel, and public transportation had been sharply reduced. Frequent blackouts and lighting restrictions in larger cities further contributed to the overall dilemma, so that many venues went to weekend hours only, and a number simply shut their doors "for the duration," a phrase commonly used from 1941 until 1945. As a final blow, the federal government decreed a 20 percent amusement tax to raise much-needed war revenue and then imposed a nationwide midnight to dawn curfew, called a *brownout,* that effectively shut down most urban areas at night.

It might also seem convenient to assign blame for the downturn in the fortunes of the swing phenomenon to two non-war-related events: first, the simmering feud between ASCAP (American Society of Composers, Authors, and Producers) and BMI (Broadcast Music Incorporated) resulted in the protracted absence of ASCAP-related recordings over the airwaves during much of 1941, an absence that included many of the popular big bands. The second event occurred in late 1942, when the AFM (American Federation of Musicians) decreed that no union musicians could participate in commercial recording sessions, although this ban did not include vocalists. Not until late 1944 did the boycott come to an end, a curious chapter in American music history. (See chapter 4, "Recordings and the Music Business," for more about both of these happenings.)

Little evidence supports the position that these boycotts and bans contributed directly to the decline of swing's popularity. The AFM restrictions on recording perhaps heightened public awareness of singers and vocal groups and may have exacerbated the problem, but the overriding cause for the erosion of the music's dominance came about because of changing tastes. Swing had run its course as the people's favorite. New approaches and new artists attracted audiences always looking for anything novel or fresh. Too many of the bands repeated their old favorites, relying on the tried and true instead of innovation, and in time, this easygoing spirit no longer attracted the multitudes it had during the music's heyday. What had been new and exciting in the 1930s now sounded old-fashioned to a new generation of musicians and listeners.

Wartime Swing Bands

Despite these growing signs of economic and personnel problems, several new bands jumped into the already crowded field. For example, in 1938, Les Brown introduced his new aggregation, the Band of Renown. Although it boasted no unique sound or style, several long hotel and club engagements gave the members some stability, and Brown managed to land a recording contract with RCA Victor's Bluebird label, a major accomplishment. In 1940, a young singer named Doris Day briefly joined the group, but soon left. She, however, returned in 1943, a move that signaled an important change in the orchestra's image. In late 1944, Day and Brown recorded "Sentimental Journey" (1944; music by Ben Homer and Les Brown, lyrics by Bud Green). An immediate hit, it stayed on the charts throughout early 1945, peaking that spring. "Sentimental Journey" ultimately emerged as the #2 song for the year and ensured the continuing popularity of the Les Brown band, at least for a while. For her part, Doris Day moved on to a solo career that culminated with remarkable success in the movies.

Woody Herman, another in the new crop of orchestra leaders, had been active in big-band music from the late 1920s onward. He had spent most of that time laboring as a reed-playing sideman. In 1936, he took over the leadership of the popular Isham Jones Orchestra and immediately faced the dilemma of whether or not to continue performing as a new Jones ensemble or branch out into untried fields. The band members chose the latter course and agreed to call the group "The Band That Plays the Blues"; at first, but only briefly, Herman's name as leader is hard to find. With a carry-over Decca contract giving them some security, the orchestra began to record, appropriately enough, a number of blues-oriented compositions.

Finally, in 1939, "The Band That Plays the Blues" attracted considerable attention with the release of "Woodchopper's Ball" (1939; music by Woody Herman and Joe Bishop). An up-tempo piece, it effectively captured the energy of the aggregation and established Woody Herman as a major new force in swing circles. In addition, he played clarinet on this tune, and the strength of his performance immediately put him into the charmed circle of clarinetists then dominated by Benny Goodman and Artie Shaw.

Up to this time, the group's theme had been an older tune, "Blue Prelude" (1933; music by Gordon Jenkins and Joe Bishop). Because of the aforementioned ASCAP-BMI dispute then reaching its peak, it could not be played on the air. To get around these restrictions, a new theme, "Blue Flame" (1941; music by James Noble), replaced "Blue Prelude" and served to introduce Herman and his sidemen. A haunting number, its distinctive mood provided an impressive opener for the band.

Numerous club dates and more recordings followed, and by 1943, the Woody Herman Orchestra—"The Band That Plays the Blues" had been dropped—boasted a loyal cadre of fans. The following year, a number of significant personnel changes took place, and Herman left Decca and signed a new contract with Columbia Records. For some time, the group had been attempting increasingly modern compositions, and critics even took to calling this latest incarnation of the orchestra the "First Herd." In time, the Second Herd would replace the First, the Third Herd the Second, and so on.

Herman's First Herd burst on the scene with several dizzying numbers unlike anything ever previously heard. "Apple Honey" (1945; music by Woody Herman), "Northwest Passage" (1945; music by Woody Herman, Chubby Jackson, and Ralph Burns), "Bijou" (1945; music by Ralph Burns), and "Wild Root" (1945; music by music by Woody Herman and Neal Hefti) serve as tantalizing samples of what the band could do. For the next several years, Woody Herman's orchestra would electrify listeners with its disciplined hysteria. Arrangers Ralph Burns and Neal Hefti deserve much credit, as do soloists Bill Harris (trombone), Pete Candoli (trumpet), Flip Phillips (tenor saxophone), and the inimitable leader himself on clarinet. The experimentation, the sharp movement away from traditional swing arrangements as the band focused more on modern jazz, would continue into the postwar period, and Herman's Herds ranked among America's favorite orchestras. By eschewing traditional swing, Herman avoided, for a few years, the collapse that occurred for those bands clinging to the past.

Another new ensemble emerged when two sidemen from the big bands of the 1930s joined forces in 1939. They named their creation "Will Bradley and His Orchestra, featuring Ray McKinley." Bradley, a trombonist, and McKinley, a drummer, quickly capitalized on the then-ongoing craze for boogie-woogie

---

BOOGIE-WOOGIE

Uncertainty surrounds both the origin of this form of instrumental piano blues and the source of its name. Some believe the music could first be heard in the early 1900s in the logging and turpentine camps of the Mississippi Delta and the oil boomtowns of Louisiana and East Texas. Regardless of its physical and linguistic origins, boogie-woogie, with its strong, relentless beat, became enormously popular in the late 1930s and early 1940s.

Pioneers in the idiom included Clarence "Pinetop" Smith, Cow Cow Davenport, Pete Johnson, Meade Lux Lewis, and Albert Ammons. When aficionado and promoter John Hammond produced his 1938 and 1939 Carnegie Hall concerts called *From Spirituals to Swing*, the programs featured boogie-woogie, among many other styles, bringing increased public awareness. Pete Johnson, along with singer Big Joe Turner, roused the audience with "Roll 'Em, Pete"; Meade Lux Lewis executed "Honky Tonk Train Blues," and Albert Ammons offered "Swanee River Boogie."

Country artists, intrigued by the insistent boogie-woogie beat, experimented with combining it with traditional Western music. Johnny Barfield, a regional favorite in the South, recorded his version of Pinetop Smith's "Boogie Woogie" in 1939; its success led to groups such as the Delmore Brothers issuing titles like "Freight Train Boogie," "Boogie Woogie Baby," "Mobile Boogie," and "Hillbilly Boogie." Bob Wills, one of the leaders of Western Swing, also experimented with the format.

Meanwhile, the big swing bands increasingly put boogie-woogie numbers in their repertoires since dancers liked them so much. Tommy Dorsey and his band in 1938 had scored with "Boogie Woogie," an adaptation of the Pinetop Smith chestnut. Will Bradley's orchestra made the charts with "Beat Me, Daddy, Eight to the Bar" in 1940 and returned in 1941 with "Scrub Me, Mama, with a Boogie Beat." The Andrews Sisters created a wartime classic with "The Boogie-Woogie Bugle Boy (of Company B)," and Freddie Slack and his band, featuring vocalist Ella Mae Morse, likewise struck gold with "Cow Cow Boogie" in 1943. After that, however, the craze began to die down, and soon boogie-woogie became a relic of the musical past.

---

by stringing together a succession of hits with titles like "Beat Me, Daddy, Eight to the Bar" (1940; music by Don Raye, lyrics by Hughie Prince and Eleanor Sheehy [pseudonym for Ray McKinley]), "Scrub Me, Mama, with a Boogie Beat" (1940; words and music by Don Raye), and "Bounce Me, Brother, with a Solid Four" (1941; music by Hughie Prince, lyrics by Don Raye). They received invaluable assistance in these efforts from their own pianist, Freddie Slack, himself a virtuoso interpreter of the boogie-woogie style.

The Bradley-McKinley orchestra enjoyed its biggest hit, however, with a novelty number incongruously called "Celery Stalks at Midnight" (1940; words and music by George Harris and Will Bradley); as imaginative as it sounds, the title, conceived on the spot, really means nothing beyond its playfulness. But listeners liked its bouncy rhythm, and "Celery Stalks at Midnight" served as one of the few charted tunes produced by this clever but swinging band.

In 1942, the ensemble played its last set, and the leaders went their separate ways. McKinley proceeded to form a new group of his own. He did reasonably well until the draft caught up with him, an event that put him in Glenn Miller's Army Air Force Band as the leader of Swing Shift, a small ensemble from within the ranks of the larger orchestra. With Miller's untimely death in 1944, McKinley and arranger Jerry Gray fronted the band while it completed its European tour of duty. After his discharge, McKinley returned to the civilian podium with yet another aggregation, one that received considerable acclaim.

After serving an apprenticeship during the 1930s as a pianist, composer, and arranger for a number of big bands, Claude Thornhill, in 1940, likewise started an orchestra. Following a rocky beginning, he found his own style, one that combined rich, sonorous dynamics with unusual instrumentation, including tubas, French horns, and several clarinets. With its tonal delicacy, his 1941 composition, "Snowfall," captured the band's unique sound well and achieved considerable commercial success. Just as he was getting established, Thornhill chose to enter the Navy, an enlistment that included playing piano with Artie Shaw's service band as well as fronting a group of his own. Fortunately, a handful of recordings he had made previously kept him in the public eye, so Thornhill soon resumed his commercial duties upon his 1945 discharge. He organized a new band and hired the immensely talented Gil Evans as his chief arranger. In no time, the Thornhill-Evans sound found a host of listeners, and the two musicians went on to become significant voices in the creation of new directions in modern American music.

With varying degrees of success, several other new bands attempted to buck the trends of the early 1940s. Most turned out to be short-lived, but they nonetheless produced, during their varying tenures, interesting variations on the ongoing swing motifs then passing from public favor. For example, Hal

McIntyre led a group that played much in the style of Glenn Miller, an approach that initially assured some club and dance hall dates, but one that also wore out its welcome in a short time. On another plane altogether, Raymond Scott led a quintet (called a "quintette," and in reality, a sextet) in the late 1930s and then a big band during the 1940s. For many, however, he will be best remembered as the man who fronted the orchestra on *Your Hit Parade* from 1949 until it went off the air (on both radio and television) in 1957.

During his earlier work with a small group, Scott proved himself a real innovator, creating such popular novelty songs as "The Toy Trumpet" and "Twilight in Turkey" (both 1937; music by Raymond Scott), plus "In an Eighteenth-Century Drawing Room" and "Huckleberry Duck" (both 1939; music by Raymond Scott, lyrics by Jack Lawrence). Remarkably complex in their composition and execution, these tunes and several others made their way to the soundtracks of Warner Bros. cartoons, the medium in which most people gained exposure to his wacky music. The quintette unfortunately broke up in 1939, and Scott switched to a big band, did arranging, and worked in radio during the 1940s. But for two years, he pioneered in the creation of offbeat novelty music that had strong jazz and swing overtones.

The All-Girl Bands

While these new bandleaders tested the uncertain waters of wartime America, the military draft went on unabated, and its consequences deeply affected the music business. Conscription created the phenomenon of more and more women instrumentalists populating the ranks of previously all-male ensembles. Although they encountered considerable resistance and discrimination from critics, the public, and often the sidemen in the bands, a few cracked the big time and achieved some success. To name but a few of the women who played with top-flight but mostly male organizations: vibraphonist Marjorie Hyams and trumpeter Billie Rogers established their credentials with Woody Herman; Melba Liston played trombone with Gerald Wilson's band; guitarist Mary Osborne played with several bands, including Buddy Rogers, Joe Venuti, and Stuff Smith; Frances Shirley took trumpet honors with Charlie Barnet; and Lionel Hampton hired Elsie Smith for his saxophone section. Countless other women labored in relative anonymity with lesser-known orchestras, but virtually all of them possessed AFM union cards and could more than hold their own with their male counterparts, despite an endless barrage of snide remarks about their abilities.

The declining pool of eligible male musicians also gave rise to the "girl bands," a situation where women formed commercial groups of their own. No one would have thought to say *women's bands* in those less gender-sensitive times; regardless of age, they were "girls" playing in all-female aggregations.

Not an entirely new phenomenon, a few girl bands had existed prior to World War II, groups that billed themselves as novelties and capitalized on gender. One of the best was Ina Ray Hutton and her Melodears, an ensemble that featured the nonplaying leader, who billed herself as the "Blonde Bombshell of Rhythm," a woman who exuded sex appeal while attired in slinky gowns. Hutton formed her orchestra in 1934, and it prospered until 1939, including several film shorts and a part in the full-length feature movie *The Big Broadcast of 1936* (1935). Shortly after dissolving the Melodears, Hutton formed an all-male group that lasted until 1944, a curious decision, since men qualified to play in a professional band were in increasingly short supply, given the pressures of World War II. With this new group, she called herself "Queen of the Name Bands." Hutton continued in the music business in the postwar era, forming another all-girl group and then moving on to television in 1950.

Entrepreneur Phil Spitalny, who had endured a nondescript career in popular music during the 1920s, emerged a pioneer in the area of promoting women for roles as competent, professional instrumentalists when he devised the gimmick—no other word adequately describes what he sought—an orchestra made up entirely of women. In 1934, the same year Hutton introduced her Melodears, he realized his dream when he unveiled a group that he immodestly called "Phil Spitalny and His All-Girl Orchestra." Unlike Hutton, Spitalny emphasized class and decorum, not sex appeal, in his productions, and it paid off. He landed a radio contract in 1935 with CBS for a music show that received the name *The Hour of Charm,* a term quickly transferred to the aggregation itself. Despite the program's title, the broadcast ran only 30 minutes, but it earned good ratings throughout the year. Archrival NBC noted its success and picked up the show for the next decade, 1936–1946, only to have CBS regain it for another two years, 1946–1948.

Hardly a driving swing band, Spitalny's crew played light classics and a lot of schmaltz, all part of his concept of "musical femininity." The Hour of Charm Orchestra at times boasted a choir, and always featured strings, harp, and piano, instruments considered more ladylike than brass or reeds, although the aggregation had the requisite trumpets, trombones, and saxophones, too. When on tour, the Hour of Charm staged elaborate production numbers. Aside from Spitalny himself, Evelyn Kaye Klein, or "Evelyn and Her Magic Violin," took honors as star of the show. The violin, reputedly a rare Italian model, received a workout from Evelyn since she preferred virtuoso numbers. Radio success led to Hollywood, first for some shorts, and then parts in two features, *When Johnny Comes Marching Home* (1942) and *Here Come the Coeds* (1945). The novelty of an all-girl orchestra eventually wore off, especially in light of similar groups performing throughout the war years, but Spitalny and his ensemble helped break the ice and survived until the early days of television. In addition, he and Evelyn, who also served as concertmaster during the heyday of the organization, wed in 1946.

INA RAY HUTTON, A SUCCESSFUL WOMAN BANDLEADER

Known as the "Blonde Bombshell of Rhythm," Ina Ray Hutton, born Odessa Cowan in Chicago in 1916, gained notoriety during the 1930s and 1940s for both her music and her seductive stage persona. But she also earned some well-deserved fame as the only prominent female bandleader during the big band era. Hutton began singing and dancing at the age of eight and, during the early 1930s, appeared in several Broadway shows and the *Ziegfeld Follies*. In 1934, with the help of producer and entrepreneur Irving Mills, Hutton organized an all-girl orchestra.

Promoters called the band Ina Ray Hutton and Her Melodears, and it toured and recorded for five years as well as having parts in several Paramount film shorts. At the end of the 1930s, Hutton broke up the group; in partnership with George Paxton, she formed an all-male orchestra. Billed as Ina Ray Hutton and Her Orchestra, the group featured Paxton on tenor sax, Hal Schaefer at the piano, and Jack Purcell playing guitar. Although the aggregation did not lack for musical talent, Hutton's seductive swaying and dancing on stage served as the band's primary drawing card.

The ensemble made several recordings for the Okeh and Elite labels during World War II, but most of its recording opportunities arose as it toured various military bases. The Armed Forces Radio Service would, on occasion, provide access to broadcast facilities for the orchestra and then send transcriptions on to American troops stationed around the world.

Given Hutton's visual appeal, she and her band appeared in a Paramount film short, *Ina Ray and Her Orchestra,* in 1943. The following year, she had a 1944 movie role in a Columbia Pictures musical titled *Ever Since Venus.* Hutton dissolved her orchestra in 1946, but two years later, she again led an all-male band. In 1950, she formed yet another all-girl orchestra, which, for several years, reached audiences through a regional television show. Her last recorded performance came in a 1974 movie called *Brother, Can You Spare a Dime?* Ina Ray Hutton died in 1984.

If nothing else, Hutton and Spitalny legitimatized the idea of women performing professionally in orchestras. Their acceptance opened the doors for others, and the later 1930s and early 1940s witnessed a number of new all-girl bands attempting to make a go of it. One of the best called itself the International Sweethearts of Rhythm. Originally an all-black orchestra, the group was formed in 1937 to raise funds for the Piney Woods Country Life School, a rural Mississippi institution for poor or orphaned minority girls. When the band toured, the members actually lived in their bus, given the racial segregation of the region. In time, their traveling took them to larger cities, and they received favorable reviews as a good, solid swing orchestra. In 1940, they severed their connection to Piney Woods School and moved to northern Virginia as a commercial act and took paid bookings.

As the performance skills and professionalism of the Sweethearts of Rhythm increased, former Count Basie arranger Eddie Durham came aboard as the band's music director, and he guided the outfit into the first rank of touring bands. Durham, by the way, went on to become the "Sepia Phil Spitalny" by working with the All-Star Girl Orchestra and the Darlings of Rhythm in the 1940s, two other swinging all-girl bands that went on the professional touring circuit.

At the end of the war, the International Sweethearts of Rhythm performed for American troops in USO (United Service Organizations) shows staged in Europe and also recorded for RCA Victor, one of the leading labels of the day.

Trombonist Glenn Miller led one of the most popular and successful swing bands of the era. He enlisted in the Air Force in 1942, and thereafter Captain Glenn Miller led a big service band until his untimely death in 1944. Library of Congress, Prints & Photographs Division.

Despite problems of prejudice, both racial and gender-based, this unusual all-woman organization, one of the most successful both commercially and artistically of its type, continued to entertain audiences until 1949.

In a similar vein, Prairie View A&M University, situated in southeast Texas, organized the Prairie View Co-Eds in 1943, a band set up as the women's counterpart to the college's all-male Prairie View Collegians. The wartime draft had taken most of the Collegians' musicians, and so the Co-Eds came into being almost as replacements. In a short time, however, the Co-Eds established themselves as a first-rate swing band and went on tour. Since Prairie View existed as a black school, the youthful players had to face the same problems of segregation and prejudice the International Sweethearts of Rhythm endured. Despite their formidable musical skills, neither group got to enjoy the perks of fame, such as bookings in posh nightclubs or movie contracts; they instead labored in relative obscurity, an endless succession of one-nighters in small towns, traveling in rickety buses to play in gyms, theaters, and small dance halls.

Even with the difficulties facing all-girl bands, the idea spread, and promoters found the talent they needed to form groups throughout the later 1930s and on into the war years. The following list does not begin to name every orchestra active during that period and serves instead to suggest the sheer numbers of women playing in organized musical ensembles.[3]

All-Girl Orchestras during World War II

- Frances Carroll and the Coquettes
- Joy Cayler and Her All-Girl Orchestra
- Herb Cook's Sweethearts
- Al D'Artega's All-Girl Orchestra
- Dixie Rhythm Girls
- Frances Grey's Queens of Swing
- Harlem Playgirls
- Ada Leonard's All-American Girls Orchestra
- Betty McGuire's Sub-Debs
- Jean Parks and Her All-Girl Band
- Rita Rio and Her All-Girl Orchestra
- The Sharon Rogers All-Girl Band
- The Syncoettes
- Virgil Whyte's All-Girl Band (later Musigals)

Whether playing with bands of their own or with male-dominated orchestras, the strong presence of women in popular music—and performing outside the traditional role of vocalist, or "canary"—lasted only for the duration of the conflict, or until the troops started coming home; at that time, the returning sidemen picked up their dusty instruments and resumed their musical employment at the expense of those women who had, it turned out, and often to their dismay, only temporarily replaced them. Sad to say, for most women in the music field, second-class citizenship accompanied their chosen profession. The accepted musicians continued to be male, a situation that has persisted into the present.

The Service Bands

Another problem, related to conscription and the attrition of personnel occurring in many aggregations, pertained to the leaders themselves. Some felt the need to enlist, and others received their draft notices from the government. Either way, a number of the most prominent bandleaders of the day were soon wearing uniforms instead of tuxedoes. In 1942, at the height of his popularity and too old for the draft, Glenn Miller donned an Army Air Corps uniform, along with the rank of captain. He had tried to join the Navy, but officials would not allow it because of his age, 38 in 1942. But the Army yielded, thus giving birth to the most successful service ensemble of them all, a huge organization consisting of a 42-piece marching unit, a jazz combo, string accompaniment, and most famously, his 19-piece Army Air Force Band. Even after Miller's death in December of 1944, the various groups carried on under the leadership of sideman Ray McKinley until they finally disbanded with the return of peace.

But Glenn Miller represented only one of many bandleaders who fronted service orchestras. Miller's civilian sidekick, vocalist and saxophonist Tex Beneke, led a Navy band in landlocked Oklahoma. After his discharge, and with the consent of the Miller estate, he took over the civilian leadership of the old Glenn Miller Orchestra, and so the dynasty continued. Beneke was not alone conducting a Navy band; for whatever reasons, that nautical branch of the various services seemed a magnet for a number of swing-oriented leaders. Artie Shaw also formed a unit, as did saxophonist Sam Donahue and pianist Eddie Duchin, while Bob Crosby wielded a baton for the Marine Corps. Clyde McCoy not only enlisted in the Navy's Special Services division, many members of his band likewise joined at the same time. On the Army side of things, Major Tiny Bradshaw led a large dance orchestra that played for the troops overseas, and "Waltz King" Wayne King, a bit long in the tooth for active duty, served at a post in Chicago with a number of good musicians in his group.

When these and other leaders and sidemen received their discharges in 1945–1946, they returned to a changed musical picture. Many once-prominent swing bands were no more, others faced discouraging economic realities, and new musical styles competed for the public's attention. During 1946, a crucial year, the accumulating problems of the war years, such as declining interest, the rise of vocalists, and new trends in music, came to a head: in short order, Les Brown, Benny Carter, Tommy Dorsey, Benny Goodman, Woody Herman, and Harry James broke up their bands. An era had come to a close, and those still hanging on faced an uncertain future.

JAZZ BACKGROUND

Older than swing, and in many ways the founding force for the style, jazz existed in the shadows throughout swing's heyday. Many fine jazz artists and groups struggled for survival during the 1930s and early 1940s, muffled by the loud applause given their boisterous stepchild. The successful (i.e., profitable) orchestras tended to be white, which meant, given the times, their fans consisted of a preponderance of white patrons. These attitudes carried with them racial implications: a white musician had a far better chance of being hired by a big-name, popular band than did his black counterpart. As a result, many black artists turned to jazz and its evolving expression.

During this time, *swing* and *jazz* often seemed synonymous terms, and the dividing line between the two formats appeared fuzzy indeed. When Count Basie and His Orchestra performed "One O'Clock Jump" (1937; music by William "Count" Basie) or Billie Holiday brought her vocal talents to "Trav'lin' Light" (1943; music by Jimmy Mundy and Trummy Young, lyrics by Johnny Mercer), the renditions delighted jazz and swing fans alike, and any discussions about jazz and swing differences carried the hallmarks of academic nitpicking more than anything else. The jazz aficionados might be dismissive—"mere swing tunes"—about Glenn Miller's "A String of Pearls" (1941; music by Jerry Gray, lyrics by Eddie De Lange) or Artie Shaw's 1938 hit version of "Begin the Beguine" (1935; words and music by Cole Porter), whereas those on the other side might be ecstatic, proclaiming them great dance numbers. Whatever one's leanings, however, most could agree that swing and jazz enjoyed a close kinship, at least until the 1940s.

The Renascence of Jazz

With the era of the highly structured and tightly arranged swing orchestras slowly drawing to a close in the waning days of World War II, jazz innovators started carving out new paths that distanced them from a style that had seemed, just a few short years earlier, destined to rule American music for the foreseeable future. The demise of many big bands simultaneously brought about the rise of countless small groups in the 1940s, especially in the area of modern (as opposed to traditional) jazz. Both all-instrumental and instrumental-plus vocalist combos flourished, and they allowed for a wide variety of musical expression.

For many jazz-oriented musicians, the early forties represented a time of artistic opportunity, but one that did not always equate with commercial success. Overwhelmed by the dominance of swing, much contemporary jazz went unheard by the listening audience. The leading record companies wanted artists like Tommy Dorsey, Benny Goodman, Harry James, and Artie Shaw—artists who would sell. The same held true for nightclubs, dance halls, and concerts. Owners depended on customers, and those customers, or so the owners assumed, wanted the leading names in swing.

Wartime restrictions on travel, along with curfews, also meant fewer people could get out to enjoy entertainment of any kind, and decreased revenues created economic hard times for both clubs and the big bands. Nightclubs, faced with shrinking audiences, replaced large ensembles with small groups and vocalists. In the midst of these problems, a renewed interest in jazz manifested itself. From a revival of traditional New Orleans styles to the most avant-garde experiments, the early 1940s served as a breeding ground for musical innovation, although the war and simple economics served to conceal much of this ferment from potential audiences until later in the decade and the return to peace.

As a result of a number of scholarly studies and record reissues, along with the ardent interest and collecting among fans during the 1930s and early 1940s, old-time jazzmen like Sidney Bechet, George Brunis, Pops Foster, Bunk Johnson, George Lewis, and Kid Ory enjoyed a spark of renewed public interest in the autumn of their careers. At the same time, a group of younger, tradition-favoring musicians, such as Wild Bill Davison, Bud Freeman, Art Hodes, Pee Wee Russell, and Muggsy Spanier, joined with these veteran players. Guitarist Eddie Condon, owner of a New York club, served as an unofficial raconteur for the East Coast factions of the revival as well as leading his own group of spirited jazzmen. As the 1940s progressed, the movement created a small but enthusiastic following.

On the West Coast, trumpeter Lu Watters and His Yerba Buena Jazz Band, an outfit that featured trombonist Turk Murphy and pianist Wally Rose, led a similar revival during this period, one that tried to stay true to the authentic music of New Orleans in its heyday. Watters' group brought, they claimed, a kind of historical purity to their music. Other musicians joined in, including Bob Scobey's band and the singing of Clancy Hayes. Many listeners, East and West Coast, lumped these efforts under the generic title "Dixieland," but the music cultivated a core of dedicated fans during the 1940s that has endured into the present. For many, the traditional revival signaled a desire to return to the roots of jazz, and the popularity espoused for New Orleans, Dixieland, or any of their variants amounted to a denial both of big-band swing and the many experiments taking place in the realm of more modern jazz styles.[4]

Expanding Jazz: Duke Ellington and Others

Amid often strident discussions about the nature of jazz that occurred during the early 1940s, composer and bandleader Duke Ellington pursued his own magisterial path, seemingly unperturbed by the swirling arguments over the proper course for jazz. He had, by the beginning of the decade, reached an unparalleled pinnacle of success: he played the best dance halls, clubs, and concerts; his records sold well, and he was turning out one classic song after another. A remarkable year, 1940 witnessed "Never No Lament" (later retitled "Don't Get Around Much Anymore" in 1943), "Ko-Ko," "Jack the Bear," "Cotton Tail," and "In a Mellotone." In 1941, he added "Just Squeeze Me" and "I Got It Bad and That Ain't Good" to his ouput. The next year saw "What Am I Here For?" and "C-Jam Blues"; he followed 1942 with his first major suite, *Black, Brown, and Beige* (1943). His 1944 compositions included "I'm Beginning to See the Light" and "Main Stem," and he welcomed 1945 with "I'm Just a Lucky So-and-So" and "Everything but You." To top things off, composer-lyricist-arranger Billy Strayhorn came onboard in 1939, creating one of the greatest artistic collaborations in jazz history. Strayhorn, incidentally, not Ellington, contributed the band's famous theme, "Take the 'A' Train," in 1941.

Ellington moved into the realm of extended compositions in 1943, premiering *Black, Brown, and Beige* at Carnegie Hall in January. Not only did he compose the music, he also wrote the accompanying libretto. He followed this work with *New World A-Comin'* in December of that same year. In 1944, he unveiled the four-part *Perfume Suite,* coauthored with Billy Strayhorn. Numerous other extended works would be forthcoming from Ellington, including *The Deep South Suite* (1946), *The Liberian Suite* (1947), and *The Tattooed Bride* (1948). Slowly, Duke Ellington came to be seen by critics and audiences alike as a significant American composer, someone "beyond jazz."[5]

Another event, in this case a single 1939 recording, also deeply influenced the development of jazz. Tenor saxophonist Coleman Hawkins, a renowned swing veteran of the Fletcher Henderson Orchestra and countless small groups, made a studio recording of "Body and Soul" (1939 [popular revival of a 1930 song]; music by John Green, lyrics by Edward Heyman, Robert Sour, and Frank Eyton) that announced to the music world that momentous changes awaited contemporary music. After touching on Green's melody, Hawkins launches into a long (two choruses, plus the coda), rhythmic improvisation that examines the harmonics of the song. Remarkably, given its abstract

The urbane Duke Ellington is shown leading his orchestra at a New York cabaret in 1943. Always an innovator, the war interfered little with his work, as compositions like "Things Ain't What They Used to Be" (1942) and "Do Nothin' 'Till You Hear from Me" (1943) attest. Library of Congress, Prints & Photographs Division.

qualities and absence of a recognizable melody, "Body and Soul" became a hit. A master instrumentalist, Hawkins presaged the bop revolution and its emphasis on chord structure and in so doing opened the boundaries of jazz to a new generation of artists.

At the same time Coleman Hawkins was dissecting "Body and Soul," a young guitarist named Charlie Christian joined Benny Goodman. He quickly became a regular in the Sextet, an extension of the former Benny Goodman Quintet (Goodman, clarinet; Lionel Hampton, vibraphone; Johnny Guarnieri, piano; Artie Bernstein, bass; Nick Fatool, drums). Christian's long, linear lines of improvisation, played over the more traditional 4/4 swing of the Goodman group, established new ways of listening to solo instruments, not unlike what Hawkins had achieved.

Drummer Gene Krupa, formerly a star with Goodman in the 1930s, formed his own band in 1941, one that spotlighted trumpeter Roy Eldridge, or "Little Jazz," and vocalist Anita O'Day. They enjoyed a hit with a 1941 effort, "Let Me Off Uptown" (1941; words and music by Earl Bostic, Roy Eldridge, and Redd Evans). O'Day's sassy singing and Eldridge's piercing trumpet work would prove strong influences on a new generation of players, and it all indicated changes ahead. Since O'Day was white and Eldridge was black, the close interplay between the two presented the evolving face of jazz in the 1940s. More and more bands and groups became racially integrated, quietly and without fuss for the most part, and this progress would continue throughout the decade.

While Gene Krupa and his orchestra opened new vistas for contemporary popular music, veteran pianist Earl Hines, a virtuoso performer in almost any style, formed a band under his own name during the 1942–1943 period. It had a young trumpet player from South Carolina, John Birks "Dizzy" Gillespie, in the brass section, and a young Kansas City alto saxophonist, Charlie "Bird" Parker, in the reeds. An equally youthful Sarah Vaughan doubled on vocals and occasional piano, and Billy Eckstine, the "sepia Sinatra," as some labeled him, carried the male singing duties. This remarkable lineup thus included some of the top names in modern jazz, and the Hines orchestra would at times perform some of the now-classic tunes associated with the musical changes of the 1940s. For example, "A Night in Tunisia" (1942; music by Dizzy Gillespie), destined to become a jazz standard, could be found in Hines's repertoire.

At the same time, bandleader Cab Calloway, perhaps most popular for his humorous vocal, or jive, renditions of tunes such as "Minnie the Moocher" (1931; words and music by Cab Calloway, Irving Mills, and Clarence Gaskill), by the early 1940s allowed considerable latitude for his musicians, a roster that also briefly included trumpeter Gillespie, among other young artists. In spite of some superior swing arrangements, Calloway's recordings give little evidence of any modernist innovations, and Gillespie merely played as part of the ensemble, but gained invaluable experience along the way.

Perhaps encouraged by his work with Earl Hines, Billy Eckstine branched out with his own band in 1944. In retrospect, this pivotal orchestra stands as a virtual who's who of modern jazz innovators, and it often presaged some of the changes ahead for traditional swing bands and also for jazz. In addition to Gillespie and Charlie Parker, both of whom had apprenticed with Earl Hines, Lucky Thompson and Gene Ammons played tenor saxophones, Art Blakey kept time on the drums, and Sarah Vaughan returned to the bandstand as a vocalist. Most importantly, Eckstine counted among his arrangers Tadd Dameron, Boyd Raeburn, Budd Johnson, and Gillespie—a stellar group of inventive writers in the evolving jazz idiom. In no way did this orchestra qualify as a traditional swing ensemble. Thanks to recording contracts with the DeLuxe and National labels, two pioneering independents, Eckstine's group survived the war years and looked toward the second half of the decade with some optimism.

The Birth of Bebop

In their after hours, many of the young and enterprising musicians who would come to fame throughout the 1940s went to Minton's Playhouse. A small club in Harlem that had opened in 1940, Henry Minton owned and ran it; he hired Teddy Hill, a musician himself, in 1941 as manager. Regulars included the aforementioned Gillespie and Parker, along with tenor players Lester Young and Budd Johnson, pianists Thelonious Monk and George Wallington, drummers Kenny Clarke and Max Roach, bassists Milt Hinton and Oscar Pettiford, and guitarist Charlie Christian. These up-and-coming artists also congregated at the many jazz clubs then lining New York City's 52nd Street between Fifth and Seventh avenues. This locale, often called "Swing Street," or more simply "the Street," had reigned as a jazz mecca for musicians black and white, traditional and modern, since the mid-1930s. Most of the establishments on 52nd Street encouraged impromptu jam sessions, where players could test their skills in a competitive, but friendly, atmosphere.

Some of the clubs featured traditional jazz, or Dixieland, but they were in the minority. The music most likely to be heard in the early 1940s came to be called *bebop*. A few at first referred to it as *rebop*, but both forms soon came to be shortened to *bop*. Etymologically, *bebop-rebop-bop* probably derives from the music itself. A musician might take several bars and rhythmically play them be-bop, be-bop, and so on. Singers, instead of articulating words when imitating instruments, might also use these terms as part of their so-called scat singing, improvisational vocalizing that replaces regular speech with made-up syllables such as "oop boop bop sha bam." Whatever its roots, *bop* became the commonplace term during 1943–1945 when referring to this new jazz format.

Bop mixes swing, gospel, stride, and the blues, but it also has silences, starts and stops, unusual rhythms, unexpected chord changes, and flatted fifths. It will mix 12-bar blues and 32-bar popular songs, as players create intricate solos that completely disguise the original melody. Whereas most swing bands relied on a steady 4/4 beat, in bop, the drummer employs the top cymbal to carry the beat, and the bass drum (or snare) drops *bombs*—explosive accents. The brass and reeds then build solos on long improvisational lines instead of short bits, but perform them in a rapid-fire manner that often consists of eighth notes. In the early 1940s, it all sounded like nothing that had come before. And not everyone liked it. Traditionalist guitarist Eddie Condon reputedly uttered a famous statement about bop at that time, "We don't flat our fifths, we drink them!" Other nay-sayers called the music dissonant, nervous, even frantic, and deemed it unlistenable. On the other side, the boppers called those who opposed their music "moldy figs"—people stuck in a musical rut, unable to move ahead.

At first, bop attracted mainly young black musicians, most of whom expressed disdain for swing, calling it "too white," too arranged, too predictable. They had also grown restive with the artificial racial restrictions they saw around them, especially in the segregated South. In time, however, a number of white artists also found it attractive, although much of the integration in bop occurred after the war years. Black or white, the players turned their backs on tradition and challenged their audience to discard the past and come along with them. Bop was revolutionary, a musical expression by youth. Concurrent with bop, and often associated with it, was the rise of zoot suits, an exaggerated style of male dress featuring severely pegged pants, long coats with equally long key chains, berets and pork pie hats, and goatees. An insiders' slang accompanied the fashion statements, giving worried parents and other adult authority figures indicators of change in the air. For the young artists, their music wasn't their parents' music, their jive wasn't their parents' jive. In the eyes of many, however, especially commercial promoters, the biggest downside to bop rested with the fact that people could not dance to it.

Some of the smaller independent record labels—Keynote, Savoy, Blue Note, Guild, Musicraft, Manor, Dial, and several others—emboldened by Decca's capitulation to the AFM's terms during the 1942–1944 recording ban, began capturing this new music in late 1943, so at least some of it got preserved. (See chapter 4, "Recordings and the Music Business," for more about the ban.) Also, a few individuals, in possession of recording equipment, taped a number of early performances. In some instances, their efforts eventually turned up in commercial markets, sometimes long after the event took place. For the most part, these early recordings, both professional and amateur, tended not to be the best examples of bop. They occasionally possess inferior sound, the performances tend to be uneven, and so they display an art in its formative period, as the musicians struggle with this often unfamiliar music.

Finally, in the fall of 1945, a few of the leading interpreters of bebop—Dizzy Gillespie, Charlie Parker, Max Roach, and several others—got to create some timeless examples of early bop when they gathered at the recording studios of Savoy Records. A teenaged Miles Davis even participated in a session or two, but his fame still lay years ahead of him. Among the tunes, "Salt Peanuts" (1944; music by Dizzy Gillespie and Kenny Clarke), "Groovin' High" (1945;

music by Dizzy Gillespie), and a song with a prescient title, "Now's the Time" (1945; music by Charlie Parker), were destined to become jazz classics, although they did not receive that kind of praise immediately. Several tunes took their structure from older, more established numbers: "Ko Ko" (1945; music by Charlie Parker; based on the chord changes of Ray Noble's 1938 swing classic "Cherokee," and not to be confused with Duke Ellington's 1940 tune bearing the same title), "Ornithology" (1945; music by Charlie Parker and Benny Harris; based on the chord structure of the 1940 tune "How High the Moon"), and "Hothouse" (1945; music by Tadd Dameron; based on the chord structure of Cole Porter's 1930 song "What Is This Thing Called Love?"). These songs received their new names in order not to pay ASCAP licensing fees for the originals, a common practice in bop during those formative days. Plus, in their reinvented forms, a casual listener would probably be none the wiser.[6]

Beyond Bebop

While the Gillespies and the Parkers and the Monks experimented with bop in small group settings, two adventuresome orchestras, with white leaders at their helms, attempted to assimilate some of the new sounds in modern jazz for big bands. Stan Kenton and His Artistry in Rhythm Orchestra entered the turbulent jazz field in 1941. An early member of the growing roster of musicians with fledgling Capitol Records, Kenton achieved modest success with cuts like "Eager Beaver," "Artistry in Rhythm," and "Artistry Jumps" (all 1943; all compositions by Stan Kenton). From the beginning, he hired the best musicians available and featured top-flight vocalists such as Anita O'Day and June Christy. Not satisfied with the status quo, Kenton sought out new avenues of expression and dubbed his efforts *progressive jazz,* not swing or bop. After the end of the war, Kenton continued to move forward and became known as an orchestral innovator of the first rank and commanded a devoted following.

On the heels of Stan Kenton came Boyd Raeburn. Another leader in the progressive jazz vein, Raeburn had led groups in the Midwest during the 1930s and moved to New York City in 1942 to play some extended club engagements. Until this time, he had performed as the leader of a straight swing orchestra; with little to lose, Raeburn made the risky choice of experimentation when a fire destroyed his existing charts. Modernist arrangers Johnny Richards and George Handy provided provocative music when Raeburn took the plunge, a move that attracted others from the jazz community. Hardly a traditional dance band any more, the Raeburn organization immediately gained critical kudos but little commercial success. He finally had to disband his orchestra in 1948 for economic reasons; he had been too far ahead of his time.

Jazz is a music that constantly mutates, evolves. Bop self-consciously grew in clubs, jam sessions, hotel rooms, and buses on the road, drawing from all that went before it—the blues, stride piano, swing, from Louis Armstrong's amazing trumpet constructions to Benny Goodman's fluid clarinet stylings. Since this old wine came packaged in a completely new bottle, it took some time to find an appreciative audience. Only toward the end of World War II did bop begin to attract the curious, and not until the postwar years did it mature into a full-fledged jazz style.

RHYTHM 'N' BLUES BACKGROUND

With the decline of swing and the rise of new jazz styles, the problem faced by musicians, especially black artists attempting to extend the boundaries of musical expression, revolved around reaching a mass audience. A newly assertive black working class, made relatively prosperous by wartime industry and plentiful jobs, found much of traditional swing overarranged and lacking in any spontaneity, but they also rejected the intellectually complex bop and modernist, or progressive, jazz then developing as undanceable and unlistenable. Tired by the war and searching for entertainment, this audience instead chose yet another style that called itself *rhythm and blues*. Fans quickly shortened the term to the more familiar *rhythm 'n' blues* during the late 1940s, and from there it went to the present-day *R&B*.

Reliant on a strong beat and eminently danceable, with a heritage of Southern and urban blues, this genre and an eager public soon found one another. Although the audience for rhythm 'n' blues was predominantly black at first, it also proved attractive to many white listeners, most of them youthful and equally dissatisfied with contemporary swing and jazz. The subsequent rise of this genre paralleled that of another style then achieving popular recognition: country music; both formats, however, experienced rapid growth during the postwar years. (See chapter 7, "Country Music," for more on this musical style.)

Early Rhythm 'n' Blues Artists

As was the case with bop, most early rhythm 'n' blues songs were initially recorded by small, independent labels. The larger companies, like Columbia and RCA Victor, shied away from what they termed "race music," operating on the assumption—later proved erroneous—that consumers (i.e., whites) would not accept this format, especially with its embrace of lusty good times and sexual innuendo.

Boogie-woogie, a popular sensation in the late 1930s and early 1940s, provided an impetus for the move toward rhythm 'n' blues. If Claude Thornhill epitomized a light, airy touch, bandleader Louis Jordan's approach to music went the other way, emphasizing a strong beat and frequent humor. A versatile reed player and singer, Jordan initially formed a group in the late 1930s that came to be called Louis Jordan and the Tympany Five (originally, the group's drummer, Walter Martin, included timpani in his setup, an unusual addition). In 1941, Jordan made a record for Decca that featured "Knock Me a Kiss" (1942; music by Mike Jackson, lyrics by Andy Razaf) on one side and "I'm Gonna Move to the Outskirts of Town" (1941; music by Casey Bill Weldon and Roy Jacobs, lyrics by Andy Razaf) on the other. The recording took off as an immediate hit; its combination of slangy lyrics (or *jive,* to use the language of the time) on "Knock Me a Kiss" and the timeless blues of "I'm Gonna Move to the Outskirts of Town" proved irresistible to record buyers and made Jordan and his band a force in the marketplace.

He followed this success with a novelty number called "Five Guys Named Moe" (1942; words and music by Larry Wynn and Jerry Bresler), another humorous tune that further solidified Jordan's popularity. In 1944, he continued his winning ways with "Is You Is or Is You Ain't My Baby?" (1944; music by Louis Jordan, lyrics by Billy Austin), a fast-paced vocal effort atop a rocking, rhythmic beat, and followed it the next year with the similarly frenetic "Caldonia" (1945; words and music by Fleecie Moore). Incidentally, Woody Herman's orchestra also boasted a big hit with "Caldonia," including a breathless vocal by Herman himself and some unison trumpet work suggestive of ongoing bebop phrasing. With this string of commercial successes, Louis Jordan went far in acquainting the mainstream listening public with the basic elements of rhythm 'n' blues. When this style became increasingly popular during the postwar era, Jordan emerged as a major presence, much imitated, in American popular culture for many years to come.

Another rhythm 'n' blues pioneer was Jay McShann. A graduate of the vibrant jazz scene in Kansas City during the 1930s, he led a group of his own in the later years of the decade; it endured until 1944. After a stint with the Army, McShann formed a new aggregation that focused on hard-rocking blues. Although he never achieved wide popularity, McShann did help point the way toward this evolving format, and he signaled a movement away from the tightly arranged numbers that had so characterized swing in its heyday. McShann also hired several promising musicians, particularly altoist Charlie Parker, and provided them their first exposure, a move that hastened the onset of modern jazz, albeit in a Kansas City-based swing and rhythm 'n' blues setting.

Although real commercial success eluded most bands attempting to emulate the rhythm 'n' blues style during the early 1940s, that did not stop other musicians such as Earl Bostic, Wynonie Harris, Big Jay McNeely, Lucky Millinder, Roy Milton, Hal Singer, Eddie "Cleanhead" Vinson, and Aaron "T-Bone" Walker from experimenting with its strong rhythmic format.[7]

CONCLUSION

When swing began to languish during the war years, jazz reasserted itself with renewed vibrancy. For many observers, swing had become tired—overly stylized, too arranged, and repetitive. Many of the big bands of the 1930s and early 1940s continued to cut recordings and play club dates. But the spirit, the excitement, of swing's formative years had dissipated, and jazz and other formats soon took up the slack.

Old-time, traditional jazz, or Dixieland, enjoyed a brief popular run, and highly experimental music, called, variously, *modern jazz, progressive jazz,* and *bebop* (quickly shortened to *bop*) began to be heard on records and in clubs. Hardly an overnight sensation, this frankly difficult, often cerebral, music challenged listeners and critics alike. Commercial acceptance proved long in coming, and by the end of the war its hold on audiences remained tentative. Not until the later years of the decade could these styles claim a substantial following, and even then resistance to modernism remained strong.

While swing and jazz struggled with changing formats, another area of popular American music, rhythm 'n' blues, began its long road to acceptance. Clearly a postwar phenomenon, rhythm 'n' blues can nonetheless trace its beginnings to the 1939–1945 period, a time of ferment and change for so much American popular music. With its emphasis on the beat, and because of its appeal to young people, rhythm 'n' blues paved the way for rock 'n' roll, arguably the dominant musical form for the last half of the twentieth century.

Collectively, these artists launched a revolution, the same as the players then taking up the new sounds of bebop and other forms of modern jazz. Without exception, however, the major accomplishments of these individuals would take place later in the decade, but they all honed their skills during the war years.

4

Recordings and the Music Business

BACKGROUND

As the 1930s drew to a close, the sales of phonograph recordings rose markedly. Led by an across-the-board demand for records of every description, manufacturers at last rebounded from the weak market they had endured since the mid-1920s and into the long, dark days of the Great Depression. An improved economy, the continuing popularity of swing in all its manifestations, the burgeoning jukebox trade, a radio in virtually every home, and a flood of musicals from Hollywood fueled this turnaround in the business. Not since the halcyon days of the early twentieth century did record companies fare so well.

Starting around 1900, the sales of record players had soared. Often styled as elegant pieces of furniture, complete with ornate horns that served as the speaker, they complemented any home décor. Companies like Edison, Columbia, Victor Talking Machines, Brunswick, Emerson, and several hundred lesser-known brands flooded an American market eager to buy. Close on their heels came countless recording companies offering music of every conceivable type, available as either cylinders or flat discs. But the bottom fell out of all this activity around 1926 with a newer craze: radio. The variety of music previously available only with recordings now became instantly accessible with the flick of a dial. Handsome radio cabinets replaced the phonographs so popular just a few years earlier. Between 1921 and 1932, the sales of recordings fluctuated, showing great strength in the early 1920s, falling with the rise in radio's

As ubiquitous as juke boxes, phonographs—old (this photo) and new—could be found in most American homes. This rapt listener, in a picture taken in 1940, resided in Mauch Chunk, Pennsylvania. Library of Congress, Prints & Photographs Division.

popularity, and then plummeting with the onset of the Great Depression. Not until the recovery of the later 1930s did sales rebound, and then they commenced an upward course that led into the prosperity of the postwar years (see table 4.1).

At the same time that the sales of records fell in the 1930s, the recording industry itself went through a number of complex and confusing changes. New labels came on the market, and old ones disappeared. Enterprising retailers, like the American Record Company (ARC), bought up old labels and

Table 4.1
Roller-Coaster Changes in Record Sales, 1921–1946

Year	Sales (Number Records Bought)	Sales (Dollars Spent)	Amount Spent in Contemporary Dollars, Adjusted for Inflation	Comments
1921	115 million	$106 million	About $1.2 billion	
1929	70 million	$75 million	About $884 million	In October of 1929, the stock market crashes, precipitating the Great Depression, but the year also witnesses the continued growth of radio, especially networks, and the overwhelming popularity of sound movies.
1930	40 million	$46 million	About $550 million	
1931	15 million	$18 million	About $244 million	
1932	10 million	$11 million	About $165 million	
1933	4+ million	$5 million	About $75 million	This year marks the depth of the Great Depression.
1934	5+ million	$7 million	About $100 million	At the end of 1933, repeal of Prohibition becomes official, and as bars and cocktail lounges reopen, jukeboxes assume an important place in part of many of them, spurring a rebound in record sales.
1935	7 million	$9 million	About $135 million	
1936	8 million	$11 million	About $163 million	
1937	10 million	$13 million	About $186 million	
1938	40 million	$26 million	About $371 million	A partial economic recovery is accompanied by the rise of swing.
1939	55 million, for both jukeboxes and home consumption	$36 million	About $520 million	Over 250,000 jukeboxes can be found in operation.

(continued)

Table 4.1 (continued)

Year	Sales (Number Records Bought)	Sales (Dollars Spent)	Amount Spent in Contemporary Dollars, Adjusted for Inflation	Comments
1940	80 million	$52 million	About $745 million	Over 400,000 jukeboxes are in operation.
1941	130 million	$95 million	About $1.3 billion	In the face of intense competition among manufacturers, record prices go down, and sales go up.
1942	130 million	$95 million	About $1.2 billion	The War Production Board sets limits on record production, but sizable inventories allow the industry to have another good year.
1946	275 million	$175 million	About $1.8 billion	With the beginning of the postwar era, predictions for upcoming years indicate a continued upsurge in consumer purchases; subsequent statistics uphold the predictions.

Note: Figures for the years 1943–1945 are not available.

Source: Much of the above information comes from Joseph Csida and June Bundy Csida, *American Entertainment: A Unique History of Popular Show Business* (New York: Watson-Guptill, 1978), 216–323.

reissued them under both their original names and newly minted ones. Innovators, such as Hit of the Day and Durium discs (a mix of paper and resins), employed various schemes to attract buyers. One of the most effective devices, lower prices, became a hallmark of the later 1930s, with 35-cent or three for a dollar (approximately $5.00 apiece, or three for $14.50 in contemporary money) discs a common item in department stores and record shops.

Despite all the stratagems, a falling-out occurred, and many small, independent labels went under financially at the close of the 1930s. American Decca, RCA Victor, and Columbia stood out as the primary survivors of this difficult decade. Decca, a relatively new company, boasted Bing Crosby on its roster of artists, and that alone seemed to assure profitability. Victor, with its vast catalogs of early recorded materials, especially in the area of classical music, was the one real veteran in this triumvirate. Columbia, an even older name, but in actuality a new venture, came into renewed being as the inheritor of the various ARC holdings. When CBS acquired the remains of ARC, it revived the Columbia name for its record division. With the arrival of the 1940s, however, still more changes in this volatile business lay in store.

Everyone in the industry began, in the days prior to the country's entry into World War II, to stockpile the various materials needed to produce phonograph

---

COLUMBIA RECORDS

Columbia Records, one of the oldest brands in recorded sound, dates back to 1888. Originally a distributor and seller of Edison phonographs and phonograph cylinders, the company derived its name from the District of Columbia. It began selling disc records and phonographs, in addition to the cylinder system, in 1901, and emerged as a major label in a crowded field. The economic problems of the 1930s, however, brought sharp sales declines, and the makers of Majestic Radios in 1931 acquired once-mighty Columbia. Three years later, the American Record Corporation (ARC) bought the label for next to nothing.

The new owners relegated Columbia to its slower-selling divisions, and it became essentially defunct in a short time. But in an ironic 1938 turnaround, the powerful Columbia Broadcasting System (CBS), which itself had been almost bankrupt in 1927, until financially rescued by the record company, bought ARC, a deal that included Columbia's vast catalog. CBS moved swiftly to resuscitate the failing label, adding new performers to its roster. In 1940, CBS sold the Brunswick division of ARC to American Decca and dropped the remaining ARC listings, with the exception of the Columbia label. At the beginning of the 1940s, a revived Columbia joined Decca and RCA Victor as part of a triumvirate that dominated the American recording field.

In its earlier heyday, Columbia Records had not limited itself to popular music, but instead had developed a classically oriented subsidiary, Columbia Masterworks Records. Returning to its former glory, in the mid-1940s, many notable musical artists recorded on the Columbia Masterworks label, including Aaron Copland, Leonard Bernstein, and Igor Stravinsky. In 1943, Columbia Masterworks became the first recording company to offer an album of an entire stage production—Broadway's revival of Shakespeare's *Othello*.

By the 1950s, Columbia Records had once more established itself as a dominant recording company and had contracted with several of that decade's biggest recording stars. In addition, it pioneered in the development of the long-playing vinyl microgroove record, making LPs commercially available to the public in 1948, a move that revolutionized the industry.

Throughout the war years, three commercial labels, along with one designed for service personnel only, tended to dominate most of the recording activities. Alphabetically, they were Bluebird, Columbia, Decca, and V-Discs. The giant RCA Victor Corporation created Bluebird as an economy label designed to compete with competitors' budget offerings. It featured many artists, perhaps the most important being Glenn Miller. The record shown here, "In the Mood," topped the charts for much of 1940 and went on to become a big-band classic. Columbia, a pioneer recording label, virtually disappeared during the 1930s, but rose from the ruins of the once-powerful ARC empire and emerged as a leading force in contemporary music. "Jingle Jangle Jingle," taken from a low-budget movie, became a hit in 1942. Decca, a new player in

the field, had its inception in the mid-1930s and boasted Bing Crosby on its roster of performers, a fact that guaranteed the fledgling company's success, given the singer's enormous popularity. The Decca record illustrated, "Beat Me, Daddy, Eight to Bar" (1940) shows another side of its offerings, a reflection of its eclectic approach to music, in this case the Boogie-Woogie craze of the early 1940s. The final label, V-Discs, resulted from labor disputes, a national recording ban, and the need for the armed forces to have access to the latest songs. A cooperative undertaking, the biggest names in American music contributed their talents to these unique pressings, as shown by this version of "St. Louis Blues March" (arranged in 1943) by Glenn Miller and his Army Air Force Band. The thousands of V-Disc tracks were almost unknown by stateside civilians, and in time became collector's items. All photographs by William H. Young.

records in case of any shortages. Alone among the major companies, RCA Victor had ample supplies of shellac, one of the primary ingredients in the manufacture of recordings, and also a strategic element for several war-related industries. The continuing high sales of discs, however, were quickly depleting existing supplies, and in 1942, the War Production Board placed arbitrary manufacturing limits on production, about 50 million records for the year. The board also froze prices at their 1941 levels, which meant a range of about 35 cents for a popular single to $1.50 for some classical compositions (roughly $4.80 to $20.60 in contemporary dollars). Fortunately, most companies had sizable inventories of songs from previous years, allowing them to sell more than their manufacturing allotment.

As the war drew to a close, the record manufacturers learned of another threat to their livelihoods. Soldiers returning from the battlefields of Europe brought with them news of a German tape recording machine more advanced than anything then on the civilian market. Called the Magnetophon, it used metallic tape that produced sound of unusual fidelity. It would be but a short time before American companies found themselves in a race to build an equivalent or superior tape recorder. Although this discovery of a new type of sound reproduction (most machines until then employed wire, not tape) did not immediately loom large as an omen of things to come, the more far-sighted in the industry realized that traditional disc recordings probably would not dominate music forever.[1]

THE ASCAP-BMI FEUD

In 1914, a group of composers and music publishers got together to draw up an organization designed to protect their musical creations from those who would perform them without acknowledgment and, more importantly, without paying any fees for the privilege. Out of those meetings grew ASCAP, or the American Society of Composers, Authors, and Producers. ASCAP signed agreements with the copyright holders for musical compositions and then collected fees from the users of those compositions for distribution to the various artists and producers involved. Within a short time, this group held a near-monopoly in the American music business, successfully demanding licensing payments for any songs written, performed, or produced by its members. Over time, the fee structure increased, the money poured in, and ASCAP became a powerful and prosperous force, holding the performance rights to most of the sheet music and recordings created in the United States from the date of the organization's 1914 inception until 1940. By the mid-1930s, some 15 established music publishers belonged to ASCAP, and they collectively controlled more than 80 percent of the most-played songs heard in the country.

With the rise of both radio and phonographs, problems of definition arose. ASCAP argued that playing a record over the air constituted a performance and demanded payment, whereas broadcasters replied that spinning a disc on the air equaled free advertising, caused listeners to purchase the recording, and therefore required no royalty. People in radio banded together in opposition to the ASCAP stance and, in 1923, formed their own interest group, the National Association of Broadcasters, or NAB. The new organization made no secret that it opposed any increases in licensing charges levied at stations or networks, which early on had been as low as $250 a year per station (about $3,000 in contemporary dollars) for the rights to play ASCAP music. The NAB argued that royalties should be paid to performers on a per-program basis, and not based on some blanket fee or whether or not they held membership in ASCAP. For many years, however, ASCAP held sway in the ongoing disputes, although the arguments continued to swirl, reaching a head in 1939.

At that time, ASCAP proposed increasing what it charged broadcasters for the right to play records by members of the organization, a decision which at that time included virtually all songwriters of any note. For their part, broadcasters felt both threatened and emboldened when, in the summer of 1939, a federal court decision ruled (1) that record manufacturers could license stations to play their recordings and that (2) radio stations could play recordings over the air and not pay any royalties to the musicians heard on them, and that such use did not constitute infringement of copyright. This complex, two-edged legal ruling, along with a long-festering dissatisfaction with ASCAP policies that broadcasters perceived as interference in their business procedures, set the stage for a showdown.

Appeals to the legal ruling followed, with a lower Pennsylvania court overturning a station's right to broadcast an artist without payment of royalties. In turn, the U.S. Supreme Court, in December 1940, refused to review a subsequent reversal of the Pennsylvania decision, in effect continuing to give radio stations the right to play music without royalty payments. Since records would be cheap programming, this decision led to the hiring of disc jockeys at most stations, a significant saving over retaining musicians for live performances.

Licensing questions, however, remained. Many radio stations, especially those affiliated with the three largest networks, the National Broadcasting Company (NBC), the Columbia Broadcasting System (CBS), and the Mutual Broadcasting System (MBS), along with the urging of the NAB, created Broadcast Music Incorporated (BMI) in 1940. The formation of this new body would, they hoped, counter the influence exerted by ASCAP and serve as a competitor by setting its own fees and issuing licensing agreements.

In an act of corporate hubris, ASCAP responded by raising its fee structure, a unilateral dismissal of any threat posed by BMI. As a result of this high-handed approach, BMI came into active being in February of 1940; it immediately announced, with near-unanimous station and network support, a radio boycott of all ASCAP artists. In effect, this meant the disappearance of most well-known popular music from commercial radio broadcasting because ASCAP furnished over 80 percent of the songs heard on commercial radio. The boycott would therefore create an odd situation: if people wanted to hear their favorite performers, they had to buy records, attend concerts, search out nightclubs and dance halls, or find other performance venues. Despite these predicted inconveniences, BMI did not back down.

When the boycott took effect in January 1941, 660 broadcasters (out of almost 800 active stations) promptly signed with BMI, as did a handful of publishers. Edward B. Marks, who held extensive catalogs of popular and Latin music, joined the new organization, as did Ralph Peer's Southern Music Publishing Company and M. M. Cole, both of which specialized in country-oriented music. As a result, broadcasters began programming considerably more country music than in the past, a situation that led to wide public exposure to the genre.

In the meantime, ASCAP immediately faced declining fees and public disappointment at the loss of many of their favorite artists on the air. Although ASCAP claimed to represent all musicians and had long collected licensing and performance fees from stations and networks, it only disbursed royalties to those with whom it had contractual agreements. That exclusivity meant that non-ASCAP musicians might have their music performed over the air, but ASCAP did not recognize them as members and denied them royalties. This kind of elitism made many artists ready for an organization like BMI, and the upstart group commenced an earnest search for people not signed with ASCAP. It also looked for songs in the public domain (no active copyright protection) that could be played on the air without dispute.

With the onset of the January boycott, American radio programming went through an overnight change. Instead of the most current popular tunes, listeners might at first hear old favorites by the likes of Stephen Foster or other nineteenth-century composers. For example, the Freddy Martin Orchestra, a moderately successful dance aggregation, arranged Tchaikovsky's *Piano Concerto in B-Flat,* a non-ASCAP classical piece, for airplay and recording. Retitled as "Tonight We Love" (1941; adaptation by Ray Austin and Freddy Martin, lyrics by Bobby Worth), it faced little competition and spent a number of weeks on the hit charts. The Glenn Miller Orchestra likewise combed the past and unearthed a traditional Russian folksong, "The Volga Burlack's [Boatmen's] Song." Arranger Bill Finegan turned this morose piece into the swinging "Song of the Volga Boatmen" in 1941, and it soon became a major hit.

Theme songs for popular radio shows likewise underwent some changes. Comedian Eddie Cantor had to replace his ASCAP-licensed "One Hour with You" (1932; music by Richard A. Whiting, lyrics by Leo Robin) with the old

"Good Night Ladies," also called "Merrily We Roll Along" (1853; music by Ferd V. D. Garretson, lyrics by E. P. Christy). *Amos 'n' Andy* dropped "The Perfect Song" (1915; music by Clarence Lucas, lyrics by Joseph Carl Breil) and used "Angels' Serenade" (c. 1860; words and music by Gaetano Braga), a non-ASCAP composition. Cigarette-maker Philip Morris, which had featured Ferde Grofe's readily identified "On the Trail" (1933; taken from his *Grand Canyon Suite*) for its commercials, substituted Tchaikovsky's *Andante Cantabile* (adapted from his *String Quartet No. 1* of the 1880s), another piece outside ASCAP's control.

On the other hand, the scarcity of usable, non-ASCAP songs spurred an interest in Latin music by writers not connected to the organization. Tunes like "Amapola (Pretty Little Poppy)" (1941 [popular revival of a 1924 song]; music by Joseph M. Lacalle, lyrics by Albert Gamse), "Green Eyes" ("Aquellos Ojos Verde," 1941; music by Nilo Menendez, lyrics by Adolfo Utrera, E. Rivera, and Eddie Woods), "Maria Elena" (1941 [popular revival of a 1933 tune]; words and music by S. K. Russell, Lorenzo Barcalata, and William H. Heagney), and "Yours" ("Quiereme Mucho," 1941 [popular revival of a 1931 song]; music by Gonzalo Roig, lyrics by Augustin Rodriguez, English adaptation by Jack Sherr) attracted considerable attention, gained airplay, and ended up as American hits. These compositions had originally been written outside the United States and thus lacked ASCAP licensing. Many other South American songs also strove to break into the profitable U.S. market during this difficult time.

But as BMI's hunt for usable music and competent musicians continued, their investigations revealed that over the years, ASCAP had regularly excluded most jazz and blues artists, folk singers, and country musicians, along with many black performers connected with the nascent rhythm 'n' blues field. It had instead sought mainstream performers, such as those in the broad areas of theater scores, movie soundtracks, classics, and popular songs, and ignored more specialized or narrow avenues of expression.

Eventually, both sides reached some uneasy understandings, and the boycott of ASCAP music effectively ended in late 1941, with many stations signing new licensing agreements. Normalcy returned to the airwaves, but BMI had, in this short time, established itself as a worthy rival to ASCAP. Emboldened, BMI sought to attract those songwriters and musicians bypassed by ASCAP, with the result that its early rosters leaned heavily toward jazz, country, and what the general public perceived as "black music." For listeners, BMI gave many of them their first exposure to jazz and country. This approach meant that BMI would contract a disproportionate share of the stars in the jazz, country, and rhythm 'n' blues areas, what in time would turn out to be a gold mine for the organization. The period also signaled the transition from tradition to the new era of pop and rock 'n' roll, and it would not take long for BMI to at last emerge in the postwar era as coequal with its once-invincible competitor.[2]

THE AFM RECORDING BAN

In the summer of 1940, James C. Petrillo won election as the national president of the American Federation of Musicians, or AFM. Petrillo, who had previously headed the Chicago local of the union, came into office with an agenda he hoped would improve the lot of member musicians, especially in regard to compensation for recordings. Soon after assuming the presidency, he urged broadcasters that utilized phonograph records in their programming to pay fees to the AFM for this privilege. These charges would be in addition to anything already paid by stations to ASCAP or BMI for playing music of any kind. He also wanted record companies to participate in his plan by reimbursing the union on a graduated scale based on the number of AFM musicians participating in a recording session. Lengthy negotiations with the concerned parties ensued, but broke down in June of 1942.

In retaliation, Petrillo ordered a complete ban, effective the beginning of August, on any recording activity by union instrumentalists or bands. He did not, however, block radio stations from playing their libraries of older discs, despite his testy relationship with the industry. In the long run, this ban, which kept musicians out of the recording studios, hurt his membership as much as it hurt the record companies. He assumed the public's desire for recorded music, either through record sales or over the air, would force record manufacturers, along with stations starved for new material, to accede to his demands. At the time, many thought the broadcasters and record companies would quickly negotiate with the AFM and reach a settlement, but their expectations were not met. Everyone involved displayed a stubbornness that no one had foreseen.

JAMES C. PETRILLO, CZAR OF THE MUSICIANS' UNION

Chicago-born James Caesar Petrillo (1892–1984) served as president of the American Federation of Musicians (AFM) from 1940 to 1958; in that time, he gained prominence as the all-powerful leader of the musicians' union. The son of Italian immigrants, Petrillo learned to play trumpet at an early age but soon realized his musical limitations; in 1919, he turned from being a trumpeter to working as a labor organizer. He rose quickly in the Chicago Federation of Musicians and became its president in 1922.

While head of the Chicago local, he took on hotels, radio stations, and any other venues that utilized live music. Through bluster and outright intimidation, he got them to boost pay scales and improve working conditions. In the case of radio, he forced stations to hire union musicians and to carry them on their payrolls for years, regardless if they actually played or not.

A short, stocky, tough-talking man, Petrillo broke into the larger American labor scene in 1942, when he took a combative stance on the lack of compensation for musicians who lost work and income as a consequence of recorded music.

He led a nationwide strike that barred musicians from making recordings, a move protested by many, until the record companies agreed to pay royalties to the union. For almost two years during the darkest days of World War II, the nation's recording business remained effectively stalled.

The ban finally ended after many failed negotiations between Petrillo and the four major recording companies. First Decca, and then Capitol, capitulated in 1943; nearly a year later, RCA Victor and Columbia agreed to his terms. He would impose a second recording ban in 1948 that lasted nearly a year. It ended when the AFM and the recording industry forged a permanent agreement in the form of the jointly administered Music Performance Trust Funds of the Recording Industry, today known as the Music Performance Fund. Royalties derived from the sale of sound recordings go to this nonprofit fund, which, in turn, pays musicians to play at free public concerts. A trustee, independent of both the recording industry and the AFM, administers the fund.

Amid dissension and acrimony, Petrillo relinquished his national presidency in 1958; in a hotly contested election, he then lost the local Chicago AFM leadership in 1962. Despite his loss, he remained active with the AFM for several years thereafter.

Time dragged on, and the various record manufacturers and distributors relied on existing inventories to meet public demand. Their releases, however, all predated the union's ban, and consumers wanted new songs and new performances, music they heard live over radio stations or as the soundtracks in movies. Since the ban did not include live—but unrecorded—music, the public could still hear their favorite bands and musicians perform, but they could not purchase new records by them.

A curious sidelight to this standoff involved singers. The AFM expressly forbade bands and its members who played instruments to record (with the exception of the lowly harmonica; Petrillo declared it did not qualify as a musical instrument, so harmonicas can sometimes be heard on vocal recordings). The union did not block vocalists, who as a rule did not belong to the AFM anyway, from making recordings. Perhaps an oversight on Petrillo's part, but it had the result that a number of a cappella sides were released by enterprising labels. Frank Sinatra, Bing Crosby, Dick Haymes, and other popular singers attempted a number of such arrangements, and consumers bought them up; both Haymes and Sinatra, for example, recorded separate solo versions of "You'll Never Know" (1943; music by Harry Warren, lyrics by Mack Gordon), the 1943 Academy Award winner for Best Song in *Hello, Frisco, Hello*. Haymes also did "In My Arms" (1943; words and music by Frank Loesser and Ted Grouya) and "Wait for Me, Mary" (1943; music by Nat Simon and Charles Tobias, lyrics by Harry Tobias), while Sinatra soloed on "Close to You" (1943; words and music by Al Hoffman, Carl G. Lampe, and Jerry Livingston), and few listeners seemed any the wiser. The Mills Brothers, a popular vocal group, likewise released "Paper Doll" in 1943, a revival of a 1915 song penned by Johnny S. Black, without any instrumentation, and it emerged as the #2 song of the year. Some enterprising singers even vocally imitated instruments to provide more of a backup to their musician-less performances.

With World War II raging overseas, pleas were made to Petrillo to lift the ban for the sake of morale, especially as regarded service personnel deprived of recorded music. The union president, however, refused to budge, although he did agree to the government-run program of V-Discs. The National War Labor Board, which oversaw the utilization of manpower, in 1944 ordered the ban lifted, but Petrillo remained adamant, and nothing happened. Even President Roosevelt, several months later, urged the feisty labor leader to drop it, again to no avail. But both the War Labor Board and Roosevelt had stepped into the discussions belatedly, and Petrillo knew full well that things would turn in his favor shortly.

In the fall of 1943, the first cracks in the defense against the union had already appeared. For some time, the record companies and several major radio stations had been working behind the scenes to solve the impasse. Led by Decca Records and several stations, a tentative agreement with the AFM was finally struck in September of 1943, some months prior to appeals made by the War Labor Board and Roosevelt. Many smaller labels likewise agreed to the terms—all in the AFM's favor—as did a number of broadcasters, but two recording giants, RCA Victor and Columbia, held out until the fall of 1944 before capitulating. In November, after more than two years' duration, Petrillo lifted the last remnants of the recording ban, and new pressings began to come onto the market. Jubilant consumers flocked to record stores to purchase the latest discs, and things returned to normal in the usually more placid world of American music. For the next several years, the victorious Petrillo continued to make demands, and relations among officials of ASCAP, BMI, music publishers, record companies, broadcasters, and the AFM remained frosty at best. Petrillo's imperious approach to labor disputes eventually led to federal laws limiting the power of unions later in the decade, although he attempted another recording ban in 1948.

With the onset of peace and the threat of television looming in the immediate future, and with the federal government looking into antitrust violations, the postwar era gave every indication of being as confusing and complex for the music industry as the tumultuous years of the early 1940s.[3]

JUKEBOXES

Although coin-operated machines date back to the end of the nineteenth and beginning of the twentieth centuries, in general, they possessed little visual appeal, frequently broke down, and thus had little impact on the music industry. By 1927, however, the forerunners to the modern jukebox began making an appearance. The Automatic Instrument Company, or AMI, introduced an early model that held eight records, and customers paid a nickel to hear a song. Eight selections soon went to 24 during the 1930s, and a nickel (worth about 60 cents in current money) still bought a single play, but a quarter (about $3.60 today) purchased six selections. By the early 1940s, a few machines boasted 16 plays for 50 cents (about $6.85 today). A few enterprising distributors, aware of all the noise at a typical jukebox location, even went so far as to offer three minutes of silence for a nickel, but little evidence exists that their idea ever took particular hold.

With the repeal of Prohibition, reopened bars and cocktail lounges installed great numbers of the increasingly attractive (some might say garish) machines. From those venues, they quickly spread to ice cream parlors, soda fountains, and restaurants—any places where music might boost business. Customers saw them as a form of cheap entertainment; proprietors saw them as drawing cards. Within a short time, three major American companies had come to dominate the jukebox field: Rock-Ola, Seeburg, and Wurlitzer. By mid-decade,

Found virtually everywhere by the 1940s, juke boxes had become a part of the American musical scene. The one in this photo was located in the Student Union at the University of Nebraska in Lincoln. Library of Congress, Prints & Photographs Division.

distributors had placed about 34,000 machines, a number that grew to 300,000 by the late 1930s. They all relied on commercially available recordings as their music sources, thereby providing an enormous shot in the arm for American record companies, especially in the later 1930s and early 1940s.

At the beginning of the 1940s, 400,000 jukeboxes dotted the land, sporting imposing names like *Night Club, Peacock, Singing Tower, Streamliner,* and *Throne of Music.* Insatiable machines, they consumed over 13 million discs a year, or almost 15 percent of the total output of the nation's record companies. One firm in particular, Decca, thanks to its lineup of stars like Bing Crosby, the Andrews Sisters, and Ella Fitzgerald, dominated the jukebox trade, at one time boasting a whopping 90 percent share of sales.

Beginning in 1944, *Billboard* magazine, a widely read trade journal, posted a weekly chart it called "Most Played in Juke Boxes," a listing of the individual songs currently available for play. This coverage of the jukebox business underscored the importance given to the coin-operated machines. What people heard on them they frequently bought, with the result that jukeboxes, thanks to their heavy use, exerted a strong influence on the acceptance and sales of individual songs.

Coupled with the continuing popularity of swing and the rise of vocalists as an important component of the contemporary music scene, jukeboxes could be found just about anywhere by 1940. Most important of all, they made money, both for the establishments willing to having them and for the music business in general. The war years dampened the enthusiasm for jukeboxes in only one way: shortages and regulations on the use of strategic materials, such as aluminum and plastics, sharply limited their production. Any large-scale increases in available markets for new jukeboxes would have to wait until the end of hostilities and the relaxation of government controls on consumption.[4]

THE RISE OF THE SMALL, INDEPENDENT RECORD LABELS

As the 1930s drew to a close, three labels had risen to dominate the recording field: RCA Victor (particularly with its less expensive Bluebird subsidiary), Columbia (born out of the dissolution of the once-mighty American Record Corporation [ARC] empire), and Decca (a relative newcomer, founded in 1934). A number of smaller companies, usually referred to as *independents* because of their lack of any connection, financial or otherwise, with their larger counterparts, competed for the remaining fragments of the market, but the Big Three accounted for the majority of sales.

Around 1932, Milt Gabler, proprietor of New York City's famed Commodore Music Shop, decided to create an independent label catering to jazz aficionados. His shop, already a mecca for collectors searching for records by specific artists, prospered with the growth of the swing era, and Gabler saw an opportunity to capitalize on their enthusiasm. He named his nascent line of recordings, at first reissues culled from other labels, after the music shop. Always an entrepreneur, he and several associates formed a fan club for like-minded jazz devotees, the United Hot Clubs of America. From that grew one of the first record clubs, with its own line of UHCA recordings.

When the larger labels saw how well Gabler's Commodore line was doing, they ceased giving him permission to reissue their material, figuring they could do the same thing themselves. Their decision prompted Gabler to move into production, and in 1938, a new line of Commodore records came into being. Hardly a major label, this independent operation, like his United Hot Clubs of America, aimed for the jazz niche market and established itself accordingly. Gabler oversaw recording sessions featuring the top musicians and vocalists of the day. Whereas Victor and Columbia might release the latest tracks by top sellers like Glenn Miller, Artie Shaw, and Benny Goodman, Commodore put out sides by such lesser-known artists as saxophonists Coleman Hawkins and Lester Young, trumpeters Hot Lips Page and Bobby Hackett, pianists Teddy Wilson and Fats Waller, and vocalist Lee Wiley. In 1939, Columbia even lent the label singer Billie Holiday (who was under contract to Columbia) so they would not be associated with the controversial antilynching song "Strange Fruit" (1939; words and music by Lewis Allan [pseudonym of Abel Meeropol]). Commodore endured until 1954 and the rise of rock 'n' roll, a movement that erased many of the older small labels but brought with it a host of new ones.

At the time, however, Commodore's success brought other independents into the field. In 1938, the Hot Record Society, another organization devoted to collectors and fans, created its HRS label. Bob Thiele's jazz-oriented Signature records soon followed suit. Blue Note, the 1939 creation of two German emigrants, Alfred Lion and Frank Wolff, emerged as one of the leading jazz producers during the postwar era. That same year also saw Solo Art, a brand that focused on boogie-woogie.

All the independent labels endured tough going since they tended to appeal to small, select audiences. Despite their considerable enthusiasm, these markets generated limited sales. To make matters worse, in April 1942, the War Production Board cut domestic shellac consumption by 70 percent. Record manufacturers had to scramble to find adequate supplies, and a search ensued to discover a suitable substitute. In the meantime, they cut back on production runs, and shoppers at times experienced shortages of new records.

It therefore took a courageous (or foolish) firm to bring out a new label. Shortages, rationing, and fickle buyers provided formidable barriers to anyone wanting to get into the record business. But newcomers nonetheless appeared, led in 1942 by a Hollywood group initially calling itself Liberty Records. Formed by songwriters Buddy DeSylva and Johnny Mercer, along with music store owner Glenn Wallichs, Liberty soon changed its name to Victory, but that seemed too close to giant RCA Victor, so they finally agreed on Capitol Records. In a short time, this upstart organization, riding on several hits, became the first major record company based on the West Coast. Capitol's rapid rise caused the big three to become the big four among record producers.

Most people in the recording industry knew about the threat of a 1943 recording ban that could paralyze production. In light of the impending strike, DeSylva and Mercer worked tirelessly at recording as many artists as they could, thereby building up a backlog of titles to see the new label through the crisis, since the union had said the ban would not apply to previously recorded material. Their ploy worked, and Capitol came through the crisis poised to make further inroads on the territory held by RCA Victor, Columbia, and Decca.

A continent away, New Jersey–based Savoy Records also enjoyed a 1942 birth. Blues and jazz-oriented, Savoy was created by the colorful Herman Lubinsky using some early Fletcher Henderson sides and a handful of miscellaneous jazz discards contributed by associates. The label soon held recording sessions of its own and served as one of the pioneers in the evolving bebop style of jazz, as well as preserving the efforts of many relatively unknown black performers of the era. Savoy would emerge, in the late 1940s and early 1950s, as a leader in rhythm 'n' blues.

Other independents that rose to some notice during the war years include Keynote in 1943 and De Luxe and National in 1944. King Records, which also came along in 1943, specialized in country music and initially did well with it. It also had a subsidiary label, Queen Records, that marketed "race records," or recordings aimed at essentially black audiences. As such, Queen offered gospel and early rhythm 'n' blues. Following the war, Queen steadily outpaced King when the latter's roster of country artists sought other outlets. For the mid-1940s, however, King Records stood as one of the few companies that specialized in country and hillbilly music. One of 1944's newcomers, Apollo Records, tested the economic waters by featuring unknown black artists. The strategy paid off handsomely after the war and the subsequent rise of blues and rhythm 'n' blues.

By the end of 1945, some estimates have as many as 200 different record labels in existence. Most, however, produced little of lasting note, struggled financially, and disappeared shortly after their founding. This figure included many tiny operations, such as religious productions, politically influenced recordings, children's tunes, and the like. Although the independents often serve to introduce new trends in music, they seldom receive the benefits of popularity. If something catches on, a larger label will usually steal the innovators away, and the smaller company must begin the search for a hit all over again.

V-DISCS

In July of 1943, despite the musicians' strike, the Office of War Information (OWI) ordered that V-Discs (the *V* stands for *Victory*) be manufactured and made available to service personnel everywhere. Under the strong urging of the U.S. Army, and fearing a publicity backlash if he did otherwise, Petrillo granted the record companies permission to employ AFM musicians. A morale booster, the recordings were sent to troops, with 90 percent of them going overseas. Fearful that fragile shellac discs would never survive lengthy transport and rough handling (plus shellac was in short supply and a valuable wartime commodity), the government utilized the RCA Victor facilities in Camden, New Jersey, and commenced pressing these recordings on a new unbreakable plastic called Vinylite, the precursor to vinyl.

Beginning in the fall of 1943, the first monthly shipment of 100,000 V-Discs went out in boxes of 30 recordings each to American soldiers in both the European and Pacific theaters of operation. The following year, the number of records in each monthly box declined to 20 so that more boxes could be shipped overseas, and then fell to 15 in the latter part of 1945. The Navy, no doubt envious of the Army, along with the other service branches, came on board the program in 1944. Riding on a wave of success, 2 million more records (or some 100,000 boxes) made their way to the armed forces in 1944, and an additional 4 million discs were shipped in 1945.

The program proved so popular that the Army developed a portable, hand-wound phonograph for personnel stationed in isolated areas lacking power. The government also thoughtfully provided new steel phonograph needles in all shipments since steel needles had a tendency to wear out quickly, especially under hard, sustained use. Recordings destined for the military continued beyond the end of the war and did not stop until mid-1949, when the evolving technology of magnetic tape recording and the Voice of America replaced them. The government ultimately shipped a total of 8 million records during the six-year life of the V-Disc program. Over 900 separate recordings, featuring some 3,000 different titles, made up this figure, with each record holding several performances.

As a rule, each V-Disc consisted of a 12-inch, 78-rpm recording that bore a distinctive red, white, and blue label. In contrast, most commercial records, with the exception of longer classical compositions, measured 10 inches in diameter. This larger size, along with smaller grooves on the Vinylite surface, increased the time available per side, usually about six minutes instead of the customary three to four minutes. Manufacturers could therefore cut two three-minute songs, instead of one, to a side. They could also include, in some cases, extended takes on selected numbers, an important consideration for many jazz numbers.

The content of a typical V-Disc package included air checks (material taken off the air from stateside radio broadcasts), occasional original variety shows the armed forces produced, older music from company masters, movie soundtracks, and lots of newly recorded pieces. In time, and given the expressed preferences of the troops, the bulk of any package consisted of fresh material, with about 80 percent of it straight popular tunes, along with a generous sampling of big-band swing and small-group jazz. V-Discs also served as a means for getting country music to soldiers and their families. In addition to mainstream pop artists, a few popular country music performers participated in this effort. Classical and semiclassical, folk, and black music rounded out the selections. Regardless of the type of music, performers often provided recorded comments to accompany their selections, usually something that they hoped would further boost the morale of the troops.

The best artists of the day participated in the V-Disc program. Bing Crosby (whose version of Irving Berlin's "White Christmas" proved the most popular single title among the troops), Frank Sinatra, Glenn Miller, Benny Goodman (the clarinetist boasted the most individual sides of any performer), Harry James, and Tommy Dorsey led the way in overall popularity, although virtually any music from home found an enthusiastic audience.

Under rules jointly established by the OWI and the AFM, the contents of V-Disc packages were reserved for the armed forces exclusively and could not be obtained by civilians. The AFM stipulated that all masters would be destroyed at war's end, since the union did not want these royalty-free performances ending up in department stores and record shops. An exception to this draconian ruling involved the Library of Congress: it possesses a complete set of V-Discs. Of course, with millions of records in circulation among the armed forces, keeping them out of the hands of civilians proved impossible. Returning service personnel brought back some of their V-Discs, either knowingly or unknowingly breaking the law, and many of the recordings made exclusively for the program have long since become eagerly sought collector's items. Several enterprising record companies, at first mainly foreign operations attempting to avoid any potential prosecution, have reissued many of these previously unheard musical takes by the leading musicians and vocalists of the day. Today, several major American distributors have also assembled V-Disc material, and the AFM has agreed to its release.[5]

DISC JOCKEYS

Despite a reluctance on the part of stations and networks, not all the music coming out of radio speakers was live; from the early 1920s onward, broadcasters had used phonograph records in their studios. The need might arise to cover dead air spaces not taken by regularly scheduled live shows or band remotes; when this situation manifested itself, interludes of recorded music often filled these voids. Soon these interludes evolved into shows of their own, often featuring specific styles or particular musicians. At some indefinite time, but probably in the early 1940s, the hosts for this kind of programming, once called *platter spinners,* acquired the name *disc jockeys,* or DJs, since many people referred to phonograph records as *discs,* and certainly these men behind the microphones jockeyed (i.e., manipulated, handled) many discs during a program.

During the war, disc jockeys rose to some importance at radio stations across the land. With few exceptions, however, they did not reach the celebrity status they would later achieve with the rise of rock 'n' roll. They instead functioned to select and cue records and engage in some innocuous patter about the sides being played. The emergence of disc jockeys nonetheless signaled a change in American radio: no longer would stations rely on live performances or studio orchestras; stations instead served as conduits for recorded music.

Two pioneering DJs, however, defied most management thinking and enjoyed successful, prosperous careers spinning discs in imaginative ways. Al Jarvis on the West Coast, and Martin Block in the East, soon established themselves as leaders in this new field of radio announcing. In 1934, Jarvis began his calling with records on the air in Los Angeles, the sounds emanating from an imaginary ballroom that he devised at the station's studio. Block, in 1935, acknowledged his counterpart's success by hosting a similar show of his own, one that he called, simply, *Make-Believe Ballroom.* Of these two pioneers, Block rose to greater fame (and wealth).

He had been hired by New York's WNEW just a few years earlier for a weekly salary of $20 (about $310 in contemporary dollars). An innovator, as well as a born pitchman, Block bought records with his own money, playing his purchases on his show, adding a little patter, and endorsing products of all kinds during breaks in the music. Audiences took to his mellifluous voice and easygoing manner, and sponsors appreciated his endorsements. As an indication of the power of radio and the importance eventually assigned disc jockeys, by the onset of World War II, Martin Block boasted annual earnings in excess of $60,000 (more than $800,000 in contemporary dollars), plus he made a percentage on the sales of products advertised on his shows. A marketable product in its own right, *Make-Believe Ballroom* eventually went into syndication.

Although many broadcasters felt relying on recordings and disc jockeys lessened the importance of the station itself, the early 1940s witnessed a shift in emphasis. The networks would struggle against the change, but when television swept away traditional radio programming in the late 1940s and early 1950s, stations were left with little to do but turn to recordings for much of their content. And with the change came the reign of the DJ, the new arbiter of radio content. All of that, however, followed the war years, a time when most radio stations paid only cursory attention to the so-called platter spinners waiting for their moment.

CONCLUSION

With the war serving as a backdrop, the music business endured a stormy four or five years. A long-festering feud between ASCAP and upstart BMI led to a situation where radio stations could not play ASCAP materials, but they could utilize anything not licensed by the organization. Once that dispute was settled, the AFM attempted to ban activities by its membership until radio stations and record companies agreed to pay higher fees to the union for music that relied on AFM artists. Under the leadership of James C. Petrillo, the AFM won most of its demands.

In the meantime, record sales increased and jukeboxes flourished, which led to the rise of many small, independent labels. The public demand for all the latest songs hastened the rise of disc jockeys at radio stations, and the government instituted its successful V-Disc program for servicemen stationed abroad.

5

Music on Radio

BACKGROUND

From the early 1930s through the early 1950s, radio claimed the largest mass audience of any medium. Growing at a remarkable rate throughout the Depression and on into the wartime era, American homes with radio receivers rose from 67 percent in 1935 to 89 percent in 1945. During that same period, the number of commercial AM (amplitude modulation) stations on the air jumped from 616 broadcasters to 933—and all this growth came about despite economic disturbances and war-imposed shortages. From the moment they awoke in the morning, until they turned off the lights at night, radio allowed Americans to "stay tuned." By the 1940s, 9 out of every 10 homes possessed at least one receiver, and proliferating stations fiercely competed for listeners. Broadcasters across the land provided a virtual nonstop menu of news, sports, and entertainment, with music occupying an important place in their offerings.[1]

With a global struggle destined to go beyond anyone's worst fears, a struggle that would consume the nation's resources and attention, American radio responded. News broadcasts increased in number, and radio journalism attained a legitimacy it had never before known. Not only did people stay tuned, they stayed glued to their sets to learn the latest from fighting fronts around the world. Radio gave World War II an immediacy unlike any previous conflict.

Table model radios came in all shapes and prices. This Chicago dealer stands proudly beside his considerable stock, but wartime scarcities would soon make such merchandise difficult to find. Library of Congress, Prints & Photographs Division.

THE BROADCAST DAY

The entertainment function of commercial radio also acknowledged the country's increasing involvement with the war. Patriotism—support your country, support the troops at home and abroad, buy bonds, save scrap, obey rationing restrictions, give blood—became repeated themes from shows of all kinds. But, by the same token, much broadcasting continued to present cheerfulness and good spirits, an aural escapism that did not dwell on the

A civilian, residing in a mobile home, turns on her radio. In a pretelevision age, radios were deemed essential for both news and entertainment. Library of Congress, Prints & Photographs Division.

gruesome realities of protracted combat. Jack Benny, Fred Allen, Bob Hope, Amos and Andy, and Edgar Bergen (along with Charlie McCarthy) all told jokes, laughed along with their guests, and generally avoided anything of particular substance. They had risen to fame doing the same thing with the Great Depression, and audiences and listeners loved it. Following a grim news report, humor, accompanied by some buoyant music, served as a good pick-me-up.

For the most part, the songs and tunes emanating from people's radios presented an aural image of business as usual. Or so it might seem. Hundreds of new songs vied for attention annually, but only a handful became hits; fewer still lingered on past a month or two. A small percentage dealt directly with the war and went on to become popular hits—"A Slip of the Lip (Can Sink a Ship)" (1942; words and music by Luther Henderson and Mercer Ellington), "Comin' in on a Wing and a Prayer" (1943; music by Jimmy McHugh, lyrics by Harold Adamson), "(There'll Be a) Hot Time in the Town of Berlin (When the Yanks Go Marching In)" (1943; words and music by Joe Bushkin and John De Vries), "The G.I. Jive" (1944; words and music by Johnny Mercer), and others—but they proved exceptions amid the welter of tunes songsmiths cranked out during this time. Most pop music concerned itself with love and romance, the old staples of the business. Many carried an aura of sadness or loneliness, such as "A Boy in Khaki—A Girl in Lace" (1942; music by Allie Wrubel, lyrics by Charles Newman) or "Goodnight, Wherever You Are" (1944; words and music by Dick Robertson, Al Hoffman, and Frank Weldon), and oftentimes they would be indistinguishable from similar tunes that had absolutely nothing to do with the conflict. Since millions of sweethearts found themselves separated by events out of their control, people could interpret them as war songs or not, depending on the situation.

Regardless of how one chose to read the lyrics of a particular song, commercial broadcasting strove to please everyone during a typical day, and music-oriented shows of all kinds appeared on most station schedules. Mornings and afternoons might be weighted toward homemakers and children, but by evening the emphases shifted to dramatic productions, comedy, and variety shows, with music occupying a large proportion of such programming. For example, people with a taste for country music met their desires with just a spin of the dial (only a few sets, usually the more expensive models, boasted push buttons then, and they differed markedly from the electronic presets found on contemporary receivers). Those wanting swing, the latest pop songs, show tunes, or some relaxing classical selections could likewise easily find their particular favorites.

COUNTRY MUSIC AND COWBOYS

Given the importance of radio in everyday life during the 1940s, most newspapers published extensive station and program listings daily. A glance at such a schedule would reveal that, for country music fans, Saturday nights meant, first, *The National Barn Dance* out of Chicago, followed by Nashville's *Grand Ole Opry*. Since the National Broadcasting Company (NBC radio) carried both shows, most listeners could pick them up on their local NBC affiliate stations. Similar in content and presentation—*The National Barn Dance* had premiered in 1924, *Grand Ole Opry* in 1925—the two live programs offered a mix of humor, skits, and lots of down-home music. The *Barn Dance* segment led off the evening with its theme, the well-known "There'll Be a Hot Time in the Old Town Tonight" (1896; music by Theodore A. Metz, lyrics by Joseph Hayden). *Grand Ole Opry*, for its part, featured the music of its legions of guest stars, and something up-tempo usually opened the proceedings after a brief commercial for Prince Albert Tobacco, a longtime sponsor.

Even in the grimmest days of World War II, these two shows, erstwhile competitors that nonetheless complemented each other in all aspects, never missed a broadcast and claimed a base of listeners remarkable in their loyalty. Country music may have appealed to a limited audience, but it made up in dedication what it lacked in numbers. The long-term success of these two shows spawned a host of imitators over the years, such as the *Renfro Valley Barn Dance* (1937; Cincinnati, Ohio), *The Iowa Barn Dance Frolic* (1931; Des Moines, Iowa), *Korn's-a-Krackin'* (1941; Springfield, Missouri), *WOWO Hoosier Hop* (1932; Fort Wayne, Indiana), *WSB Barn Dance* (1940; Atlanta, Georgia), and *WWVA Jamboree* (1933; Wheeling, West Virginia).

Capitalizing on their movie fame, several cowboy stars who also sang parlayed popularity into continuing radio productions. Gene Autry and Roy Rogers, probably the best known of this group, enjoyed high ratings with their shows. Autry, "America's Favorite Cowboy," led the way with *Melody Ranch* in 1940, a fast-moving mix of humor, tales, and music. Throughout much of the war and amid considerable publicity, since Autry took time out in 1944 and 1945 for military service, the series delighted his fans, the Columbia Broadcasting System (CBS radio), and Wrigley's Doublemint Gum, his continuing sponsor. The show eventually survived for 16 years as a regular network offering, finally going off the air in 1956.

Autry's chief rival, Roy Rogers, the "King of the Cowboys," likewise made the transition to radio, premiering *The Roy Rogers Show* in 1944, a time when Autry was away in service. The Mutual Broadcasting System (MBS radio) carried it. Accompanied by the Sons of the Pioneers, a popular Western singing group of which Rogers had been a founding member, the program mixed music, comedy, and drama, but never as successfully as Autry's *Melody Ranch.* Burdened by an erratic schedule and far fewer affiliates, *The Roy Rogers Show* sputtered along until 1955. (See chapter 7, "Country Music," for more on this kind of music on radio.)

CLASSICAL PROGRAMMING

If country and cowboy tunes failed to meet a person's expectations, a further twist of the dial would reveal endless additional musical choices. Radio may have been perceived by many as appealing to the lowest common denominator, but in reality, both the networks and local stations aimed at a wide range of listeners. Unlike today, many broadcasters, including the networks, felt that programming featuring serious music increased the prestige behind the call letters, with the result that even tiny, low-power stations usually carried some classical offerings.

Friday evenings during the war years provided *The Cities Service Concerts* (called *Highways of Melody* after 1944), half an hour of quality popular songs and light classics. Late afternoons on Sundays, NBC, together with sponsor Coca-Cola, offered *The Pause That Refreshes on the Air,* featuring an orchestra led by Andre Kostelanetz. CBS countered with *Great Moments in Music* on Wednesdays, and Mutual featured the Longines Symphonette several evenings a week. Monday nights, however, belonged to NBC. At 8:00 P.M. (changing to 9:00 P.M. after 1942), *The Bell Telephone Hour,* from 1940 until 1958, blended renowned artists and genres, playing to an audience estimated in the millions nationwide. Immediately following came *The Voice of Firestone* (which, after 1942, actually preceded *The Telephone Hour*), a venerable series that had premiered on the network in 1928. Together, the two productions provided listeners a spirited musical mix that ranged from spirituals to show tunes to light classics in back-to-back 30-minute segments.

On a more serious musical note, NBC had its own NBC Symphony Orchestra, under the baton of the famed Arturo Toscanini from 1937 until 1954, usually on weekends. Because of contractual details, the equally renowned Leopold Stokowski often conducted in Toscanini's absence. Not to be outdone, CBS arranged with the New York Philharmonic Orchestra, led by John Barbirolli (1936–1941) and Artur Rodzinski (1942–1947), for broadcasting rights. The show aired on Sunday afternoons.

Other classically oriented performances could also be found, including such groups as the distinguished Boston Symphony Orchestra (NBC, Saturday evenings), the Cleveland Symphony Orchestra (NBC on Wednesday evenings until 1943; Saturday afternoons on CBS until 1947), the Indianapolis Symphony Orchestra (CBS, 1938–1943, various times and days), Alfred Wallenstein's Sinfonietta (Mutual, 1935–1945, various times and days), and *The Treasure Hour of Song* (Mutual, 1942–1947, usually Thursday evenings). Of course, no mention of classical music on radio would be complete without acknowledging Saturday afternoons and performances by the Metropolitan Opera. Premiering in 1931 on NBC, this show became a ritual for opera lovers everywhere and continued broadcasting throughout the war years and thereafter. Hosted by the urbane Milton Cross from its beginnings until 1975, and sponsored by Texaco from 1940 onward, *The Metropolitan Opera* became one of the longest-running shows in radio history, a tribute to its unstinting quality of production.[2] (See chapter 8, "Classical Music," for more on such programming.)

MAINSTREAM PROGRAMMING

Popular formats, such as jazz, swing, top hits of the day, and light instrumentals and vocals, occupied a vast middle ground in radio programming and claimed by far the greatest share of the radio audience. True, country and

Orchestra leader Tommy Dorsey performs at a typically large radio studio in front of a "live" audience. Most stations of any size boasted such elaborate facilities. Courtesy of Photofest.

classical music in the war years attracted their share of dedicated listeners, but they stood as two extremes on radio's musical spectrum.

During the early 1940s, the big swing bands continued their dominance, but the demands of the military draft depleted the pool of available male musicians. Large orchestras reduced their rosters, and small groups often had to break up following the loss of key players. The "girl bands," a product of the war, also filled in for their missing male counterparts, with groups like the Prairie View Co-Eds, the Darlings of Rhythm, the Sharon Rogers All-Girl Orchestra, Ada Leonard and Her Girl Band Revue, and the International Sweethearts of Rhythm touring dance halls and military bases, gaining appearances in occasional movies, and playing various radio shows. These shifts in personnel had little effect on programming, although Phil Spitalny's All-Girl Orchestra (The Hour of Charm), which had actually formed in 1934 as a novelty act, enjoyed a long-running 30-minute spot on NBC from 1936 to 1946. By and large, however, stations and networks did little to accommodate the changes brought about by the war, and radio remained a male-dominated medium, from conductors to bandleaders, from vocalists to instrumentalists. (See chapter 3, "Swing, Jazz, and Rhythm 'n' Blues," for more on the all-girl phenomenon.)

In addition to all the other shows that could be heard on any given night, NBC carried music of a distinctive sort with broadcasts by Fred Waring and his glee club, the Pennsylvanians. In a series of top-rated daily network shows during this period called, variously, *Chesterfield Time, Pleasure Time, Songs of Freedom,* and *Victory Tunes,* the Pennsylvania-born Waring warmed the hearts of legions of listeners by arranging old favorites and standards for both voices and orchestra. During the war years, his producers saw to it that these 15-minute shows always contained a generous serving of patriotic songs such as "The Marines' Hymn" (1867 [1919]; music by Jacques Offenbach, lyrics by L. Z. Phillips), "Don't Sit Under the Apple Tree (With Anyone Else But Me)" (1942; music by Sam H. Stept, lyrics by Lew Brown and Charlie Tobias), "Sky Anchors" (1942; words and music by Fred Waring), and "Praise the Lord and Pass the Ammunition" (1942; words and music by Frank Loesser). This approach further burnished his reputation, one he worked diligently to maintain.

Waring had established his orchestra and glee club format early in the 1930s when he first got into radio and recording, and from that time, he opened his broadcasts with a tune called "I Hear Music" (c. 1930; words and music by Fred Waring, Roy Ringwald, and Jack Dolph) and closed them with "Sleep" (1923; words and music by Adam Geibel and Earl Burtnett). His astute melding of lyrics and music made the Pennsylvanians the real stars, with the orchestra providing a discreet background without ever upstaging the glee club. It may have been syrupy music for some, but for his fans, Fred Waring could do no wrong.[3]

RADIO AND THE BIG BANDS

The period 1939–1945 must also be seen as the final cresting of the swing era, a time when big bands ruled and radio stations attempted to take advantage of their popularity. Except for a few stars like Bing Crosby, Frank Sinatra (and he owed his meteoric rise to big bands, especially Tommy Dorsey's), and Kate Smith, vocalists played second fiddle to the orchestras backing them. But the Duke Ellingtons, the Benny Goodmans, the Glenn Millers, the Artie Shaws remained dominant at least into the early years of World War II. It would eventually all change; roles would reverse, but not overnight. In the meantime, most bandleaders (and vocalists as well) paid lip service to war efforts both at home and abroad, but they directed the bulk of their music and singing at dancing, relaxing, and romancing. Ellington's "I Got It Bad (and That Ain't Good)" (1941; music by Duke Ellington, lyrics by Paul Francis

Webster), Goodman's "Slipped Disc" (1945; music by Benny Goodman), Miller's "A String of Pearls" (1941; music by Jerry Gray, lyrics by Eddie DeLange), and Shaw's enduring "Begin the Beguine" (1935; words and music by Cole Porter) hardly qualify as war songs, and they have maintained their popularity long since the cessation of hostilities.

In September of 1939, things fell apart in Europe; the German march into Poland dispelled any last, faint hopes for peace. But it would take time for current events to filter down into the world of popular music. At that same time, Glenn Miller, after a lackluster career, boasted a big hit in "Over the Rainbow" (1939; music by Harold Arlen, lyrics by E. Y. Harburg), as noncontroversial a song as anyone could wish, coming as it did from the smash 1939 movie *The Wizard of Oz*. Miller's success on the charts led CBS to offer him and his band a place on the network's schedule. Calling the program *Chesterfield Time,* it consisted of a 15-minute evening slot, three nights a week. He quickly graduated to other shows, such as *Sunset Serenade* (1941–1942) on NBC and *I Sustain the Wings* (1943–1944) on CBS and, later, NBC. At the

Guy Lombardo (on the left, before a microphone) fronts his band in a studio setting. Continuing sponsors often had flags and posters advertising their products to a studio audience. Courtesy of Photofest.

peak of his popularity, only his unfortunate death in 1944 on a military flight over the English Channel prevented Miller from furthering his success on radio.

Although the success of the Glenn Miller Orchestra hardly typified other swing bands, many aggregations also enjoyed both radio and recording exposure. Swing and the overwhelming popularity of the big bands came about in good part because of radio. As early as the 1920s, orchestras established themselves as fixtures at the larger stations, while smaller operations relied on the latest recordings. However the music came across the ether, it provided a background for a variety of programming. Soon the bands had their own time slots, and their selections, from romantic ballads to up-tempo numbers, characterized a significant percentage of the broadcast day.

By the late 1930s, band remotes—direct wires from a radio station to a hotel or dance pavilion—were old hat for many in the entertainment business. Remotes allowed the music to be transmitted to a participating station, which in turn would broadcast it to unseen listeners, often recording the proceedings in the process. If a band got lucky, the station would have a network affiliation, and so the program went out to countless stations and helped mightily in making the orchestra known to a wide audience. In fact, just such a remote setup assured the success of Glenn Miller. He and his band had played innumerable dances and had even cut some forgettable recordings for the Brunswick label. Despite the activity, the group seemed unable to inspire any great enthusiasm among listeners. In the summer of 1939, Miller landed a contract to play the Glen Island Casino, an elegant restaurant and ballroom on Long Island Sound. Some new charts from his arrangers clearly helped—including "Over the Rainbow"—but it took a series of remote broadcasts of the orchestra to capture the attention of millions. That, in turn, sparked a flurry of best-selling Bluebird records, and soon, Glenn Miller rocketed to the top in terms of popularity.

Prior to Miller's success, radio had already taken more than cursory note of swing and the big bands. *Let's Dance,* the show that made clarinetist Benny Goodman the "King of Swing," first began in 1934, so the roots for this kind of programming had been long established. In 1936, CBS premiered *The Saturday Swing Club,* and NBC made room for the long-running *Fitch Bandwagon* on Sunday evenings beginning in 1938. With a global conflict in the offing, the energy and optimism inherent in swing made for an effective contrast with the grim reality of war. Soon, the networks contracted dozens of orchestras, some sweet and some hard-driving, to capitalize on the overwhelming popularity swing had engendered. One of the outstanding examples of this approach involved *The Victory Parade of Spotlight Bands* (1941–1942, Mutual; 1942–1945, NBC; 1945–1946, Mutual), a constantly changing array of orchestras that played rousing music for servicemen and anyone else who liked swing.

With heady nightly salaries in the thousands of dollars (allowing for inflation, $1,000 in 1942 equals roughly $12,400 in contemporary dollars)—and sponsors and networks willing to pay these sums—everyone profited in the boom years of swing. Plus, the greater a band's importance on radio, the higher the fees it could charge for appearances. The following listing, hardly complete, suggests how eagerly radio promoted the big bands and swing during the war years. Only a few of the better-known leaders receive mention.[4]

Many additional orchestras played ballrooms, one-night stands, nightclubs, dining rooms, and the like, and the two major networks—NBC and

Table 5.1
Big Bands and Their Leaders Appearing on Radio during World War II

Bandleader	Shows	Dates	Networks
Cab Calloway	*The Cab Calloway Orchestra*	1941 1942	Mutual NBC (both shows summer replacements)
Tommy Dorsey	*Tommy Dorsey's Variety Show*	1942–1943	NBC
Duke Ellington	*A Date with the Duke*	1943 1945–1946	Mutual ABC
Benny Goodman	*The Benny Goodman Orchestra*	1942 1943	Mutual CBS
Glen Gray	*Glen Gray and the Casa Loma Orchestra*	1943	Mutual
Harry James	*Chesterfield Time*	1942–1944	CBS
Sammy Kaye	*The Old Gold Program,* *The Sammy Kaye Sunday Serenade*	1943–1944 1944–1948	CBS ABC
Guy Lombardo	*The Guy Lombardo Orchestra*	1941–1943 1944 1945–1946	CBS NBC ABC
Vincent Lopez	*The Vincent Lopez Orchestra*	1941–1943	NBC
Freddy Martin	*The Freddy Martin Orchestra*	1941–1942 1942–1943	CBS NBC
Glenn Miller	*Chesterfield Time,* *Sunset Serenade,* *I Sustain the Wings*	1939–1942 1942 1943 1943–1944	CBS Mutual CBS NBC
Raymond Scott	*The Raymond Scott Orchestra*	1940–1944	CBS

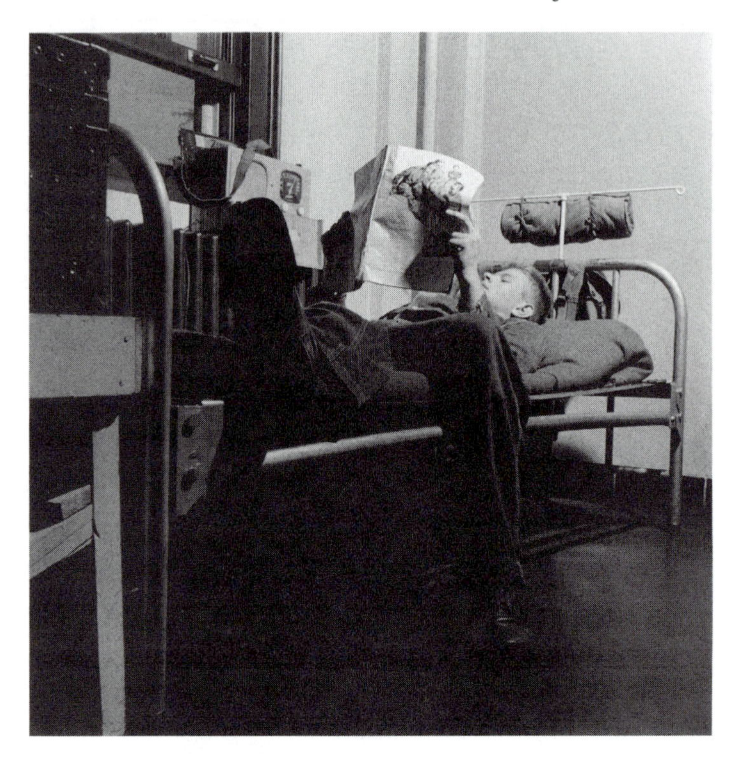

Radio provided American troops a vital link to the civilian world. Here a soldier relaxes with a magazine and his radio on a bunk at a Virginia military base in the fall of 1942. Library of Congress, Prints & Photographs Division.

CBS—maintained house bands, resident musical aggregations that were available much of the broadcast day. Made up of musicians of the first rank, these bands seldom traveled anywhere, but remained at the network studios to back up a variety of shows. Thus NBC had Les Brown leading his orchestra for *The Fitch Bandwagon* in 1944, Al Goodman and his band backed *The Fred Allen Show* from 1940 to 1944 (CBS), and Gordon Jenkins led the orchestra on *In Person, Dinah Shore* (1942–1943, NBC) and then took over on *The Colgate Program* (1942–1943, CBS). So it went at the busy studios, with a virtual game of musical chairs occurring as shows changed, along with orchestra personnel.

Although they played a major role in disseminating swing and jazz, black American bandleaders and musicians unfortunately found few opportunities to play on any commercial radio shows. In the listing above, only Cab Calloway and Duke Ellington crossed the invisible color line that blocked almost all black performers at stations and networks everywhere. On a brighter note, the federal government had created Armed Forces Radio, a War Department agency that worked to maintain morale among army personnel. Officials renamed the group the Armed Forces Network (AFN) in 1943. When it first began, the AFN provided both previously taped network programming and original shows for rebroadcast to military personnel based overseas.

Among its transcribed series of broadcasts was a show called *Jubilee* (1942–1953). Consisting of recorded appearances by top black artists for black service personnel, *Jubilee* could not be heard within the United States. Despite this ludicrous restriction, *Jubilee* allowed musicians of the caliber of Count Basie, Nat King Cole, Lionel Hampton, Teddy Wilson, Ella Fitzgerald, and Lena Horne, all at the peak of their creative powers, the chance to play and be appreciated by those few who could hear them.

MALE VOCALISTS

Vocalists, who had been but a small part of large aggregations in the 1930s, found themselves in demand during the 1940s, often at the helm of bands of their own. For example, Bing Crosby, one of the most popular entertainers of the 1930s and 1940s, took the reins of *The Kraft Music Hall* in 1936, replacing another major male star of the era, Al Jolson. A Thursday night tradition that opened with Crosby's theme, "Where the Blue of the Night (Meets the Gold of the Day)" (1931; music by Fred E. Ahlert, lyrics by Rou Turk and Bing Crosby), this NBC offering had made its debut in 1933 and ultimately ran until 1949. During Crosby's tenure, which lasted until the spring of 1946, its variety format presented a cross section of American popular music. John Scott Trotter, a close associate of Crosby's for many years, served as overall music director throughout World War II and saw to it that musicians of all kinds made the guest lists. Top-ranked jazz personalities performed their specialties, as did esteemed classical artists, and everyone considered it an honor to perform with Crosby on *The Kraft Music Hall.*

YOUR HIT PARADE

Billed as "an accurate, authentic tabulation of America's taste in popular music," *Your Hit Parade* debuted on NBC radio on April 20, 1935. Such was the show's popularity that in March of 1936, it commenced airing on both NBC and CBS, with NBC carrying a Wednesday evening segment and CBS airing it on Saturday nights. That arrangement did not last, and by 1937, CBS had exclusive rights to *Your Hit Parade.* But NBC regained the program in 1947 and would have it until its demise in 1957.

Employing a simple format, the program aired the nation's top tunes of the week, counting down to the #1 song, according to polls of disc jockeys, radio stations, dance halls, jukebox owners, and record stores. To add to the suspense, Lucky Strike cigarettes, the show's longtime sponsor, kept the results under wraps until the actual broadcast.

Initially, the program included 15 songs, but that number changed to 7, followed by 10 (the figure most people seem to recall), and finally stabilized at 9 in 1943. The songs varied from the latest pop tunes to novelty numbers to seasonal offerings. A jazz composition could occasionally be heard, and genteel rhythm 'n' blues crept in as the 1940s progressed. Some tunes made but one appearance, while others stayed at the top for months. An old favorite or standard might at times show up as a "Lucky Strike extra."

More than 50 singers or groups, along with 19 orchestra leaders, appeared at one time or another, and they ranged from the fairly well known (Frank Sinatra sang the hits from 1943 to 1945) to relative unknowns (Gogo Delys, Barry Wood, for example). As a rule, the top three songs received the greatest attention, each preceded by a drum roll, with the final song introduced as the "top song in the country, number one on your Lucky Strike hit parade." A show that enjoyed huge popularity during the 1940s, it clearly served as a barometer for American musical preferences.

In the early part of the 1940s, Frank Sinatra, 11 years Crosby's junior, challenged his older counterpart's show business dominance. The younger singer had rocketed to fame with the Tommy Dorsey Band at the end of the 1930s and, by 1941, rode a crest of popularity propelled by thousands of adoring fans. Seeing his potential to attract a youthful audience, CBS, in the fall of 1942, scheduled *Songs by Sinatra* for network distribution. Fifteen minutes long, as were many music shows at that time, it featured Sinatra, along with celebrity guests, in a mix of music and patter that strongly resembled, but on a smaller scale, the successful *Kraft Music Hall.* By early 1944, the network extended *Songs by Sinatra* to a full half hour and blocked it into the Wednesday night schedule, where it would remain until 1947. While ensconced at CBS, Sinatra, in 1943, also became one of the lead singers on the popular *Your Hit Parade,* a long-running Saturday night show that tracked the musical hits for the preceding week. He remained with *Your Hit Parade* for almost two seasons, and the added exposure made him an even bigger star as the postwar years dawned.

While these two giants vied for popularity, other male singers continued with careers of their own. During the late 1920s and early 1930s, veteran crooner Rudy Vallee had actually enjoyed greater popularity than Bing Crosby. But times and tastes change, and Crosby eventually eclipsed him, emerging as the most significant male vocalist of the later 1930s and into the war years. Vallee, however, remained an important presence on the music scene, especially on radio. A pioneer in the medium, his *Fleischmann Yeast Hour* (1929–1936, NBC) had blazed new paths in broadcasting. In 1940, he and NBC created *The Rudy Vallee Show* for Thursday evenings. Primarily a comedy offering, it boasted its fair share of music. When Vallee enlisted in the Coast Guard in 1943 to lead a service band, the series changed its format, devolving into *The Sealtest Village Store,* a situation comedy. Vallee returned to civilian life and other radio work in mid-1944, but his days as a singing star had passed.

Dick Haymes achieved considerable acclaim as a vocalist by performing with several top bands in the late 1930s and early 1940s, especially stints with Harry James, Tommy Dorsey, and Benny Goodman. Promoters groomed him as the natural rival to Crosby and Sinatra, and in 1943, CBS gave him a contract to do *Here's to Romance* alongside singer Helen Forrest, another popular singer and also a graduate of the Harry James Band. The following year, NBC offered him a 30-minute slot for a new production, *The Dick Haymes Show,* a series that ran until 1948. It also carried an alternative title, *Everything for the Boys,* a reference to the war. A smooth interpreter of ballads, his biggest hit came in 1944 with "I'll Get By" (originally 1928; music by Fred E. Ahlert, lyrics by Roy Turk), an older song that his version revived. Never successful in reaching the very top, Haymes nevertheless remained an engaging singer with a good radio personality.

Many other males took to the airwaves in the 1940s, but most have been forgotten today. Al Jolson, another enormously popular entertainer from the prewar era, performed more or less continuously on radio from 1932 onward, but the 1940s saw his career in decline. He did, however, host *The Colgate Show* over the 1942–1943 season. Similarly, the veteran vaudevillian Eddie Cantor had variety shows—*The Chase and Sanborn Hour, Camel Caravan, Time to Smile,* and others—on either NBC or CBS from 1931 until 1949, and popular music played a major role in all of them. In addition, Cantor stressed patriotic music and uplifting messages throughout the war years, much more so than most of his fellow entertainers.

Additional male vocalists gracing the airwaves during World War II included names like Jack Berch (many 15-minute slots during the 1940s), Morton Downey (the "Irish Troubador," his tenor voice was featured widely on radio during the 1940s), Vaughn Monroe (a regular guest and performer on numerous shows), Lanny Ross (the "Troubador of the Moon" enjoyed his largest radio audiences while starring in various shows under his own name between 1939 and 1942), and Jack Smith (after breaking into the big time with *The Kate Smith Hour,* he worked a variety of programs, including his own, from 1943 until 1952). Whether fresh young talent or fading stars of yesteryear, these artists kept the music coming and spirits up throughout the conflict, although none of them ever achieved any particular fame or association with tunes relating to the war.

FEMALE VOCALISTS

On the distaff side, singer Kate Smith carried an already successful radio career on into the 1940s. She had broken into broadcasting in 1931, quickly achieving major network status, and her enduring CBS show, *The Kate Smith Hour* (1936–1945), made her a household name. The "Songbird of the South," as her many fans knew her, entertained listeners mainly with music, sprinkling in comedy and light drama for variety. Graced with a strong contralto

Most major entertainers could be heard on network radio. Here vocalist Dinah Shore, accompanied by orchestra leader Paul Whiteman, in 1943 rehearses at a National Broadcasting Company studio prior to going on the air. Courtesy of Photofest.

voice, Smith created a repertoire of nostalgic, folksy tunes that appealed to an older audience. Her theme, "When the Moon Comes Over the Mountain" (1931; music by Harry Woods, lyrics by Howard Johnson), became a fixture that audiences immediately associated with her.

As the threat of a new worldwide conflict grew, composer Irving Berlin dug out of a trunk a long-forgotten song he had written for a musical comedy called *Yip, Yip, Yaphank*. Composed in 1918, the closing days of World War I, it bore the title "God Bless America." His resurrected composition emerged as one of the most inspiring songs of World War II. Impressed with Kate Smith's singing and personality, Berlin granted her exclusive rights to the music and lyrics of "God Bless America." In 1938, she sang it publicly on her show. It spurred an overwhelming audience response that soon made Berlin's forgotten number into a virtual second national anthem. Smith performed it countless times thereafter for war bond drives and any other occasion that called for stirring people's patriotic feelings.

Smith cut her first recording of "God Bless America" in 1939, and it received heavy airplay on stations everywhere, and soon became a weekly staple on *The Kate Smith Hour.* Throughout the conflict, her rendition brought her the admiration of millions. In 1943, Warner Bros. released *This Is the Army,* one of those star-studded flag-wavers that Hollywood did so well during World War II. Featuring Irving Berlin's music, the movie contains an episode that allows Kate Smith and a chorus to once again perform "God Bless America." When she died in 1986, her grave bore the inscription, "This Is Kate Smith—This Is America."[5]

Although Kate Smith may be the best-remembered female vocalist from the era, other women also achieved considerable fame. The Andrews Sisters (LaVerne, Maxine, and Patty) were arguably the most popular vocal group of the period. With a string of hits, including "Beat Me, Daddy, Eight to the Bar" (1940; music by Don Raye, lyrics by Hughie Prince and Eleanor Sheehy), "Boogie Woogie Bugle Boy (of Company B)" (1941; music by Hughie Prince, lyrics by Don Raye), "Ac-Cen-Tchu-Ate the Positive" (1944; music by Harold Arlen, lyrics by Johnny Mercer), and "Rum and Coca-Cola" (1945; music by Paul Baron and Jeri Sullavan, lyrics by Morey Amsterdam), the trio made the rounds of most music shows and even had their own, *The Andrews Sisters Eight-to-the-Bar Ranch,* on the American Broadcasting Company (ABC) from 1944 to 1946. They appeared in seven movies between 1941 and 1944, trifles that ranged from *Buck Privates* (1941) to *Hollywood Canteen* (1944).

Dinah Shore, another popular vocalist of the era, appeared on many of the top-ranked music shows and finally landed her own network program, *The Dinah Shore Show* (NBC), in 1939. From there she moved to the irreverent *Chamber Music Society of Lower Basin Street* (1940), a unique, satirical show that mixed jazz and humor. That job led to *Songs by Dinah Shore* (NBC, 1941–1942) and *In Person, Dinah Shore* (NBC, 1942–1943), plus several other variety shows.

THE BIRTH OF ABC

The American Broadcasting Company, better known as ABC, came into being in 1943 after lengthy legal maneuvering. In 1938, the Federal Communications Commission (FCC) had undertaken an investigation into the charge that radio networks, particularly NBC's Red and Blue divisions, had created a monopoly situation that blocked competition. The agency published a report that cited problems and suggested solutions and, in 1941, proposed a licensing regulation that would result in the breakup of NBC as it then existed.

Although the FCC could not regulate or license networks directly, it could influence their operations by virtue of its authority over individual radio stations. Consequently, the agency ruled that no licenses, new or renewed, would be issued to stations affiliated with a network that maintained multiple divisions. In short, the FCC targeted the Red and Blue branches of NBC.

NBC argued this indirect approach to regulation violated communication law and appealed to the courts. But the FCC won its case, and NBC had to sell one of its divisions; the network opted for NBC Blue, the smaller of the two. After dividing the assets of NBC Red and NBC Blue, including some programming, NBC's parent company, the Radio Corporation of America (RCA), set an asking price of $8 million for a package containing leases on landlines and studio facilities in New York, Washington, Chicago, and Los Angeles; contracts with personnel associated with about 60 affiliates; licenses for three stations; and the trademark and good will associated with the Blue name.

Edward Noble, owner of Life Savers candy and the Rexall drugstore chain, bought the Blue Network from RCA in the fall of 1943. He had formed a company for this purpose, which he called the American Broadcasting System. Several months later, Noble renamed his network the American Broadcasting Company and began acquiring more stations with established programs such as *The Lone Ranger, Sergeant Preston,* and *Sky King*. He also prerecorded shows, an innovation that proved attractive to busy stars. In addition, Noble established a production base in Hollywood, another imaginative move because NBC and CBS remained situated in New York City. The new network grew; by the mid-1940s, ABC, while not yet the equal of its larger rivals, could claim national network legitimacy.

Shore's contemporary, singer Jo Stafford, likewise achieved some attention in the early 1940s, first as a vocalist with the Tommy Dorsey Band, and then in many appearances on a variety of musical programs such as *The Colgate Program* (1942–1943), *The Johnny Mercer Music Shop* (1943), *The Chesterfield Supper Club* (1944–1949), and many others. Like a number of other performers from the early 1940s, Stafford's career blossomed in the years following the war.

Connee Boswell, one of the three singing Boswell Sisters (Connee, Martha, and Helvetia, or "Vet"), a group that competed with the Andrews Sisters for hits, frequently appeared as a soloist on Bing Crosby's *Kraft Music Hall* as well as the popular wartime variety show *Stage Door Canteen* (1942–1945). The "Sweetheart of the Armed Forces," Jane Froman, also had stints on *Stage Door Canteen*, plus she hosted a show under her own name in 1942. A serious 1943 airplane accident while en route to a USO performance interrupted Froman's career for the remainder of the war years.

Singer Ginny Simms starred in her own series, which ran from 1941 to 1952, and quickly became a major radio entertainer. One of her productions, much loved during World War II, bore the title *The Purple Heart* because she interviewed wounded servicemen and women while on the air.

And the list of performers goes on: Ella Fitzgerald, Marion Hutton, Helen O'Connell, Connie Haines, Peggy Lee, Doris Day, and Judy Garland are but a few of the female vocalists who also enjoyed time on radio. A star-studded lineup, many of them would go on to multifaceted careers in movies, recordings, and that new medium of the postwar years, television. (See chapter 3, "Swing, Jazz, and Rhythm 'n' Blues," for an extensive listing of big-band vocalists, both male and female.)

CONCLUSION

Music of all kinds, live, on radio, or recorded, appealed to listeners throughout the 1940s. As far as radio went, war-oriented songs tended to receive considerably less airplay than more traditional fare like "Skylark" (1942; music by Hoagy Carmichael, lyrics by Johnny Mercer), "People Will Say We're in Love" (1943; music by Richard Rodgers, lyrics by Oscar Hammerstein II), or "Sentimental Journey" (1944; music by Ben Homer and Les Brown, lyrics by Bud Green).

Recordings took on greater importance in the mid-1940s with the decline of the big bands and decreased live radio broadcasting of any kind. Radio stations increasingly became conduits for recorded music and little else, and the disc jockey filled that need. After 1945, the once mighty stations and networks cut back sharply on all original programming, substituting recorded music whenever possible; with the onset of the postwar era, the Golden Age of American radio slowly drew to a close.

6

Music on Stage and Screen

BACKGROUND

As the 1930s drew to a close, the musical had long been an established vehicle on both stage and screen. Generally speaking, musicals provided audiences a few moments of escapism since they seldom dealt with current events or social issues. Instead, the thrust of these entertainments involved love and romance, comedy, and music, music, music. Elaborate dance routines, lush sets, and creative costumes heightened the illusory quality they projected, and the public responded favorably.

Year in and year out, the numerous Hollywood studios released hundreds of feature movies of all varieties, whereas Broadway, following the Great Depression, served up a few dozen plays in the best of seasons. Both theater and film, however, displayed a reluctance to tackle the looming war, although most executives and producers knew full well that America would eventually be drawn into the conflict. On stage, *Margin for Error* (1939), *There Shall Be No Night* (1940), and *Watch on the Rhine* (1941) stand out among the nonmusical dramatic offerings that refer to ongoing events abroad.

A mere handful of motion pictures, such as *The Last Train from Madrid* (1937), *Blockade* (1938), and *Foreign Correspondent* (1940), take on world affairs, and gingerly at that. Comedian Charlie Chaplin ridicules European tyranny with *The Great Dictator* in 1940, a humorous look at Hitler and Mussolini unusual for its or any time. It took Warner Bros., whose feisty *42nd Street*

(1933) had sparked the popular revival of film musicals back in the depths of the Great Depression, to again lead the way, but this time, in a rather different direction. The company's production of *Confessions of a Nazi Spy* (1939) clearly identifies the enemy and warns audiences about subversion in their midst. Modestly successful at the box office, *Confessions of a Nazi Spy* spurred other studios to attempt some references to reality, but with mixed results.

Most American-made motion pictures from the period 1939–1941 reflect a changing view of the country, one that encourages military preparedness and the growing presence of sailors, soldiers, and airmen in everyday life. The imagery, unlike that in *Confessions of a Nazi Spy,* acknowledges no outside threats, but instead reassures audiences that little likelihood of war exists and that strong armed forces will keep the nation safe and out of foreign conflicts.

Looking at musicals as a type, the output of movies fitting this genre greatly exceeds anything attained by the Great White Way. When World War II erupted in September of 1939, that numerical differential remained in place. Space restrictions forbid discussing every individual play and film that came out during those years and fit the category of musicals, but Appendix A lists the yearly titles for both stage and screen productions in the genre. It provides an idea of the great popularity musicals enjoyed during the period.

In brief, the numerical breakdown by year in musicals, both stage and screen, can be seen in table 6.1.[1]

Table 6.1
Broadway and Hollywood Productions, 1939–1945

Year	Broadway Musical Productions	Hollywood Musical Films	Totals
1939	13	22	35
1940	13	33	46
1941	10	37	47
1942	12	44	56
1943	13	54	67
1944	10	55	65
1945	16	38	54
Totals	87	283	370

The figures in table 6.1 show that, during the war years, over three times as many movie musicals came out as did theatrical ones, averaging 40 new films a year, as against Broadway's average of 12 annual productions. For audiences, those numbers translate as 52 new stage and screen musicals a year, a remarkable figure.

Looking at these totals on a yearly basis (1939–1945), motion picture musicals begin the survey at a low 22 new films released in 1939, a number that then begins sharply climbing in 1940, rising steadily from 1941 to a figure of 54 in 1943, peaking at 55 in 1944, and dropping rapidly in 1945. Theatrical openings, on the other hand, remain consistent throughout the seven-year period. Should the figures be extrapolated into the times prior to, and following, World War II, they would reveal that the musical genre had entered the war years in a strong position, with Broadway annually averaging 11 new musical productions in the late 1930s, and the film industry 50 new musical titles. In the immediate postwar period, stage musicals remained at their earlier figures, but the movie industry continued to fall, averaging only 20-odd new musical films each year. Despite the ups and downs in the motion picture figures, the musical nevertheless demonstrated considerable popularity, especially during wartime.

BROADWAY: 1939–1941

Neither stage plays nor motion pictures took little overt notice of the war that grew in intensity in Europe and the Far East, instead choosing to reflect the prevailing feelings of the majority of the population. Most Americans favored neutrality, with many retreating into isolationism, a desire to stay out of foreign wars altogether. Broadway clearly went along with this attitude, entertaining its audiences with two entries by Cole Porter, *Du Barry Was a Lady* and *The Man Who Came to Dinner* (both 1939). *Yokel Boy* (1939), by the team of Sam Stept, Lew Brown, and Charles Tobias, and *George White's Scandals* (1939; the seventh edition of this venerable series), featuring music by Sammy Fain and Jack Yellin, were also among the new shows on stage. But the humorous "Well, Did You Evah!" (Porter's *Du Barry*) hardly qualifies as reflective of current events, nor do "It's Me Again" (*Yokel Boy*) and "Are You Havin' Any Fun?" (*George White's Scandals*). The same could be said for virtually any number of other tunes performed in the remaining nine musicals gracing New York theaters in 1939.

The following year, 1940, saw the same situation repeated: "Life Was Pie for the Pioneer" (1940; music by Burton Lane, lyrics by E. Y. Harburg) in *Hold On to Your Hats* delivers its message in its title, as does "You Can't Put Catsup on the Moon" (1940; music by Sammy Fain, lyrics by Irving Kahal) in *Boys and Girls Together.* Perhaps *Cabin in the Sky* (1940) contained the greatest substance among the season's musicals. Starring an all-black cast and dealing with the issue of race, albeit veiled in metaphor, its score, including the title song, was the creation of the white team of Vernon Duke (music) and John Latouche (lyrics) and featured the classic "Taking a Chance on Love," interpreted by the show's star, Ethel Waters. Their approach did not rely on stereotypes or pseudo-jazzy music, and as a result, *Cabin in the Sky* introduced audiences to a new dimension in American musical theater, that of a serious, dignified portrayal of black characters.

The entry of the United States as a combatant in World War II marked 1941, but it did not occur until the end of the year, with the Japanese attack on Pearl Harbor on the 7th of December. Several days later, Germany formally declared war, and America responded in kind. For the preceding 11 months, however, peace reigned on Broadway, although *Let's Face It* (1941), another Cole Porter vehicle, based some of its shenanigans around an Army base and included "Jerry, My Soldier Boy." More characteristic during this time of waiting, shows like *Best Foot Forward* (1941; music by Hugh Martin, lyrics by Ralph Blane) offered "Just a Little Joint with a Jukebox," and *Sons o' Fun* (1941) brought back the team of Sammy Fain and Jack Yellin for a bit of fluff called "Let's Say Goodnight with a Dance." And *Lady in the Dark* (1941), more of a sophisticated comedy than a true musical, even though it boasted the combined talents of composer Kurt Weill and lyricist Ira Gershwin, furnished a plot that revolved around psychoanalysis, not the threat of war. Nevertheless, *Lady in the Dark* did offer "My Ship," one of those standards that never goes out of fashion.

HOLLYWOOD: 1939–1941

While Broadway remained steeped in tradition, the movie industry likewise continued on its own tried-and-true path. The precocious Mickey Rooney and Judy Garland sing and dance in an unusual 1939 film adaptation of Richard Rodgers-Lorenz Hart stage musical, *Babes in Arms*. Unfortunately, about all that remains of the original 1937 Broadway production is the title; most of the memorable songs are absent, including such sophisticated standards as "The Lady Is a Tramp," "My Funny Valentine," and "Where or When." What plays on screen is a mishmash of old songs and several new ones, but not much by Rodgers and Hart. The two teenagers sing Stephen Foster's "Oh, Susanna" (composed in 1847), "I'm Just Wild about Harry" (1921; music by Eubie Blake, lyrics by Noble Sissle), and "Good Morning" (1939; music by Nacio Herb Brown, lyrics by Arthur Freed), one of the few contemporary tunes in the completely revised score. Although *Babes in Arms* lost its Broadway heritage, the movie version clearly appealed to audiences, and the energy Rooney and Garland bring to their roles makes up in part for the juvenile story.

On a more adult plane, *The Story of Vernon and Irene Castle* (1939) reunites Fred Astaire and Ginger Rogers for the ninth time during the 1930s (the dancing duo would make one final film together, *The Barkleys of Broadway*, in 1949).

Nostalgia dominates *The Story of Vernon and Irene Castle,* a cinematic biography about two popular dancers active in the early twentieth century. In the process, the score revives such hoary chestnuts as "Come, Josephine, in My Flying Machine" (1910; music by Fred Fisher, lyrics by Al Bryan) and "By the Light of the Silvery Moon" (1909; music by Gus Edwards, lyrics by Edward Madden), but studiously avoids, just as in *Babes in Arms,* anything topical or contemporary.

The Marx Brothers, a trio of zany comedians, also evade the present amid jokes and sight gags in *At the Circus* (1939). Groucho performs the hilarious "Lydia, the Tattooed Lady" (1939; music by Harold Arlen, lyrics by E. Y. Harburg), a song destined to reappear in 1940's *The Philadelphia Story.* At the same time, the Ritz Brothers, occasional rivals to the Marx Brothers, enliven *Argentine Nights* (1940). Another bit of escapism, the movie features Latin music as interpreted by the Andrews Sisters, a fast-rising singing trio that immersed itself in swing tunes of the day, such as the movie's "Rhumboogie" (1940; music by Don Raye, lyrics by Hughie Prince). *Down Argentine Way* (1940) also offers a Latin soundtrack (along with a similar title) and includes Betty Grable and the unique Carmen Miranda in its roster of stars. But as far as concerned these motion pictures, World War II played no role.

Even the Bob Hope–Bing Crosby film, *Road to Singapore* (1940), despite its title, has little to do with the Far East. A rollicking comedy featuring tunes like "Captain Custard" (1940; music by Victor Schertzinger, lyrics by Johnny Burke) and "Sweet Potato Piper" (1940; music by James V. Monaco, lyrics by Johnny Burke), this "exotic South Seas romance" positions itself for fun, not a lesson in current events, and ignores the growing threat to Singapore and surrounding Asian nations with the rise of Japanese imperialism at that time.

They might not be topical, but the road pictures of Bing Crosby and Bob Hope certainly provided a bright spot in the dark days of World War II. This long-running cinematic franchise would eventually total seven comedy features: *Road to Singapore, Road to Zanzibar* (1941), *Road to Morocco* (1942), *Road to Utopia* (1945), *Road to Rio* (1947), *Road to Bali* (1952), and *Road to Hong Kong* (1962). Exercises in frivolity, the movies also boast the presence of the lovely Dorothy Lamour, more often than not clad in a sarong, and she provides the romantic interest, along with a bit of sex appeal. Musically, the series has little to offer, aside from pleasant pop tunes from Crosby, Hope, or Lamour. Sometimes all three harmonize together during the course of the silly plots. *Road to Morocco,* however, does offer "Moonlight Becomes You" (1942), while *Road to Utopia* has Crosby crooning "Sunday, Monday, or Always" (1943; music and lyrics for both tunes by Jimmy Van Heusen and Johnny Burke).[2]

As world conditions worsened with the arrival of 1941, Hollywood began to take more notice of events. The year saw the release of a spate of service-oriented productions bearing titles like *Caught in the Draft, Dive Bomber, Great*

Guns, and *Tanks a Million.* On the musical side, the studios decided to make up for lost time. In short order, marquees advertised *Buck Privates, In the Navy, Keep 'em Flying, Kiss the Boys Goodbye, Navy Blues, Rookies on Parade,* and *You'll Never Get Rich,* all of which drew attention to the military draft (also known as Selective Service, or conscription), instituted in 1940. More and more men, along with a handful of women, entered the various service branches, and motion pictures began to reflect the nation's attempts to attain readiness for any emergencies. Most of these movies, however, show young people having a good time, and their titles suggest as much. The truly military side of things receives little serious coverage other than lots of uniforms on screen. But the sheer numbers of films, including dramas—this shift in themes did not limit itself to musicals—indicated changes in the thinking of producers and directors.

Of course, the usual quota of escapist musicals also came from the studios during this momentous year. *Babes on Broadway* again teams Judy Garland and Mickey Rooney for another round of adolescent fantasy, the seventh picture together for the two young stars. At the time, Rooney was all of 21, Garland 19. Their previous *Babes in Arms* had proved so popular with audiences that MGM doubtless felt compelled to capitalize on its success as quickly as possible. Aside from an embarrassing (for today) rendition of "Babes on Broadway" (1941; music by Burton Lane, lyrics by Ralph Freed) done in blackface, the picture effectively skirts important issues. With forgettable songs like "Minnie from Trinidad" (1941; words and music by Roger Edens) and some old vaudeville numbers, the movie coasts along with its amiable stars, a pleasant diversion.

Hardly a musical in the traditional sense, *The Lady Eve* (1941) provides some nice old Rodgers and Hart melodies, including 1932's "Isn't It Romantic" and "Lover," as background. Despite the melodic soundtrack, the film stands as a strident screwball comedy from director Preston Sturges. It upends romance and makes its manic way to a happy conclusion, more of an echo of productions from the 1930s than anything from the 1940s. On the other hand, *Birth of the Blues* (1941), cast in a more customary mode, offers both old and new numbers, with "The Waiter and the Porter and the Upstairs Maid" (1941; words and music by Johnny Mercer) being a standout. By this time, songwriter Mercer had emerged a Hollywood favorite and a potent force in popular music, and his scores embellished many a motion picture.

BROADWAY: 1942

By the early months of 1942, the United States had gone from professed neutrality to all-out war against the Axis powers. On Broadway, composer

Irving Berlin offered his patriotic *This Is the Army* (1942). From the syrupy "I Left My Heart at the Stage Door Canteen" to the humorous "Oh! How I Hate to Get Up in the Morning" (1918) to the flag-waving "This Is the Army, Mr. Jones" (1942), the show proved a hit. Although it had a limited New York run, audiences reacted so positively that the musical went on the road, touring Army bases everywhere until 1945 and the return of peace. Berlin himself often attended these performances, even occasionally stepping on stage to

---

WAR BOND DRIVES

As the United States inched closer to active involvement in World War II, President Franklin D. Roosevelt urged the nation to begin purchasing the newly issued Series E savings bonds as a means of helping to finance military expenditures. On May 1, 1941, he personally initiated a defense bond drive by buying the first Series E U.S. savings bond from Henry Morgenthau, the secretary of the treasury. Promptly renamed *war bonds* after the December 7, 1941, attack on Pearl Harbor, citizens everywhere rallied to the cause. For example, children were given cards with slots that held 75 quarters. A completed card, or $18.75, would purchase one $25 E-bond; they proved extremely popular among youngsters and ultimately raised millions of dollars.

The entertainment industry offered time and a host of talents to promote bond sales. Musical stars such as Roy Rogers, Bing Crosby, Judy Garland, Eddie Cantor, and others worked tirelessly to raise money for the war. Singer Kate Smith alone raised over $600,000 in bond sales (or almost $7 billion in contemporary dollars). In 1941, composer Irving Berlin penned "Any Bonds Today?" and the popular Andrews Sisters made a hit recording of the tune. It all worked; over 85 million Americans (or 64 percent of the national population of 132 million) invested in war bonds.

Between 1941 and 1946, government and business urged Americans to contribute to the war effort by providing posters, along with print and radio advertising, and patriotic newspaper and magazine stories about the virtues of buying bonds. When the U.S. Treasury, at the beginning of 1946, received the last proceeds from the many bond campaigns, more than $185 billion (over $2 trillion in contemporary dollars, when adjusted for inflation) in Series E bonds had been sold.

The primary intention of the Series E bond campaign had been to help finance the war. But the bond drives also brought Americans from all walks of life together in a common cause. Clearly they had a positive impact on the morale of those on the home front. The purchase of a war bond served as an expression of patriotism, allowing the buyer to contribute to the war effort through an act of financial sacrifice.

Irving Berlin, one of most patriotic of American songwriters, penned "Any Bonds Today?" in 1941, a time when massive bond drives were becoming more commonplace as the nation geared for war. Picture by William H. Young.

enthusiastic applause. Quickly adapted for the screen in 1943 with an all-star cast (including a future president, Ronald Reagan), both versions raised millions for the Army Relief Fund and demonstrated that even musicals could be important components in the war effort.

This Is the Army evolved from *Yip, Yip, Yaphank*, a 1918 play that Berlin wrote while serving in the U.S. Army during World War I. In the songwriter's words, "a military 'mess' cooked up by the boys" of his unit, he adapted the earlier work mainly in spirit, and only "Oh! How I Hate to Get Up in the Morning" survived intact. Together, *Yip, Yip, Yaphank* and *This Is the Army* illustrated Berlin's innate ability to entertain, while at the same time stirring the audience's patriotic feelings.[3]

Despite the clear success of *This Is the Army*, the remainder of the 1942 Broadway season reverted to tradition, although here and there references about the growing conflict popped up in scripts and songs. *Banjo Eyes* (1942)—the title a reference to star Eddie Cantor, whose ability to appear wide-eyed earned him this nickname—featured "We Did It Before (and We Can Do It Again)" (1941; words and music by Cliff Friend and Charles Tobias), the message of which cannot have gone unnoticed by theatergoers: we were victorious in World War I, and we'll repeat the victory in the present struggle. The short-lived *Count Me In* (1942; 61 performances) likewise brought the war to mind with the seldom-heard "All Out Bugle Call" and "On Leave for Love" (1942; music and lyrics for both by Ann Ronell). *New Faces of 1943* (title aside, the show opened late in 1942), a spirited, periodic Broadway revue with different performers, included "We'll Swing It Through" (1942; music by Lee Wainer, lyrics by John Lund), another allusion to ongoing events.

Finally, *By Jupiter*, the last original show written by the team of Richard Rodgers and Lorenz Hart, ignored the war completely. A musical comedy with classical roots, its dealt with conflict, but of a kind entirely different from anything experienced in the twentieth century. The plot focused on the ancient Greeks and their clashes with the Amazons, those women warriors of myth. But Rodgers and Hart managed to give contemporary audiences two classics: "Nobody's Heart" and "Wait Till You See Her."

HOLLYWOOD: 1942

On the movie side of things, a song originally written in 1931 came to signify many of the hopes and dreams of people everywhere more than a decade later. Composer Herman Hupfield had contributed this number to a Depression-era play titled *Everybody's Welcome*, but it elicited little notice at the time. Then, in November of 1942, Warner Bros. released *Casablanca* in New York City, with national distribution occurring in January of 1943. A romantic saga starring Humphrey Bogart and Ingrid Bergman as lovers that the fates of war have thrown together, it attracted audiences immediately. Since it came out at the end of the year to qualify for the Academy Awards, many people consider *Casablanca* a 1942 movie, but others call it a 1943 picture because of its belated national release. Regardless of which year, the plot involves a song that the Berman/Bogart characters recognize as their own. In the film, Dooley Wilson sings it to remarkable effect, both for the lead actors and the audience—it is, of course, "As Time Goes By," Herman Hupfield's forgotten tune. Wilson's rendition stands as one of those movie moments that everyone who has seen it will remember.[4]

Overnight, "As Time Goes By" rose on the 1943 hit charts, eventually spending 41 weeks on the lists in recorded versions by several vocalists, the most popular being Rudy Vallee's interpretation. It may have been ignored in 1931, but this resurrected composition's belated success illustrates the impact popular films could have on audience reactions. The movie itself won Academy Awards for Best Picture, Best Director (Michael Curtiz), and Best Screenplay (Julius Epstein, Philip Epstein, and Howard Koch), along with five additional nominations, in 1943. Since it dated back to 1931, "As Time Goes By" did not qualify for Best Song, and so the judges' choice went to "You'll Never Know" (1943; music by Harry Warren, lyrics by Mack Gordon), a number from the score of the Alice Faye musical *Hello Frisco, Hello.*

A fine popular tune in its own right, and one that has come down to the present as a standard, "You'll Never Know" has never kindled the intense feelings about romantic love that "As Time Goes By" continues to engender. But that intensity goes with the experience of having seen, at some time or another, *Casablanca.* Song and movie will always be inextricably linked for legions of viewers. Remembered today as one of the best motion pictures to come out of World War II, *Casablanca* and its resurrected melody bring a sad but lushly romantic perspective to the conflict, and both continue life in endless television replays and strong movie rentals over a half century after the picture's release. (See chapter 2, "Popular Hits and Standards," for more on this iconic song.)

Among the many 1942 movies that fit the more traditional expectations about wartime musicals—upbeat, patriotic, fast-moving, with laughs and lots of music—*Call Out the Marines, The Fleet's In, Iceland, My Favorite Spy, Priorities on Parade, Private Buckaroo, Ship Ahoy, Star Spangled Rhythm, Swing It Soldier, When Johnny Comes Marching Home,* and *Yankee Doodle Dandy* should fit the definition nicely. The war had just begun, and few people realized what a fierce struggle it would become. But Hollywood, under the urging of several government agencies, wanted to portray the nation's participation in positive, winning terms, and that is exactly what these pictures attempt. The formula would not appreciably change for the duration of World War II, a conflict that would drag on, steadily growing in intensity for almost three more years.

During the false optimism of 1942, when most Americans thought the country would sweep to victory in a short time, the movie industry did its part in fostering that view. Both the dramas and the musicals cranked out that year usually supported illusions that completely ignored the present. For example, *Song of the Islands* (1942) has Betty Grable dancing in a grass skirt in the Hawaiian Islands, the same locale as Pearl Harbor. But these islands display tropical splendor, exotic scenery, a paradise where sneak attacks and bombings cannot possibly occur. Songwriters Mack Gordon and Harry Owens collaborated on a score that reinforces any and all stereotypes about Hawaii, presenting songs like "Down on Ami Ami Oni Oni Isle," "Sing Me a Song of the Islands," and "Maluna Malolo Mawaena," the kind of fluff that best belongs in travel brochures.

Similarly, *Pardon My Sarong* (1942) stars Bud Abbott and Lou Costello, two popular slapstick comedians of the day, as bus drivers who get hopelessly off course and end up in another tropical paradise. As a chorus of natives serenade, vocalist Nan Wynn performs such lackluster tunes as "Lovely Luana" and "Vingo Jingo" (1942; both composed by the team of Don Raye and Gene DePaul). On the other hand, this kind of escapism took audiences' minds off the increasingly grim headlines that awaited them outside the theater, and so movies like this did react to the war, but on their own entertainment terms.

One final 1942 movie musical merits discussion: *Holiday Inn*. Featuring a score by Irving Berlin, it serves to soften even the coldest heart around Christmastime, especially that particular Christmas with the country mired in a war with no clear indication of victory. For this picture, which stars Bing Crosby and Fred Astaire, Berlin penned a number he called "White Christmas," and Crosby sings it on screen. With more and more men going overseas, with families separated during the holidays, and with people looking back fondly on more peaceful times, "White Christmas" turned out to be a runaway hit. Millions of records sold—so many that Decca wore out the master disc and had to have Crosby rerecord it in 1945—and it became, in time, the top-selling single of the twentieth century. With "God Bless America" in 1938–1939 and "White Christmas" in 1942, Irving Berlin probably plucked more patriotic heartstrings than any other songwriter of the era. (See chapter 2, "Popular Hits and Standards," for more about "White Christmas.")

BROADWAY: 1943

Broadway greeted 1943 with a musical destined to rank among the great accomplishments of American theater: *Oklahoma!* This show marked the beginning of the long collaboration between composer Richard Rodgers and lyricist Oscar Hammerstein II. Rodgers entered the partnership following his long and illustrious career with Lorenz Hart, and Hammerstein came to it with a string of successes with numerous composers that dated back to the early 1920s. Together, Rodgers and Hammerstein would create some of the most successful and enduring musicals the stage has seen.

Oklahoma! did not address the ongoing war, but instead presented a warm story about the American heartland, where the mornings are beautiful, the corn grows high, and all the surreys have fringe on top. The bright, soaring score made the show an enormous hit, and it would continue to run on Broadway for an unprecedented 2,212 performances, finally drawing the closing curtain in the spring of 1948. It has since been revived countless times, and although clearly destined for the screen, it did not make the cinematic transition until 1955.

If *Oklahoma!* ignored the ongoing world of 1943, it did so by creating an alternative one that spoke to deep-seated American beliefs, suggesting that here were values worth fighting for. Its innovative dancing, all choreographed by the renowned Agnes de Mille, included a lengthy "Dream Sequence" ballet at the end of the first act that further set it apart from other musicals of the day. In many aspects, the show served as an eloquent antidote to World War II, and audiences clearly responded in kind.

Anything else that Broadway offered for the 1943 season paled beside the overriding success of *Oklahoma!* Only in retrospect can it be seen that other good musicals came out that same year. *One Touch of Venus,* featuring music by Kurt Weill and lyrics by the poet Ogden Nash, played a respectable 567 performances. It also offered a classic song, "Speak Low." A movie adaptation came out in 1948. Another popular show, a revival of Rodgers and Hart's 1927 *A Connecticut Yankee,* brought such evergreens as "My Heart Stood Still" and "Thou Swell" (both 1927) back to the stage, and the nostalgia of the entire production found a receptive public.

Something for the Boys took the opposite tack and reminded theatergoers about the war, but in an upbeat way. One of Cole Porter's lesser efforts—no lasting tunes came from his score—it nonetheless offered laughs and dancing to the audience. A silly story about a group of young service wives living together near a military base, it allowed for plenty of shenanigans and even had Ethel Merman in the lead. A more serious musical, *Carmen Jones,* took Georges Bizet's classic opera *Carmen* (1875) and restaged it in a wartime parachute factory. Oscar Hammerstein II created contemporary lyrics to grace the original libretto, and Robert Russell Bennett wrote the orchestrations to Bizet's music. Featuring an all-black cast, the final result worked remarkably well and led to an acclaimed movie adaptation in 1954. Some of Hammerstein's lyrics, set in a dated and artificial black patois, might not ring true to contemporary listeners, but he remained faithful to the tragic love story.

HOLLYWOOD: 1943

While Broadway gloried in *Oklahoma!* the film industry went into overdrive and turned out 55 musicals for 1943. Most of them had little impact and disappeared after short runs, forgotten in the glut of movies of all kinds that flooded the market that year. Who recalls *Campus Rhythm?* Or *Gals, Incorporated?* Or *Larceny with Music?* In a year with 55 movie musicals, however, a few ultimately escaped the crowd and established themselves as memorable motion pictures, worthy of note. The much-anticipated film adaptation of Irving Berlin's *This Is the Army* came to screens everywhere, and it proved just as stirring in this medium as it had on stage. *Cabin in the Sky* took the celebrated 1940 stage vehicle and, if anything, improved it. The cinematic version again stars Ethel Waters, reprising her Broadway role of Petunia, and also boasts Lena Horne, Louis Armstrong, Duke Ellington and His Orchestra, plus a bevy of other distinguished black performers. The score adds "Happiness Is Just a Thing Called Joe" (1943; music by Harold Arlen, lyrics by E. Y. Harburg), a number of such quality that it received an Academy Award nomination for Best Song 1943, but it lost out to the equally memorable "You'll Never Know," discussed above.

The Gang's All Here brings together the talents of famed choreographer Busby Berkeley (also as director, in this instance) and bandleader Benny

The Stage Door Canteen, located in the heart of New York City and operated by the American Theatre Wing, provided free Broadway entertainment for service personnel for the duration of the war. Library of Congress, Prints & Photographs Division.

Goodman and his orchestra, plus Alice Faye and Carmen Miranda. Mostly music and dance, this bit of froth has Faye warble "No Love, No Nothin'" (1943; music by Harry Warren, lyrics by Leo Robin), and the inimitable Miranda wears one of her outrageous head adornments in "The Lady in the Tutti Frutti Hat" (1943; music by Harry Warren, lyrics by Leo Robin). At the same time, Mickey Rooney and Judy Garland paired up yet again, this time for a cinematic remake of the immensely popular 1930 stage musical *Girl Crazy*. Originally a collaboration between George and Ira Gershwin, the movie version retains much of their lilting original score, including such gems as "I Got Rhythm," "Bidin' My Time," "Embraceable You," and "But Not for Me." Busby Berkeley codirected the film and also choreographed the dance sequences.

The war colors much of *Hers to Hold,* a vehicle for the talents of singer Deanna Durbin. Reprising her character of Penny Craig, seen previously in *Three Smart Girls* (1936) and *Three Smart Girls Grow Up* (1939), Durbin now works on an aircraft assembly line and wears a drab factory outfit. But she can still sing, including "Begin the Beguine" (1935; words and music by Cole Porter), a song that remained a popular favorite throughout the war years, and a moving "Say a Prayer for the Boys Over There" (1943; music by Jimmy McHugh, lyrics by Herb Magidson), a poignant reminder of the times.

Fred Astaire gets to show off his dancing skills with *The Sky's the Limit,* this time with Joan Leslie instead of Ginger Rogers. The background of the plot has Astaire as a pilot (with the famed Flying Tigers, no less) on leave, anxious to forget the war for a few days. He, of course, goes back to his squadron at movie's end, but in the meantime, he and Leslie have a brief romance supported by a fine score from composer Harold Arlen and lyricist Johnny Mercer. Standout numbers include Leslie singing "My Shining Hour" and Astaire singing and dancing "One for My Baby (and One More for the Road)" while breaking glasses atop a bar. It all provides a moment of escapism for both the characters and the audience, yet the war remains the focal point of much of the story.

Thank Your Lucky Stars has Eddie Cantor and Joan Leslie as the ostensible leads in this star-studded musical from Warner Bros., a picture that allows the studio to parade most of its contract players—Humphrey Bogart, Olivia de Havilland, John Garfield, Dinah Shore, along with many others—as themselves for brief cameos. The film demonstrates some originality when none other than Bette Davis sings "They're Either Too Young or Too Old," a cute number about the shortage of eligible males in wartime, and action hero Errol Flynn warbles "That's What You Jolly Well Got" (both 1942; music by Arthur Schwartz, lyrics by Frank Loesser), doubtless a surprise for most of his fans.

Finally, *Stage Door Canteen* brings together much of Hollywood, Broadway, and musical stardom for a brief tale about soldiers interacting with theatrical luminaries at New York's famed wartime canteen. The endless cast features people like Tallulah Bankhead, Katharine Cornell, Helen Hayes, Katharine Hepburn, Gypsy Rose Lee, and Johnny Weissmuller all under their own names. Bandleaders Count Basie, Xavier Cugat, Benny Goodman, Kay Kyser, Guy Lombardo, and Freddy Martin make cameo appearances and provide a lively soundtrack, with many of the compositions by the team of James V. Monaco (music) and Al Dubin (lyrics). Fun for everyone as they take a much-needed breather from the ongoing hostilities.

BROADWAY: 1944

With the arrival of 1944, the nation sensed the tide of World War II had turned. The Axis powers suffered more defeats than victories, and Allied troops marched forward on all fronts. Many grim battles still lay ahead, and casualties would continue to be horrific, but at some time it would all end, although no one could yet predict how soon. Broadway, in the meantime, offered a limited musical menu for the season, just 10 new productions, and only a few of them achieved much distinction, musically or dramatically.

With such paltry pickings, little wonder that few memorable songs emerged from 1944's stage musicals. *Bloomer Girl,* a tale set during the American Civil War, offered a score by the renowned Harold Arlen (music) and E. Y. Harburg (lyrics), but somehow they failed to work their customary magic with the material. "When the Boys Come Home" might be read in contemporary terms—when the soldiers of World War II finally return—although such a reading seems unlikely, given the show's setting.

The most successful musical of the year was *Follow the Girls,* a raucous tale about burlesque that ran for over 800 performances. Somewhat topical, since it dealt with servicemen and their desire to see pretty girls, preferably unclothed, *Follow the Girls* remains pretty much forgotten today, although it seemed suitably daring for its time. The music has likewise fallen through the cracks, featuring as it does such titles as "Thanks for a Lousy Evening," "You're Perf," and "Today Will Be Yesterday Tomorrow" (1944; all with music by Philip Charig and lyrics by Dan Shapiro and Milton Pascal). On the other hand, the music probably played well amid lots of dancing and abbreviated costumes. The show also introduced audiences to the antics of Jackie Gleason, a player destined to make his name in just a few short years in the new medium of television.

Cole Porter, who almost always opened a new musical with each Broadway season, offered his many fans *Mexican Hayride,* yet another Latin-flavored vehicle in keeping with popular tastes on both stage and screen. Not even the redoubtable Mr. Porter, however, seemed able to reach his usual heights; although the romantic "I Love You" has come down to the present as a standard, not much else from the score has survived. All in all, theatergoers might well look forward to 1945 and hope for some improvement over 1944.

HOLLYWOOD: 1944

While Broadway floundered, Hollywood flourished. Movie marquees advertised, at one time or another during the year, another 55 new musicals, the same as in 1943. Not only did the studios remain in high gear, many of their releases clearly continued to reflect the war. Universal released *Follow the Boys,* a picture that had nothing in common with the concurrent stage production of *Follow the Girls* other than a similar title. It instead boasts a star-studded cast led by Marlene Dietrich, Orson Welles, the Andrews Sisters, the Delta Rhythm Boys, George Raft, W. C. Fields, and just about anyone else in the studio's stable. Virtually nonstop in its action and music, this picture mixes old favorites like "I'll Get By" (1928; music by Fred E. Ahlert, lyrics by Roy Turk) with current material such as "Shoo Shoo, Baby" (1943; words and music by Phil Moore) and "Is You Is or Is You Ain't My Baby?" (1944; words and music by Louis Jordan and Billy Austin). The backdrop of USO (United Service Organizations) clubs and the efforts to entertain the troops gives *Follow the Boys* a topical air, while providing audiences some of the best entertainers of the day.

Twentieth Century Fox, another major studio, did not allow rival Universal to reap all the credits; *Four Jills in a Jeep* in many ways mirrors *Follow the Boys.* The picture allows a host of entertainers, ranging from Alice Faye to Carmen Miranda, to perform their specialties, with comic bits tying together this tale of USO units overseas. Faye reprises "You'll Never Know" (1943; music by Harry Warren, lyrics by Mack Gordon), an Academy Award–winning Best Song she originally performed in *Hello Frisco, Hello* a year earlier. For her part, Miranda shines in "I Yi Yi Yi Yi (I Like You Very Much)" (1941; music by Harry Warren, lyrics by Mack Gordon), while once more garbed in an outlandish costume.

Another all-star picture, Warner Bros.' *Hollywood Canteen,* not only complements *Follow the Boys* and *Four Jills in a Jeep,* it also provides a response to the previous year's *Stage Door Canteen,* a United Artists release. Whereas *Stage Door Canteen* focuses on the justly famous New York canteen and features many Broadway performers, *Hollywood Canteen* celebrates the film capital's own roster of celebrities. Comedians like Jack Benny, Joe E. Brown, and Eddie Cantor provide the requisite light touch, and groups like Jimmy Dorsey and his band, Carmen Cavallero and his orchestra, Roy Rogers, and the Sons of the Pioneers contribute the music. Rogers, in fact, sings Cole Porter's "Don't Fence Me In" (1944 [popular revival of a 1934 song]; words and music by Cole

THE USO AND USO CAMP SHOWS

Shortly before the country's entry into World War II, President Roosevelt asked six civilian agencies—the Salvation Army, the Young Men's Christian Association, the Young Women's Christian Association, the National Catholic Community Services, the National Travelers Aid Association, and the National Jewish Welfare Board—to coordinate their resources to form a new organization with the purpose of reaching out to those in uniform. Thus, on February 4, 1941, the USO (United Service Organizations) was chartered as a private, nonprofit agency.

Between 1941 and 1944, as the number of people in the armed forces skyrocketed, the USO worked to open facilities that would welcome those serving their country. In 3,000 communities nationwide, and housed in everything from churches and museums to barns and storefronts, these centers became known as welcoming places for lonely service personnel. They provided a chance to dance, chat, write letters, watch movies, or simply find quiet solace. Plus, they always served hot coffee and doughnuts.

As with the ongoing bond drives, entertainers from stage, screen, and radio participated in the USO endeavors. In New York City, the Stage Door Canteen was staffed by Broadway's leading lights, while the movie industry offered the Hollywood Canteen and movie stars. At both, famous entertainers willingly served the coffee and mingled with the GIs. Canteens also popped up in other large cities, although they could seldom match the celebrity quotient of their New York and Hollywood counterparts.

The USO quickly recognized a need for more than just places where soldiers could gather and, in May 1941, sent seven traveling show buses to entertain enlisted men in Army camps east of the Rocky Mountains, while a similar Hollywood group staged several large shows in California. Demand for this kind of service grew, and on October 30, 1941, USO Camp Shows, Inc., a separate corporation, launched a troop entertainment program.

The USO Camp Shows organized into four circuits: the Victory Circuit took full-sized revues and concerts to the larger military installations, and the Blue Circuit sent smaller touring companies to perform at Army and Navy sites. The Hospital Circuit provided entertainment at military hospitals, and the Foxhole, or Overseas Circuit, the most dangerous of the four, went as close to the front lines as possible. When the group disbanded in 1947, USO Camp Shows had presented more than 428,000 performances in the United States and had sent some 7,000 performers overseas.

Porter [with Robert Fletcher]), a tune that ranked #2 for the year. For the rest of the movie, many Hollywood stars appear uncredited on screen, and audiences can try to match names with faces. As in any undertaking with so many diverse performers, the music comes across as uneven, although "What Are

You Doing the Rest of Your Life?" (1944; music by Burton Lane, lyrics by Ted Koehler), written for the film, has emerged a standard.

Most of Hollywood's 1944 musicals, however, pursue less ambitious goals—a handful of songs and two or three stars usually suffice. *Carolina Blues* fits this definition nicely; Kay Kyser and his popular band headline the film, along with dancer Ann Miller. The plot involves a defense plant and attempts at arranging a dance date, while the music, hardly distinguished, allows for a few production numbers. Similarly, *Here Come the Waves* carries a thin plot held together by the music. Another story of people entering service and the complications that arise, it stars Bing Crosby and allows Betty Hutton to shine in a dual role. The movie rambles along pleasantly enough, thanks to composer Harold Arlen and lyricist Johnny Mercer. This polished duo provides, among several tunes, "Let's Take the Long Way Home" and "Ac-Cen-Tchu-Ate the Positive." Unfortunately, the latter number is done in blackface,

One of the most successful and prolific of American lyricists, Johnny Mercer set the words to dozens of standards, such as "Blues in the Night" (1941), "Ac-Cen-Tchu-Ate the Positive" (1944), and the humorous "G.I. Jive" (1944). Courtesy of Photofest.

an uncomfortable echo of minstrel shows, but the performance must be seen in light of 1944 standards, not the present.

Universal sought to profit from the previous popularity of *Babes in Arms* (1939) and *Babes on Broadway* (1941) by producing *Babes on Swing Street*. Perhaps a good idea, but the studio had neither Mickey Rooney nor Judy Garland under contract. This newest *Babes* entry thus lacks stars, along with much of a plot, and it additionally fails to provide a memorable score. *Babes on Swing Street* soon sank from sight, one of those B-pictures doomed to obscurity.

An exception to mediocrity occurred with *Meet Me in St. Louis*. A nostalgia-filled story about turn-of-the-century America, it tells of a family about to be uprooted by the father's job change. It stars Judy Garland, who doubtless gave thanks she avoided *Babes on Swing Street*. *Meet Me in St. Louis* permits her to sing several outstanding numbers: "The Boy Next Door," "Have Yourself a Merry Little Christmas," and "The Trolley Song" (all 1944; all with music by Hugh Martin and lyrics by Ralph Blane). Solidly ensconced as a classic musical, the picture builds on the idea that despite difficulties, the American family can overcome all obstacles. As such, the picture reinforces a view popular during World War II. And in "Have Yourself a Merry Little Christmas," Garland's wistful rendition doubtless brought a tear to many an eye with its wartime themes of loneliness and separation, emotions similarly expressed in 1942's "White Christmas" (music and lyrics by Irving Berlin).

BROADWAY: 1945

By the time 1945 rolled around, everyone knew that what they had sensed in 1944 would soon be realized. The Allies rolled across Europe and into Germany itself, while American forces were poised to invade Japan. The Axis mounted last-ditch actions, but they eventually had to face unconditional surrender, Germany in May, Japan in August. The great struggle had finally ended.

On the musical front, 1945 saw Broadway mount 16 new musicals, a significant increase over the previous year's 10 shows. Two productions in particular distinguished the offerings: *On the Town* and *Carousel*. Both have gone on to be considered classics of the American musical theater.

Strictly speaking, a 1944 show, *On the Town* opened on December 28, but its run encompassed 1945 and two months into 1946, with a total of 463 performances. Quibbles aside, it brought together four people who would have a profound influence on Broadway in the postwar era: Leonard Bernstein wrote the music, Betty Comden and Adolph Green supplied the book and lyrics, and Jerome Robbins staged the choreography. The impetus for the show came from Bernstein's ballet *Fancy Free*, an exercise in both modern composition and dance which had opened in the spring of 1944 and introduced Jerome

Robbins as both choreographer and lead dancer. A portrait of three sailors on 24-hour shore leave in New York City, *Fancy Free* translated easily into a musical comedy with the capable assistance of Comden and Green.

The upbeat tone of *On the Town* reflected the changing mood of the nation. With victory in sight, a happy picture of servicemen seemed more appropriate than a grim one. Both the dancing and the music ignored the war, as this trio of sailors cavorted through New York City, "a helluva town." The girls they encountered were equally joyous, a mood transmitted to the audience throughout the production. Among the memorable songs Bernstein, Comden, and Green contributed, "New York, New York," "Carried Away," and "Lonely Town" stand out as gems, standards today in the American songbook. Revived many times, *On the Town* has aged well. A film version, shot in 1949, casts Frank Sinatra, Gene Kelly, and Jules Munshin as the three sailors; an immediate hit, it set new standards for Hollywood musicals.

Just four months later, *Carousel*, the second Broadway show for the team of Richard Rodgers and Oscar Hammerstein II, further brightened the Great White Way. The production used a 1909 drama, *Liliom*, by the French writer Ferenc Molnar, as its source, and rewrote the rule book about musical comedies. Hardly a happy story, both the original and the Rodgers and Hammerstein adaptation employed suicide, marital unhappiness, prejudice, and violence as themes. Despite these unusual motifs, *Carousel* worked, and its score has supplied several standards. "If I Loved You," "June Is Bustin' Out All Over," and "You'll Never Walk Alone," major numbers performed in the play, have become part of the Rodgers and Hammerstein canon and known to millions. Even with its explorations of the darker sides of human nature, *Carousel* proved an enormous hit.

Meanwhile, *Oklahoma!* continued its record-breaking run, and Rodgers and Hammerstein knew that, in a sense, they would be competing with themselves. They need not have worried; *Carousel* played for almost 900 performances and did not close until May 1947; *Oklahoma!* ran until May 1948. In 1956, 20th Century Fox released a film version of *Carousel* that also received critical and popular acclaim. With the remarkable successes of both shows, Richard Rodgers and Oscar Hammerstein II emerged as the most successful practitioners of the musical on Broadway.

While *On the Town* and *Carousel* reenergized the theatrical musical, two other 1945 openings delved into tradition. *The Red Mill*, a 1906 operetta by composer Victor Herbert, once again amused audiences in the fall of the year. Operettas, usually staged with lots of costumes, innocuous plots, and frothy music, serve as exercises in escapism, and *The Red Mill*, in both its 1906 and 1945 incarnations, satisfied on all counts. Another composer who excelled in this form was Sigmund Romberg. He had made his name years earlier with hit shows like *Maytime* (1917), *The Student Prince* (1924), and *May Wine* (1935), and it therefore came as no surprise that he had crafted a new operetta with *Up in Central Park.* A bit of fluff that showcased lyrics by the estimable Dorothy Fields, the show revolved around New York City in the latter half of the nineteenth century. Since it featured the period costumes and romantic songs so beloved by buffs of this form, it gave Romberg yet another hit. *Up in Central Park* went promptly to film in 1948.

HOLLYWOOD: 1945

While Messrs. Bernstein, Rodgers, and Hammerstein were bringing the musical theater into a new era, the movie business underwent few changes. People bought tickets at a record clip, the studios churned out hundreds of features each year, and the future seemingly looked rosy. No one foresaw the rapid changes—and decline—that awaited the motion picture industry just a few years down the road. Blissful in their ignorance, the studios' 1945 crop of 38 new musicals closely resembled those of preceding years.

The war continued to rage in January, but the sense that peace might soon become a reality clearly colored the year's productions. Hollywood offered fewer new releases that reflected the conflict, and they tended to be inconsequential, such as *Bring on the Girls* (sailors and gold diggers), *Sing Your Way Home* (war correspondent and group of all-girl entertainers on board a ship), *Thrill of a Romance* (war hero and married woman), and *Tonight and Every Night* (the show must go on, despite bombings).

But one picture rose above the others and showed that, in the right hands, good movies could still be made about topical material. *Anchors Aweigh,* a lighthearted MGM production, stars Gene Kelly, Frank Sinatra, and Kathryn Grayson. The plot, which echoes *On the Town,* then playing on Broadway, involves two sailors (Kelly and Sinatra) on leave and their adventures. A good score further enlivens events and includes Sinatra crooning "I Fall in Love Too Easily" (1945; music by Jule Style, lyrics by Sammy Cahn) surrounded by a sea of pianos. But the standout number has to be Gene Kelly singing and dancing to "The King Who Couldn't Dance" (1945; music by Sammy Fain, lyrics by Arthur Freed), and what makes it memorable is Kelly's partner: Jerry the Mouse from the *Tom and Jerry* cartoons of the day. Using almost seamless special effects, it appears this odd couple, one live, one animated, is having a wonderful time together. *Anchors Aweigh,* like its Broadway counterpart, brings a cheeriness to its story of servicemen in time of war that never spills over into sentimentality.

If *Anchors Aweigh* surpasses the other war-oriented musicals of 1945, *State Fair* doubtless steals the scene from the year's remaining musical films. Not only does it boast a splendid score, it also marks the one and only time Richard Rodgers and Oscar Hammerstein collaborated on a major motion picture.

Based on a 1932 novel, and filmed the following year as a vehicle for the folksy Will Rogers, this warm, family based story has long been a popular favorite. In its 1945 movie version (it would be remade in 1962), Rodgers and Hammerstein wrote such memorable songs as "It Might As Well Be Spring," "It's a Grand Night for Singing," and "Isn't It Kind of Fun?" Playing in movie theaters concurrently with their two Broadway smashes, *Oklahoma!* and *Carousel,* the success of the cinematic *State Fair* gave the songwriting team a unique dominance in show tunes for the time.

The remainder of the 1945 movie menu provided audiences many additional choices, but little of outstanding quality. *Earl Carroll's Vanities* and *George White's Scandals of 1945* merely re-create, and not altogether successfully, the long-running series that had years earlier become fixtures on Broadway. *Incendiary Blonde* features the energetic Betty Hutton in a biography of entertainer Texas Guinan, and *Rhapsody in Blue* attempts to do the same for George Gershwin. Fortunately, the latter film has a fine Gershwin score that partially overcomes its biographical shortcomings. Finally, a few all-star movies—*Week-End at the Waldorf, Diamond Horseshoe, Radio Stars on Parade,* and others—present a lineup of current studio and musical celebrities in stories that exist to allow them to perform, albeit briefly.[5]

CONCLUSION

In retrospect, both Broadway and Hollywood responded to the war years in one of two ways: either by creating shows that use World War II as a background, or by providing entertainment that serves as escapism, ignoring anything topical. It can, of course, be argued that disregarding current events functions as a response in its own right; this approach takes the audience's mind off anything unpleasant and provides a much-needed break. In both attitudes, stage and screen gave the nation some splendid music, much of which has endured well. Virtually every form of musical expression—country, sweet, swing, jazz, popular, classical—had its day at one time or another. The period 1939–1945 certainly must rank as a rich one in American music for the stage or screen.

7

Country Music

BACKGROUND

Country music, not as well known in 1939 as the songs created by Tin Pan Alley and other popular producers, gained listeners and fans with each passing year of the 1940s. It originally carried the name folk and, later, hillbilly music, evolving from hymns and ballads brought to North America by English, Scottish, and Irish immigrants in the late 1700s. Other influences, such as waltzes, ragtime, and commercially oriented tunes, later began to affect its content. Initially confined to small towns and rural areas in the South and Southwest, country music, before the days of radio and recordings, survived around the home and in the fields. It also served as an important component of family, school, church, and social gatherings.

The widespread introduction of recordings and radio into everyday American life during the 1920s and 1930s gradually broadened the influence of this music beyond its original southeastern and southwestern boundaries. At the end of the 1930s, however, country music continued to claim rural white Southerners as its primary audience. But during World War II, with demographic changes occurring everywhere, it emerged as a national phenomenon and big business.

Several factors contributed to country's explosive growth. Recording firms such as Decca searched the nation for new singers in an attempt to build a large hillbilly catalog and then aggressively marketed its discs by selling them at unusually low prices. At the same time, professional promoters developed the careers of country musicians, as well as their own, by advancing hillbilly performers through recordings and personal appearances.

The growing numbers of jukeboxes offered countless sources of increased exposure since these machines accounted for a sizeable portion of record sales. On the West Coast, Hollywood discovered some country artists, who then appeared in a number of Westerns and singing cowboy movies. These pictures introduced new audiences to the genre. Meanwhile, on the East Coast, business and labor disputes within the music industry, coupled with a resultant recording ban, caused a shortage of much new popular mainstream music from 1940 to 1943 and created an entrée for country artists. (See chapter 4, "Recordings and the Music Business," for more on industry disputes.)

Other opportunities further expanded country's potential. World War II caused major population shifts in the United States, and rural residents in search of jobs moved to urban industrial complexes and towns near military bases. Since a large number of these sites could be found in the South and Southwest, many people previously unacquainted with the music moved to regions where country already had an active following. Frequently heard on local radio stations and at public gatherings, the music gained new fans as listeners and performers shared their favorites with neighbors and members of the armed forces. Finally, country songwriters have historically featured tunes with plaintive lyrics and simple melodies, a musical format that held great psychological appeal for Americans in wartime.

COUNTRY MUSIC BEFORE 1939

Early in the twentieth century, a large percentage of rural Americans played one or more instruments—parlor organs, pianos, fiddles, guitars, banjos—to accompany singing and dancing. Live entertainment by musicians and singers, both amateur and professional, quickly became standard fare for leisure activities. Their songs remained true to the heritage of British ballads, with the story, frequently a long narrative poem, being the essence of the performance; the voice of the singer and the arrangement of the music took a back seat.

By the 1920s, recordings and radio programs offered listeners in many parts of the United States a variety of musical genres. The poor in rural sections of the country often enjoyed hillbilly songs and preferred sheet music over recordings since it allowed those who possessed instruments an opportunity to perform the compositions. Furthermore, they frequently considered radios and phonographs expensive novelties owned by the affluent and not something they could or would purchase for themselves.

But in mid-June 1923, a Georgia mill hand by the name of Fiddlin' John Carson made a recording, "Little Old Log Cabin in the Lane" (n.d.; traditional), in Atlanta, Georgia. He set in motion events that eventually led to a change; hillbilly music went from a homemade product for local consumption to its status in the 1940s as a commercial endeavor. Ralph Peer, who represented Victor Records as one of the first A&R (artists and repertoire) men in the business, initially decided against a national release of Carson's record, viewing it as an inferior and nonsaleable product. Instead, he supplied a local distributor 500 copies for the Atlanta region. These sold within days, as did an additional 1,000 pressings. Peer quickly realized the potential of this untapped market and brought Fiddlin' John Carson to New York to cut additional recordings.

Music company executives took note, and in 1927, Ralph Peer, again representing Victor Records, traveled to Bristol, Tennessee, where he built a portable studio and recorded several soon-to-become successful hillbilly artists. One, Jimmie Rodgers, a yodeler and railroad man, became known as the "Singing Brakeman." He recorded two songs true to the Southern hillbilly music tradition and gained remarkable popularity in a relatively short period. Rodgers emerged as the first country singing star and achieved his place in history as the Father of Country Music. At this same session, Peer recorded A. P. Carter, his wife Sara, and sister-in-law Maybelle, the first members of what evolved into the Carter Family musical dynasty. The pressings made by Rodgers and the Carter Family did well enough that Victor continued to record them, allowing their recognition to spread well beyond rural southwest Virginia, West Virginia, and east Tennessee. These pioneers laid a firm foundation for the future growth of country music. (See chapter 1, "Music about World War II," for more details on country music's contribution to songs directly about the war.)

THE NATIONAL BARN DANCE AND *GRAND OLE OPRY*

Radio programs with a barn dance format offered listeners some comedy and square dance music; they also helped to prepare the nation for country music's coming of age during the 1940s. Prior to these shows, and before the release of recordings by early hillbilly stars and Hollywood's production of singing cowboy movies, radio station WBAP in Fort Worth, Texas, on the evening of January 4, 1923, premiered its own kind of weekly barn dance music program.

Shortly after this airing, announcer George D. Hay played a significant role in the success of two other barn dance shows. He had worked first at Sears, Roebuck and Company's Chicago station, WLS (for *World's Largest Store*), and next at WSM, a newly opened station in Nashville, Tennessee. His radio work at these venues promoted hillbilly music in ways that gave it national recognition, eventually bringing about a name change, from hillbilly to country music.

At WLS, Hay announced for *The National Barn Dance,* a weekly barn dance show that ran from April 1924 until April 1960. From its first broadcast, the program gained a large following. Hay soon moved to WSM and every Saturday evening aired an hour or two of old-time folk tunes performed by amateur performers. The program's success convinced him that the station should change its format. Management agreed, and the show became a barn dance featuring authentic rural musicians before a live audience. In 1927, his venture officially acquired the name of *Grand Ole Opry* and has continued as a highly popular twice-weekly program from WSM.

By 1935, approximately 5,000 radio programs across the country presented some type of country music played by local musicians in a stage show format (see table 7.1). One broadcaster, WWVA in Wheeling, West Virginia, reached

Table 7.1
Representative Barn Dance Radio Shows from 1930 through 1944

Date	Show	Station	Location
1930	*Old-Fashioned Barn Dance*	KMOX	Saint Louis, MO
1931	*Iowa Barn Dance Frolic*	WHO	Des Moines, IA
1932	*Hoosier Hop*	WOWO	Fort Wayne, IN
1933	*World's Original WWVA Jamboree*	WWVA	Wheeling, WV
1934	*Crazy Barn Dance*	WBT	Charlotte, NC
1935	*Barn Dance*	WMCA	New York, NY
1935	*Brush Creek Follies*	KMBC	Kansas City, KS
1936	*Mid-Day Merry-Go-Round*	WNOX	Knoxville, TN
1936	*Boone County Jamboree/ Midwestern Hayride*	WLW	Cincinnati, OH
1937	*John Lair's Renfro Valley Barn Dance*	WHAS	Renfro Valley, KY
1938	*Old Dominion Barn Dance*	WRVA	Richmond, VA
1938	*Saddle Mountain Roundup*	KVOO	Tulsa, OK
1938	*Brush Creek Follies*	KMBC	Kansas City, KS
1940	*WSB Barn Dance*	WSB	Atlanta, GA
1941	*Korn's-a-Krackin'*	KWTO	Springfield, MO
1942	*Tennessee Barn Dance*	WNOX	Knoxville, TN
1942	*Los Angeles County Barn Dance*	KRKD	Los Angeles, CA
1944	*Bluff Creek Roundup*	KOMA	Oklahoma City, OK
1944	*Dinner Bell Roundup*	KXLA	Pasadena, CA
1944	*Hollywood Barn Dance*	KNX	Los Angeles, CA

audiences outside the South and into the Northeast because of its strong signal. Collectively, these broadcasts added to the growing national awareness of country music and its Southern roots.[1]

By 1933, an hour of *The National Barn Dance*'s five-hour show could be picked up by the National Broadcasting Company's (NBC radio) network affiliates. At the outbreak of World War II, innumerable stations around the country regularly presented hundreds of musicians performing traditional country dance tunes as well as folk music provided by fiddle bands and balladeers. But these productions also included a high proportion of sentimental pop tunes and heart songs, as well as comedy routines, giving them broader audience appeal.

The National Barn Dance boasted performers who became well known within the growing genre. A WLS scout discovered Clyde Foley, usually called Red Foley because of his hair, who first appeared on the show as a vocalist for John Lair's Cumberland Ridge Runners, a group that dressed in hillbilly costumes and played guitars, banjos, fiddles, and mandolins. Foley left WLS in 1937 to assist with the founding of the *Renfro Valley Barn Dance* and, in 1938, became a member of the cast for NBC radio's *Avalon Time*. Described as a variety and comedy show and a vehicle for Western music, he briefly costarred with comedian Red Skelton before returning to *The National Barn Dance* in 1940.

Having made several recordings with the Cumberland Ridge Runners, Foley signed an individual contract with Decca Records in 1941 and hit it big with his first recording, "Old Shep" (originally written in 1933; words and music by Red Foley), a song that became a country classic recorded by many artists, including Hank Snow and Elvis Presley. Another recording by Foley, "I'll Be Back in a Year, Little Darling" (1941; words and music by Ben Shelhamer Jr., Claude Heritier, and Russ Hull), had been cut a couple of months earlier by the Prairie Ramblers and held the distinction of being the first patriotic World War II piece recorded by a *National Barn Dance* act.[2] At this time, Foley made his film debut with Tex Ritter in a Monogram Pictures Western called *The Pioneers* (1941).

During the war, Red Foley performed before military and civilian audiences and, in 1944, experienced another success with a recording of "Smoke on the Water" (1943; words and music by Zeke Clements and Earl Nunn [not to be confused with the 1973 tune of the same name]). In January of 1944, *Billboard* magazine, a music trade journal, introduced a folk chart that included country songs. Foley's first *Billboard* chart achievement with "Smoke on the Water" began in September 1944, when he held the #1 spot for 13 consecutive weeks and also appeared on *Billboard*'s list of most played jukebox pop music between September 30 and December 16, 1944, for 11 weeks, with 4 weeks in the Top 10.

In January 1945, Red Foley became the first major country performer to record in Nashville. Additionally, he cut some discs with Lawrence Welk and his orchestra, a sweet band of the day. Foley followed these accomplishments by signing on as a regular member of the *Grand Ole Opry* and soon became the perfect candidate to replace Roy Acuff as the show's headliner.

He had gained recognition as a country performer because of regular appearances on *The National Barn Dance.* Lulu Belle and Scotty Wiseman likewise enjoyed national popularity from their slots on the show. Lulu Belle joined the program in 1932 and Scotty in 1933. Until their departure in 1958, they played novelty pieces, folk songs, and current country compositions sung to their own guitar and banjo accompaniments. During her first year with WLS, Lulu Belle sang with Red Foley. After she met and married Scotty, *The National Barn Dance* dubbed them the show's sweethearts, and they became the leading husband-wife duo in country music. They could be heard weekly, often performing numbers composed by Scotty.

Like many of *The National Barn Dance* and *Grand Ole Opry* acts, Lulu Belle and Scotty participated in traveling country music shows, weekday performances housed in tents or auditoriums throughout the country. Soon, other established radio barn dances, such as Cincinnati's WLW Barn Dance and the Renfro Valley Show in Kentucky, also offered road performances. Personal appearances at these events garnered significant box-office receipts and drew huge crowds that contributed to a growing awareness of country music. For example, Lulu Belle and Scotty typically made $500 plus transportation (approximately $7,200 in contemporary dollars) for a weekday public event. WLS road shows played thousands of performances and, between 1939 and 1942, earned over a half million dollars (approximately $7 million in contemporary dollars). Each weekend, everyone returned to the radio studio for the regularly scheduled weekend broadcasts.

Over the course of their careers, Lulu Belle and Scotty recorded for a variety of labels, such as Conqueror, Vocalion, Columbia, Bluebird, Mercury, and Starday, and remain best known for their classic "Have I Told You Lately That I Love You?" (1946; words and music by Scotty Wiseman). At the peak of their fame, the couple appeared and sang in the films *Village Barn Dance* (1940), *County Fair* (1941), *Hi, Neighbor* (1942), *Swing Your Partner* (1943), *Sing, Neighbor, Sing* (1944), and *National Barn Dance* (1944).

Other female artists, including Patsy Montana and Louise Massey, both from *The National Barn Dance,* also enjoyed commercial success. Montana began her affiliation with the show in 1933 as the vocalist for the Kentucky Ramblers, a group that played string band music with a Western flair and soon changed its name to the Prairie Ramblers. Not the first singing cowgirl, but the first to have any national impact, she composed and recorded "I Want to

Be a Cowboy's Sweetheart" (1935), a number that went on to be her signature song and country music's first million-seller by a female artist.

In 1939, Montana sang this hit in Republic Pictures' *Colorado Sunset,* a film starring none other than Gene Autry. She recorded for both RCA Victor and Decca and released many songs such as "I Wanna Be a Western Cowgirl" (1939; words and music by Gene Autry). For the war effort, she recorded "Goodnight, Soldier" (1943; words and music by Harry Johnson) and appeared in a Hollywood musical short, *The Chime Bell Ring* (1944). Her work continued to define her image as a cowboy pal, who yodeled and dressed in full Western regalia.

Another woman, Louise Massey Mabie, better known as Louise Massey, sang and played the piano and first performed on *The National Barn Dance* in 1933. The whole family got into the act. Her husband, Milt Mabie, played bass, and the group featured brothers Allen (guitar and banjo) and Dott (fiddle and trumpet). Louise, as the singer and yodeler, stood out from the other members of the Musical Massey Family. To capitalize on her growing popularity, the quartet changed its name to Louise Massey and the Westerners in 1939. They recorded many songs for Vocalion, Okeh, and Conqueror, with their most famous during the World War II era being "My Adobe Hacienda" (1941; words and music by Louise Massey and Lee Penny). It attained notice on *Billboard*'s hillbilly and pop charts simultaneously.

In the fall of 1941, merchandiser Montgomery Ward, seeking to profit from this rising star, offered a guitar, the Louise Massey Model, with a reproduction of her signature painted in brown just below the bridge. For $8.95 ($123 in contemporary dollars), the purchaser received, in addition to the signed guitar, a pick, neck cord, Spanish guitar instruction book, and the *Louise Massey and the Westerners* songbook. That same year, the NBC network contracted the group for a 15-minute radio show called *Reveille Round-Up;* it also aired on the Armed Forces Radio (AFR) from 1943 to 1945.

Not all of *The National Barn Dance* acts dealt solely with straight country music; some incorporated comical components. The Hoosier Hot Shots, consisting of brothers Ken and Paul Trietsch, along with Gabe (Otto) Ward and Frank Kettering, provided audiences of the 1930s and 1940s with tunes characterized by novel arrangements, comic lyrics, red hot rhythm, and sometimes pleasant harmony. Playing an unusual variety of instruments, such as washboards, bulb horns, a hand-pushed klaxon, clarinet, bass, and guitar, their music, whether current popular fare or one of their zany numbers like "From the Indies to the Andes in His Undies" (c. 1931; words and music by the Hoosier Hot Shots), started with Ken questioning his brother Paul, "Are you ready, Hezzie?"

As a comedy music act, even during the war years, they continued to inject novelty and humor into their repertory of songs. In addition to being regulars on *The National Barn Dance,* the Hoosier Hot Shots appeared in a number of

Hollywood films, seven from 1939 through 1945, including *In Old Monterey* (1939) starring Gene Autry, *National Barn Dance* (1944), and *Rhythm Round-Up* (1945), with Bob Wills and His Texas Playboys. Like many country artists, the Hot Shots performed in USO (United Service Organizations) shows, which offered a moment of respite for military personnel. They played for troops stationed in North Africa and Italy, and their act achieved enough fame that the Douglas Aircraft plant in Long Beach, California, christened one of its bombers the "Hoosier Hot Shot."

The Williams Brothers Quartet (Bob, Dick, Andy, and Don) joined *The National Barn Dance* in the late 1930s, having first starred on WHO's *Iowa Barn Dance Show.* Widespread radio exposure garnered them enough attention to catch the interest of Bing Crosby, with whom they made their first professional recording and a big hit, "Swinging on a Star" (1944; music by Jimmy Van Heusen, lyrics by Johnny Burke). One member of the quartet, Andy Williams, later achieved particular fame in the popular music recording industry and on television.

Not all *National Barn Dance* acts consisted of groups. Little Georgie Goebel joined WLS at the age of 13 in 1933, just one year after Gene Autry came aboard. Billed as the "Little Singing Cowboy," he rendered cowboy ballads while wearing an oversized 10-gallon hat and strumming a ukulele. By the 1940s, he had his own touring troupe, Georgie Goebel's Barn Dance Band. He served in the Army Air Corps during World War II and, after the war, dropped the first *e* in his last name, became George Gobel, turned to comedy, and later headlined on television.

Songwriter Jenny Lou Carson obtained recognition in radio. She appeared with two different female vocal groups on WLS and composed some of their songs. During World War II, she wrote popular numbers about soldiers and home; her first major hit, "Jealous Heart" (1944), made it to the country charts in a Tex Ritter recording that remained listed for 23 weeks. Lesser known is "Dear God, Watch Over Joe" (1944). In 1945, she had a second hit, "You Two-Timed Me One Time Too Often," also recorded by Ritter; it appeared in the Top 10 for 20 weeks and stood at #1 for 11 of those weeks.

The National Barn Dance also featured a number of other performers during the war years: Luther Ossenbrink, a hillbilly comedian known as Arkie the Arkansas Woodchopper, played guitar, sang, and called the square dances on the show; the DeZurik Sisters specialized in an unusual repertoire of high, haunting yodels and yips; and Pat Buttram enjoyed a regular comedy spot from 1933 until 1946. He played himself in the movie *National Barn Dance* (1944) but became famous for his many roles as Gene Autry's sidekick in postwar movies.

Grand Ole Opry quickly achieved long-lasting popularity after its first 1927 airing. Over the next decade, this program, aired live, moved to several Nashville locations in an attempt to accommodate its growing audience. In 1939, the show gained the biggest exposure ever for country music when it

NBC's popular radio show, *Grand Ole Opry,* helped spur interest in country music. This caricature depicts singer Red Foley, one of the regulars on the program during the war years. Library of Congress, Prints & Photographs Division.

obtained national network status as a 30-minute weekly Saturday night offering spot on NBC sponsored by Prince Albert Tobacco. It moved to coast-to-coast broadcasts in July 1940.

The enthusiastic outpouring of fan mail following a 1938 rendition of "Great Speckled Bird" (1936; words and music by Roy Carter and Guy Smith) by Roy Acuff and the Crazy Tennesseans led the show to headline a top performer supported by other acts, including comedians such as Minnie Pearl and Lazy Jim Day. Acuff, with his signature song, "Wabash Cannonball" (1940; words and music by A. P. Carter), became that central figure and *Grand Ole Opry*'s first solo singing star. Acuff's group changed its name to the Smoky Mountain Boys and, unlike many country music acts, avoided wearing Western and hillbilly outfits, opting instead for casual clothing.

During the war years, Roy Acuff and *Grand Ole Opry* became virtually synonymous, and the broadcasts featured traditional mountain (hillbilly)-style melodies along with sacred songs, all rendered in a plaintive and sincere manner. Acuff's many successful tunes at this time included "Night Train to Memphis" (1942; words and music by Owen Bradley, Harry Beasley Smith, and Marvin Hughes), "Fireball Mail" (1942; words and music by Floyd Jenkins), "Precious Jewel" (1943; words and music by Roy Acuff), "The Prodigal Son" (1944; words and music by Floyd Jenkins), "I'll Forgive You But I Can't Forget" (1944; words and music by Joe Frank and Pee Wee King), and "Blue Eyes Crying in the Rain" (1945; words and music by Fred Rose).

Country music grew in popularity during the war years. One of the leaders in the genre was Roy Acuff, seen here singing, accompanied by his group called the Smoky Mountain Boys. Library of Congress, Prints & Photographs Division.

Roy Acuff's interests, however, went beyond performing. Reporters noted that Governor Prentice Cooper of Tennessee announced in the early 1940s that "hillbilly music is disgraceful," causing Acuff to decide to run for that office. He failed to make it to the governor's mansion, but did become known as the "King of Country Music." In 1942, Acuff and Fred Rose joined forces to form the Acuff-Rose Publishing Company in Nashville, the first such house exclusively devoted to this form of music. He also traveled to Hollywood and portrayed himself in *Grand Ole Opry* (1940), *Hi, Neighbor* (1942), *Cowboy Canteen* (1944), and *Sing, Neighbor, Sing* (1944). In *O, My Darling Clementine* (1943), Acuff plays a singing sheriff. With singing, acting, and personal appearances, in 1944, he earned $200,000 (a little over $2 million in contemporary dollars).[3]

Grand Ole Opry also contributed to the war effort. In 1941, under the sponsorship of the R. J. Reynolds Tobacco Company, the producers organized the Camel Caravan, borrowing on the name of a popular radio show also sponsored by Reynolds' Camel cigarettes. This traveling unit of performers entertained troops at military bases in the United States and the Panama Canal region and introduced country music to people who had never before experienced it.

Eddy Arnold, the "Tennessee Plowboy" and a member of the Camel Caravan, originally came to *Grand Ole Opry* in 1940. He served as the vocalist for Pee Wee King and the Golden West Cowboys, a group that played a significant role in the spread of country music following World War II. From the security of a regular spot on the show, Arnold emerged in 1943 as a solo star and signed with Decca Records. In December 1944, he cut his first record, "Mommy, Please Stay Home with Me" (1943; words and music by Eddy Arnold, Wally Fowler, and Graydon J. Hall), followed in 1945 with "Cattle Call" (1943; words and music by Tex Owens).

At the beginning of his career, Arnold's singing style reflected the influence of the many singing cowboys, especially Gene Autry, but he quickly moved to a smoother and more melancholy delivery without the nasality, causing many to call him a country crooner. Arnold experienced moderate success and continued to record; in 1946, he hit it big with "That's How Much I Love You" (1946; words and music by Eddy Arnold, Wally Fowler, and Graydon J. Hall) and supplanted Roy Acuff as the nation's best-known country singer. He adopted an increasingly polished style of singing, and by the mid-1950s, no one considered him a hillbilly singer.

Redd Stewart, another musician with Pee Wee King, found himself drafted into military service shortly after the attack on Pearl Harbor. While stationed in the South Pacific, he wrote his first hit, the morbid "Soldier's Last Letter" (1944; words and music by Redd Stewart and Ernest Tubb), a song that Ernest Tubb, another major country singer, recorded and took to the *Billboard* charts for seven weeks. It rose to the top for four of those weeks. When Stewart returned from his tour of duty, he reconnected with King and became the group's lead singer. In 1948, Stewart and King wrote one of the most successful country songs of all time, "Tennessee Waltz."

Ernest Tubb had commenced his career in the 1930s by imitating his idol, Jimmie Rodgers; he even played Rodgers' guitar while yodeling. The removal of Tubb's tonsils in 1939 took away his ability to yodel and caused him to develop his own vocal identity. He signed on with Decca and began touring and appearing on Fort Worth's KGKO. In 1940, Universal Mills, makers of Gold Chain Flour, bought the station, giving Tubb the role of the "Gold Chain Troubadour." His big break came with "Walking the Floor over You" (1941; words and music by Ernest Tubb); as a million-selling item, it turned out to be his signature song. The tune also gave him easy entrée in 1943 to *Grand Ole Opry* as a singer who dared to use an electric lead guitar. Because of this, many consider Ernest Tubb as the trendsetter for honky-tonk music, which dominated country music during the postwar years.

In the early 1940s, Tubb toured with Pee Wee King, but by 1944, he fronted the Texas Troubadours, his own band. He also played himself in the movie *Jamboree* (1944) and had minor roles in *The Fighting Buckaroo* (1943) and *Riding West* (1944). Tex Ritter sang Tubb's "Try Me One More Time" (1941) in the 1945 film *Three in the Saddle.* Riding high, Tubb went to Nashville in 1946 to cut a disc, the second country music artist to do so; Decca had recorded Red Foley there the previous year.

At the same time that Nashville became a force in country music, Hollywood also lured a number of aspiring artists. They performed in clubs and made movies, establishing a West Coast country beachhead. In recognition of the fact, radio station KNX in Los Angeles inaugurated the *Hollywood Barn Dance* in 1944, a show that soon went with the CBS network. Considered the *Grand Ole Opry* of the West, it featured countless country and cowboy singers and offered still more choices for music fans.

"TUMBLING TUMBLEWEEDS," A WIDELY PERFORMED COUNTRY SONG

Canadian-born Bob Nolan performed as one of the original members of the Sons of the Pioneers, a popular singing group that remained together from the days of the Great Depression onward. In 1932, before his association with the Pioneers, Nolan had penned a tune he initially titled "Tumbling Leaves." No one knew about it until the Sons of the Pioneers came on the music scene as a vocal group in the mid-1930s. Nolan rediscovered his composition in 1934, when it was performed by Gene Autry in the motion picture *Tumbling Tumbleweeds,* a low-budget Republic Pictures release.

Audiences took to the music, and the Sons of the Pioneers soon recorded it and adopted it as their theme song. Their own interpretation of "Tumbling Tumbleweeds" can be seen and heard in *Hollywood Canteen* (1944), a star-studded musical that revolves around the fabled USO canteen. Before that, however, Bing Crosby had recorded the song in a 1940 release on the Decca label; it became a hit for the popular singer, who was no stranger to Western tunes. Roy Rogers, another of the original Pioneers (when he was still known as Leonard Slye), sings it in *Silver Spurs,* a 1943 opus that also has the vocal group on board.

If a song did well, it often reappeared in other movies, and "Tumbling Tumbleweeds," by the war years a Western standard, did just that. The Sons of the Pioneers repeated their efforts in a 1945 offering, *Don't Fence Me In,* which ostensibly stars Roy Rogers but does not have him performing it. Over the years, "Tumbling Tumbleweeds" has been recorded by other country stars such as Hank Snow, the Gatlin Brothers, and Willie Nelson. Pop artists, including Perry Como, Diana Ross and the Supremes, Jo Stafford, and Patti Page, have also appropriated the song.

SINGING COWBOYS

Throughout the twentieth century, American culture has romanticized the cowboy. With the advent of sound movies, Hollywood in the 1930s and 1940s expanded on the potential of this image and allowed actors to sing and strum their guitars while astride their horses or seated around the campfire. Dubbed *singing cowboys,* three of them—Tex Ritter, Gene Autry, and Roy Rogers—achieved star recognition during these two decades and at the same time advanced the popularity of country music. These Westerns, in addition to recordings and radio, influenced who listened to what kind of music; in response, country music performers across the country donned appropriate clothing and added cowboy themes to their songs.

One of the most successful of the "singing cowboys" was Gene Autry. He starred in many Western films, wrote music, and had a long-running (1940–1956, with time out for military service, 1943–1945) radio show called *Melody Ranch.* Library of Congress, Prints & Photographs Division.

The well-named Tex Ritter had played a cowpoke in Broadway plays and recorded Western songs before he made his 1936 motion picture debut with *Song of the Gringo*. Highly regarded as a Western movie star, Ritter appeared in 45 films between 1939 and 1945; *Flaming Bullets* (1945) served as his last picture in a long-running series, in which he played Ranger Tex Haines, although he would remain active as an entertainer until 1973.

Once in Hollywood, Ritter continued to record, primarily songs from his many films. Although his record sales, when compared to Gene Autry's, were at best modest, he experienced top hits with "I'm Wastin' My Tears on You" (1944; words and music by Frank Harford and Tex Ritter) and "You Two-Timed Me One Time Too Often" (1945; words and music by Jenny Lou Carson). These two songs came out on the new Capitol label (he had previously been with Decca), which was founded in 1942. Ritter's presence helped significantly in the company's early success.

Of all the Western actors of the 1930s and 1940s, Gene Autry perhaps most deserved the title of singing cowboy. From 1932 until 1934, he appeared regularly on radio's *The National Barn Dance*. At this time, he cut his first major hit, "That Silver-Haired Daddy of Mine" (1931; words and music by Gene Autry and Jimmy Long), and soon landed a role as a singing cowboy in 1934's *In Old Santa Fe*. During the war years alone, Autry made 27 Westerns. Along with his busy Hollywood schedule, he continued to record hits such as "South of the Border (Down Mexico Way)" (1939; words and music by Jimmy Kennedy and Michael Carr), "It Makes No Difference Now" (1939; words and music by Floyd Tillman and Jimmie Davis), "You Are My Sunshine" (1940; words and music by Jimmie Davis and Charles Mitchell), "(I've Got Spurs That) Jingle Jangle Jingle" (1942; music by Joseph J. Lilley, lyrics by Frank Loesser), and "Don't Fence Me In" (1944 [popular revival of a 1934 song]; words and music by Cole Porter [with Robert Fletcher]).

Autry also hosted a long-running Columbia Broadcasting System (CBS radio) series, *Melody Ranch,* using a 1939 tune, "Back in the Saddle Again" (words and music by Ray Whitley), as his theme song. The show ran from 1940 until 1956, although Autry took time out for military service in the Army Air Corps from 1942 until 1945. Because of his widespread fame, and for good public relations, service officials broke with military tradition and allowed him to wear his cowboy boots with his uniform. Following his honorable discharge, Autry immediately resumed his recording and movie careers. Prior to enlisting, Autry had finished filming Republic Pictures' *Ridin' on a Rainbow* (1941). His rendition of "Be Honest with Me" (1941; words and music by Gene Autry and Fred Rose) in that movie received an Academy Award nomination for Best Song that year. It lost, however, to "The Last Time I Saw Paris" (1940; words and music by Jerome Kern and Oscar Hammerstein II), a non-country song featured in *Lady Be Good* (1941) and one that reflected growing apprehensions about World War II.

Despite his cowboy outfits and omnipresent guitar, it is debatable as to whether or not Gene Autry's many recordings can be categorized as authentic country music. He initially employed a creaky hillbilly style similar to that of Jimmie Rodgers and Jimmie Davis. By 1940, however, he had moved on, developing his own approach to a song, and the instrumentation in his work balances steel guitar and fiddle with horns and strings, a much more commercial style. His lyrics focus on Western imagery devoid of Southern hillbilly traditions. True country music or not, his work paved the way for many other performers to blend hillbilly and pop music and strengthened the broad-based popularity of music with rural roots.

During the early 1940s, another singing cowboy, Roy Rogers, served as Autry's chief rival. Rogers began his musical career under his given name of Leonard Slye and performed with a group called the International Cowboys. From there he founded and led the Pioneer Trio, which, in 1934, became the Sons of the Pioneers. Experiencing some success, the group appeared on radio shows and cut several records as a quartet. In 1937, Rogers successfully auditioned for a newly created singing cowboy series with Republic Pictures. His movie career, however, lagged behind Autry's, until the latter got involved in a financial dispute with Republic. As a result, Autry failed to report for the first day of shooting a film to be called *Washington Cowboy*. Republic Pictures immediately contracted with Roy Rogers for the lead role and changed the title to *Under Western Stars* (1938). It served as a breakthrough for Rogers.

Roy Rogers' chance to become the top singing cowboy increased even more when Autry suspended his movie career in 1942 to enlist in the Army Air Corps. Rogers remained a civilian because being the father of several children qualified him for a deferment and allowed him to keep working. By 1943, he had achieved the status of the leading Western actor at the box office. Known as the "King of the Cowboys," during his years with Republic Pictures, he starred in 50 films between 1939 and 1945. Most are song-filled adventures with Western-tinged numbers like "Rocky Mountain Lullaby" (1942; words and music by Roy Rogers). Some of his pictures, however, such as *Man from Oklahoma* (1945), contain more commercial music. For example, that movie features "I'm Beginning to See the Light" (1944; words and music by Duke Ellington, Johnny Hodges, Harry James, and Don George) and carries a more inclusive popular classification. He also makes an appearance in the star-filled *Hollywood Canteen* (1944), singing "Don't Fence Me In" (1944 [popular revival of a 1934 song]; words and music by Cole Porter [with Robert Fletcher]), while his famed horse Trigger dances. Throughout the war years, in addition to a busy movie schedule, Rogers participated in USO tours, raising millions of dollars for the war effort through the sale of war bonds.

COUNTRY MUSIC AND THE RECORDING INDUSTRY

Two events occurred between 1940 and 1943 that challenged the recording industry and at the same time created opportunities for expanded awareness and popularity for country music. In 1939, the American Society of Composers, Authors, and Publishers, better known as ASCAP, proposed doubling the licensing fees charged to broadcasters for the use of ASCAP copyrighted material. The National Association of Broadcasters (NAB) responded by forming a rival publishing company, Broadcast Music Incorporated (BMI). On December 31, 1940, when the stations' and networks' contracts with ASCAP lapsed, the organization said that broadcasters could not play its songs. In response, stations everywhere turned to non-ASCAP sources for music to play on the air. (See chapter 4, "Recordings and the Music Business," for more details on these events.)

As a new organization, BMI initially struggled to acquire holdings. Established songwriters were reluctant to go with a fledgling organization, causing BMI to have to rely on new and inexperienced musicians and lyricists. BMI, instead of following ASCAP's practice of excluding country music songwriters because of a perceived lack of quality in their work, opened its doors to them

---

"YOU ARE MY SUNSHINE," A WELL-KNOWN COUNTRY MUSIC SONG

"You Are My Sunshine," a tune written in 1940 by Jimmie Davis and Charles Mitchell, has come down to the present as an American classic. Sung by millions of schoolchildren over the years, it may have been inspired by a composition widely performed and recorded by the renowned Carter Family. One of the staples in their repertoire was "Keep on the Sunny Side," a 1906 composition with music by Theodore F. Morse and words by Jack Drislane. A. P. Carter, the founder of the group, was always on the lookout for old music suitable for the trio; he saw great possibilities in the tune, and it soon became associated with the Carter Family.

Both "Keep on the Sunny Side" and "You Are My Sunshine" express similar sentiments: when you have those dark moments, remember that you can also have a sunny side to view. Davis and Mitchell's "You Are My Sunshine" depicts the singer waking from a dream, only to discover that his sweetheart, his "sunshine," has left him to love another. Most listeners, however, only recall the upbeat chorus—"you are my sunshine...you make me happy when skies are gray"—and do not remember the larger context of the lyrics. The song has become a country standard that has long since crossed over into the popular music mainstream. Dozens of country and pop artists, ranging from Gene Autry to Bing Crosby to Ray Charles, have recorded "You Are My Sunshine," and it enjoyed a revival in the 2000 movie hit, *O Brother, Where Art Thou?*

---

and soon acquired significant members such as Ralph Peer's Southern Music, with his sizable country music catalogs, and Fred Rose, one of the founders of Acuff-Rose Publishing. The ASCAP ban, which lasted 10 months, meant a time of increased airplay for a variety of hillbilly and country songs. Even though ASCAP and the radio networks eventually resolved their differences, BMI had secured a prominent spot in the broadcasting and entertainment fields, and thereafter far more songwriters and producers from all over the United States had an opportunity to be published and heard on the radio.

Shortly after the settlement of the ASCAP-BMI dispute, the American Federation of Musicians (AFM) and its members went on strike because of a disagreement over royalties. AFM announced that as of August 1, 1942, union musicians could no longer make recordings until the various companies involved agreed to the union's terms. Curiously, this ruling did not affect vocalists, only instrumentalists. Resolution of the problems finally began in 1943, and the strike ended late in 1944. As if these squabbles did not cause enough problems, a shortage of shellac, the material from which most records were made, created additional difficulties for the industry. Fewer recordings meant fewer jobs for everyone.

Despite many hardships, the musicians' strike actually proved a boon for many small and independent record firms that had not been targeted by the AFM, particularly companies that specialized in hillbilly music. These two events, coupled with the popularity of the radio barn dance programs, caused country music records to attract attention all over the country and enabled country music songwriters and singers to produce hits. In fact, Decca's first release after the resumption of recording was Bing Crosby and the Andrews Sisters' version of "Pistol Packin' Mama" (1942; words and music by popular country composer and singer Al Dexter). Originally recorded by Dexter, the two versions jointly sold 3 million copies during 1943 and soon reached first place on the new *Billboard* country chart.

In October 1943, *Time* magazine declared that this form of music had strengthened its foothold in the nation, creating "the biggest revolution in U.S. popular musical taste since the swing craze began in the middle '30s." From the magazine's perspective, it all started in 1939 with a song titled "It Makes No Difference Now" (words and music by Floyd Tillman and Jimmie Davis), along with a shrewd marketing ploy by Decca Records.[4] Within a few months of Jimmie Davis's successful release of the song, Decca had a version by Bing Crosby in stores. The same thing happened with one of country music's most memorable songs, "You Are My Sunshine" (1940; words and music by Jimmie Davis and Charles Mitchell), first recorded by Jimmie Davis and soon thereafter by Bing Crosby. Decca continued to practice this strategy of taking songs that experienced success among country music fans and recording them by bigger non-country names, especially Bing Crosby.

Although Jimmie Davis did not have the national following enjoyed by Crosby, he had recorded many sides for Victor Records during the late 1920s and early 1930s. He then signed with Decca Records in 1934, concentrating on sentimental and Western songs. In addition to his music career, he decided to run for public office in his home state of Louisiana and developed a successful campaign style of following a brief speech with songs backed by a hillbilly band. He was elected public safety commissioner in Shreveport in 1938, to the state public service commission in 1942, and governor in 1944. After leaving public office, he continued to record and also appeared in Hollywood musicals and Westerns such as *Strictly in the Groove* (1942), *Riding through Nevada* (1942), *Frontier Fury* (1943), and *Cyclone Prairie Rangers* (1944).

BLUEGRASS, WESTERN SWING, AND HONKY-TONK

Bluegrass Music

The term *bluegrass* comes from the name of Bill Monroe's string band, the Blue Grass Boys, which he formed in 1938. Monroe and his brother Charlie had previously performed as the Monroe Brothers on WBT out of Charlotte, North Carolina, but went their separate ways. The Blue Grass Boys soon joined *Grand Ole Opry* as regular performers and made their first recording, "Mule Skinner Blues" (1931; words and music by Jimmie Rodgers), in October 1940. The group consisted of Bill Monroe on both guitar and mandolin, along with Cleo Davis and Art Wooten on guitar and fiddle, while Amos Garren played string bass and Tommy Millard handled the jug, bones, and spoons. At this time, the band did not include a banjo, an instrument considered today as a basic component of the bluegrass style.

The Blue Grass Boys initially played music that was reminiscent of traditional hillbilly string bands and frequently presented Monroe's mandolin as the lead instrument. They quickly rose to be one of *Grand Ole Opry*'s strongest attractions and gained a regular spot on the NBC network's half-hour broadcast portion. Bill Monroe, today considered the Father of Bluegrass, became a familiar name across the country.

Monroe cut songs for RCA Victor's Bluebird label during 1940 and 1941,but did not record again until 1945, and then for Columbia Records. By that time, a radical change in his band and the consequent development of bluegrass music had occurred. First, Lester Flatt, who played rhythm guitar and sang heartfelt vocals, joined the group in early 1945. Earl Scruggs, who offered a new instrument for the group and a different playing style with his three-finger banjo picking, came on board a few months later.

The talents of Flatt and Scruggs captivated listeners and gave the group the final elements now associated with bluegrass music: a faster pace (too fast for dancing) than that played by traditional country music groups, high-pitched singing with an emphasis on multiple vocal parts, and just a touch of the blues. The guitar and fiddle took a diminished role, while the mandolin and banjo carried the lead, and individual instrumental embellishments, including the human voice, exchanged solo choruses.

Not as famous as the Monroe Brothers, the Delmore Brothers also actively participated in the bluegrass movement. Music historian Alan Lomax described this alternative approach as "folk music in overdrive with a silvery, rippling, pinging sound," music whose postwar tight rhythmic drive laid the groundwork for the rock 'n' roll of the 1950s.[5]

Western Swing

When swing became the nation's most popular music format in the 1930s, young people from coast to coast danced to the music of Benny Goodman, Tommy Dorsey, Sammy Kaye, and a long list of other dance bands. At the same time, small groups in the Southwest traveled within their regions to play at barn dances, house parties, and county fairs. The music, usually provided by a string band of fiddle, guitar, mandolin, and banjo and shaped primarily by the demands of dancing, consisted of a combination of one- and two-step dances, jitterbug, several foxtrots, along with cowboy waltzes, all showing a jazzy influence brought about by the public's enthusiastic reception of swing. Vocalists even sang in a crooner style reminiscent of Bing Crosby.

Two Fort Worth–based musicians, Bob Wills and Milton Brown, cofounders of the Aladdin Laddies, later called the Light Crust Doughboys, in the early 1930s created this stylistic blend. Old-time fiddle tunes, when expertly played, always served as crowd pleasers, but the citizens of Fort Worth liked to dance to the swing style then in vogue. Originally referred to by some as *hot string bands, hillbilly swing, country swing,* and *Texas Swing,* by the end of World War II, everyone simply called it Western Swing.

For a 1940 recording session, Wills assembled a band of 18 musicians, the largest aggregation he had ever gathered in a studio. Guitars served as the only string instruments. He utilized saxophones, trumpets, and clarinets, along with a drum set, the first time such percussion was used in a Western Swing recording. One of the songs, "New San Antonio Rose" (words and music by Bob Wills), made the year's top hit list of country songs. For copyright reasons, Wills had to add the word *new* to the title; the 1940 version is, in actuality, his 1938 tune, "San Antonio Rose." Its success marked the beginning of a growing popularity across the nation for this style of music, and "San Antonio

Rose" (new or old) became known as a Western Swing classic. A recording of this same song by Bing Crosby in 1941 went to the Top 10 on the *Billboard* country chart.

With success under their belts, Bob Wills and His Texas Playboys immediately appeared in two movies as themselves, one with Tex Ritter in *Take Me Back to Oklahoma* (1940) and the other with Glenn Ford in *Go West, Young Lady* (1941), followed by eight more Westerns during the war years. Having relocated from Texas to Oklahoma, Wills, until he enlisted in the Army at the end of 1942, and his Playboys played regularly at Cain's Ballroom in Tulsa. They frequently drew crowds between 2,000 and 4,000 people and also broadcast from the city's KVOO radio station. "Take Me Back to Tulsa" (1941; words and music by Bob Wills and Tommy Duncan) and "Cherokee Maiden" (1942; words and music by Cindy Walker) can be counted among their list of hit recordings.[6]

In June 1942, KRKD's *Los Angeles County Barn Dance* broadcast its inaugural show from a ballroom on Venice Pier. The following week, the station booked Bob Wills and brought in a crowd of 8,600. Western Swing had arrived in California, and because of the enthusiasm, four more Western Swing ballrooms opened in the area. KRKD also aired the *Western Hit Parade,* a show that ranked the popularity of songs by listeners' mail.

Most Western Swing fans, in addition to Bob Wills and His Texas Playboys, rank Spade Cooley at or near the top for influencing the development of the genre. Cooley worked as a musician and an actor during the 1930s and recorded as a sideman for Gene Autry and Roy Rogers. He did not make a disc of his own until 1941. A year later, he took control of the house band at the popular Venice Pier Ballroom, where he showcased country string band instruments—fiddle, guitar, string bass—along with drums and an accordion, and created a sound closer to conventional dance-oriented pop orchestras than even the tunes coming from Bob Wills. Still considered to be Western Swing with some country string band influences, Cooley's music gained popularity with mainstream audiences and greatly increased his number of fans.

In 1943, he signed with Columbia Records, and two years later, the first single made by Spade Cooley and His Orchestra, "Shame on You" (1945; words and music by Spade Cooley), became the second most popular country song of the year. For this recording, the bandleader used his usual instruments, with additional fiddles, steel and electric guitars, and harp, creating a large string band that indeed could be labeled an orchestra. Vocals provided by Tex Williams added an essential ingredient to the band's success. Following the war, Cooley continued with his music career as well as branching out into television. Tex Williams's primary recognition came in the postwar years after he had left Cooley and formed his own group.

Yet another aggregation, Cliff Bruner and the Texas Wanderers, initially played as a band in 1936 and cut their first Decca record one year later. They changed their name to Cliff Bruner and His Boys in 1939 and, like his counterparts Leon Selph's Blue Ridge Playboys and Bob Dunn's Vagabonds, focused on Western Swing, with lyrics that spoke of disillusionment and hard luck, of swindles, gambling, and sex, conditions frequently equated with city life.

Bruner challenged the members of his group to produce improvised solos to highlight their abilities, a departure from the conventional Western Swing practiced by the Bob Wills band. They recorded "It Makes No Difference Now" (1939; words and music by Floyd Tillman and Jimmie Davis) and "Star Dust" (1927, 1931; music by Hoagy Carmichael, lyrics by Mitchell Parish). Next came a recording of Ted Daffan's "Truck Driver's Blues" (1940), their best-known effort. Shortly after the war, Bruner left the music business, but he had changed the face of Western Swing.

Many other musicians and groups successfully represented the genre, at least regionally. Among these are Bill Boyd (not to be confused with the William Boyd of Hopalong Cassidy fame), who remained true to his Western roots by featuring only a pure string band. Another, the Cowboy Ramblers, recorded with Bluebird/RCA both before and after the war and appeared in six Western films in 1942. Adolph Hofner of San Antonio, Texas, formed a band, Adolph Hofner and the Texans, in 1939. They soon began cutting discs for Okeh and Columbia, and changed their name to the San Antonians. They enjoyed a hit in the early 1940s with "Maria Elena" (1941 [popular revival of a 1933 tune]; words and music by S. K. Russell, Lorenzo Barcalata, and William H. Heagney).

Western Swing reached its peak during the World War II era. The music coming out of Southern California revolutionized the style that had originally emanated from Texas and parts of the Southwest. The emerging country music industry paid keen attention to the innovations popularized on the West Coast, and it all gave rise to a blending of Texas fiddling with pop and jazz instrumentation.

Honky-Tonk

First played by country bands in and around Texas during the early 1930s, honky-tonk used electric instruments and had a louder sound and heavier beat than other country styles. Initially associated with rural people who had moved to cities, the songs reflected their problems and social status and told of both the good times, such as the fun on Friday night after being paid, and the guilt that followed. Many credit Al Dexter, a singer and songwriter who operated a beer joint in Texas following the repeal of Prohibition, as the originator of honky-tonk because of his use of barroom imagery.

Although honky-tonk did not come into its own until after World War II, a pair of Southwestern country music artists during the war years contributed significantly to its development and popularity. Floyd Tillman took up songwriting in addition to playing regularly with Western Swing bands. During the war, his selections reflected both his Texas background in string bands and a tendency toward a pop style. He scored his first big songwriting hit with "It Makes No Difference Now" (1939; words and music by Floyd Tillman and Jimmie Davis), a tune cut by Cliff Bruner and the Texas Wanderers, Jimmie Davis, Gene Autry, and Bing Crosby. Many consider this to be the first great classic of the honky-tonk genre. In addition, Tillman both wrote and sang "Each Night at Nine" (1944), a number that appealed to Americans separated from loved ones because of the war. But after 1945, Tillman left mainstream music and went back to his Texas roots, releasing some of the best honky-tonk songs of the postwar period.

Another Texan, Ted Daffan, worked as a bandleader, musician, singer, recording artist, and songwriter. He pioneered the use of the electric steel guitar as a lead instrument, establishing a distinctive sound that combined blues and swing, an interest that carried over into his songwriting. His first big break came when Cliff Bruner recorded "Truck Driver's Blues" (1940; words and music by Ted Daffan). It sold more than 100,000 copies, making it a significant hit. His lyrics in songs such as "Worried Mind" (1941; words and music by Ted Daffan and Jimmie Davis) and "Headin' Down the Wrong Highway" (1945; words and music by Ted Daffan) clearly capture the moods of working-class Southerners. He also enjoyed winners with songs he did not write but nonetheless recorded. "No Letter Today" (1943; words and music by Frankie Brown), a tune with wartime echoes, topped the charts, competing with the likes of Roy Acuff and Gene Autry.

FOLK MUSIC

In the United States, a predecessor to country music goes back to the earliest days of the nation: folk music. Much in this genre can be traced to the Appalachian Mountains of the Southeast. An area rich with hymns and ballads brought to the New World by the first settlers, folk songs survived by oral transmission, going from person to person and generation to generation. Originally created and performed primarily by rural people, folk music most often tells a story of legendary or historic importance or conveys some incident or lesson about everyday life. The songs tend to be simple so that anyone can memorize, sing, or play them, but because they are not written down, the music and lyrics, even whole verses, can change over time.

As towns and cities grew in the region, popular music completely overshadowed folk music, especially in the early 1920s, when radio and recordings permitted nationwide distribution of the latest hits. There were those, however, who saw commercial potential in folk music. For example, Ralph Peer, representing Victor Records, wanted to expand the company's already extensive offerings to include new formats. As a part of his plan, he went into the Southern mountains to record folk musicians whose songs the business called *hillbilly music,* a term that initially became interchangeable with folk music. Slowly, more and more people referred to the tunes that Peer recorded not as folk, but as hillbilly, which evolved into the various 1930s and 1940s kinds of country music discussed earlier in this chapter.

In the meantime, traditional folk music resurfaced in the mid-1930s. Protest songs written about the hardships of the Great Depression and the Dust Bowl, as well as those compositions about labor disputes within the coal mining and textile industries, added a spark. For example, coal miners' demands for better wages and working conditions, along with their attempts to allow union membership, brought about the infamous Harlan County, Kentucky, strikes. From these disputes arose a rich collection of protest music. Textile workers in both the South and Northeast likewise attempted to organize, thereby creating another source of materials used in the writing and singing of songs that commemorated those struggles.

Woody Guthrie, a traditional rural folk singer, as a young married man in the 1930s directly experienced difficulties caused by the Depression, the Dust Bowl, and labor unrest and emerged as a prominent protest singer and composer. He penned numerous pieces about his life and living conditions that RCA Victor Records issued as a 1940 album, *Dust Bowl Ballads.* Guthrie did the singing on this production, along with much of the writing. These pieces rank among his best as a songwriter and include "Dust Bowl Blues" and "I Ain't Got No Home in This World Anymore" (both c. 1935–1938), "The Ballad of Pretty Boy Floyd" (1939), and his first rendering of "So Long, It's Been Good to Know Yuh (Dusty Old Dust)" (1940). Two years later, Guthrie offered this last song in a second version as a World War II tune telling about soldiers leaving their towns to go first to training camp and then across the sea to a "fighting shore." As they departed, they sang, "So long, it's been good to know you, there's a mighty big war that's got to be won, we'll get back together again."

Along with the cutting of *Dust Bowl Ballads,* Guthrie recorded four hours of songs and stories for the Library of Congress's Archive of American Folk Song, a project directed by Alan Lomax for the U.S. Department of the Interior. He also wrote what is probably his best-known piece, "This Land Is Your Land" (1940), in reaction to Irving Berlin's "God Bless America" (1938 [popular revival of a patriotic song penned in 1917 and performed throughout World War II]; words and music by Irving Berlin), a song he heard sung

Folk musician Pete Seeger, who had been drafted into the Army, entertains an audience with "When We March into Berlin" in Washington, D.C. The 1944 event celebrated the opening of the Washington Labor Canteen, a venture cosponsored by several labor unions. Library of Congress, Prints & Photographs Division.

daily over the radio in a recording by vocalist Kate Smith. Guthrie considered Berlin's tune unrealistic, that it glossed over the lopsided distribution of land and wealth in the United States, and originally titled his opposing song "God Blessed America for Me." Although written in 1940, Guthrie did not record "This Land Is Your Land" until 1944. Artists outside the folk arena followed Guthrie's version with cuts of their own, including Bing Crosby.[7]

Following Lomax's project, the U.S. Department of Interior commissioned Guthrie in 1941 to write songs to be used in a public information film promoting the building of the Bonneville Dam on the Columbia River in the state of Washington. Well-known titles from this collection of 26 numbers include "Hard Traveling," "Pastures of Plenty," and "Roll On Columbia." The last uses lyrics written by Guthrie but employs a melody composed in 1936 by Leadbelly (b. Huddie Ledbetter) called "Goodnight, Irene." This crossover illustrates the kind of borrowing and changing that exemplifies the folk genre.

Guthrie had relocated from the West Coast to New York in 1940 and actively participated in a folk music revival occurring there. In 1941, in addition to his recordings and work for the U.S. government, he joined the Almanac Singers, a folk trio formed earlier that year by singer Pete Seeger, Lee Hays, formerly a song leader at a radical labor college in Commonwealth, Arkansas, and Millard Lampell, a writer. The group took its name from the *Farmer's Almanac,* a book they believed all farm families owned, along with the Bible. The Almanac Singers jointly composed many of their songs and shared equally in the credits and profits, if any. Initially, they wrote and performed for labor and political rallies, believing that music played an important role in the class struggle and could have a part in subsequent social action. They held their first major, and successful, public appearance in May 1941 at Madison Square Garden for the striking Transport Workers' Union. They followed this by recording four albums—one of antiwar songs (this concert predated Pearl Harbor), one of union songs, and two of traditional folk songs.

In addition to this performance in New York and the recordings, the Almanac Singers took their show on the road, driving a beat-up car and singing at colleges, union meetings, migrant camps, antifascist rallies, and on street corners. Through the course of their work, other performers joined them, including Josh White, Arthur Stern, Agnes "Sis" Cunningham, Gordon Friesen, Baldwin "Butch" Hawes, Bess Lomax Hawes, Cisco Houston, Brownie McGhee, and Sonny Terry. A typical show consisted of protest numbers like "Which Side Are You On?" (1931; words and music by Florence Reese), "Talking Union" (1941; words and music by Pete Seeger, Lee Hays, and Millard Lampell), "The Union Maid" (1940; words and music by Woody Guthrie), antiwar songs, and traditional rural folk material.

After being on the road, the Almanac Singers returned to New York in 1941 and established the Almanac House, a co-op apartment in Greenwich Village, where they lived and held weekly *hootenannies,* an old word revived by Guthrie and Seeger to describe evenings of music with political commentary. For these gatherings, some Kentucky labor protest musicians, such as Sarah Ogan Gunning and Aunt Molly Jackson, frequently joined them. By this time, the Almanac Singers and their friends were also using their music to protest U.S. involvement in the war developing in Europe.

Because of the attack at Pearl Harbor and the country's entry into World War II, the Almanac Singers switched from protest to support of their country's efforts and interrupted their careers to serve in the armed forces. Pete Seeger joined the Army, and Woody Guthrie enlisted with the Merchant Marine. Seeger, discharged as a corporal in 1945, returned to civilian life and worked as the national director of People's Songs, Inc., a musicians' union that started a publication, *People's Song,* the first magazine devoted exclusively to folk music. In 1948, he recruited Lee Hays, one of the original Almanac Singers, Fred Hellerman, and Ronnie Gilbert to form the Weavers, a group that immediately emerged as a popular concert act and became one of America's favorite folk singing attractions. After the war, Guthrie and most other urban folk protest musicians remained active in music and contributed to folk's entrance into the pop music mainstream during the late 1940s.

Burl Ives, another performer active in New York City in the early 1940s, played guitar and banjo and described himself as a grassroots folk singer, and indeed, at a young age, his grandmother taught him songs she had learned from her Scottish-Irish-English forefathers. Ives traveled across the country in the 1930s and said that he learned songs from farmers, cowboys, and others whom he met as he performed odd jobs. Leaning more toward an acting career than a musical one, he accepted small parts in two Rodgers and Hart musicals, first a nonsinging role in an out-of-town run of *The Boys from Syracuse* (1938), followed by a part in a traveling production of *I Married an Angel* (1938–1939). Shortly after this work, Ives returned to music, making his first recordings for Alan Lomax at the Library of Congress.

In 1940, the actor-singer signed a contract to broadcast on both NBC and CBS radio. He aired weekly on various days and in many time slots under different program names, including *Back Where I Came From, The Burl Ives Coffee Club,* and *God's Country.* Most often, he used the title *The Wayfaring Stranger,* named after one of his ballads, a traditional folk song of unknown origin and frequently used "Jimmy Crack Corn" (another title for "Blue Tail Fly," which possibly dates from the Civil War era) as a theme. During these programs, he sang and told stories from his years of traveling and, in 1944, hosted a special theme broadcast for CBS highlighting folk songs of the United Nations.

Through his radio shows, Ives popularized several traditional folk songs such as "Lavender Blue," also known as "Lavender's Blue" (a lullaby probably from the seventeenth century), "Foggy Foggy Dew" (a folk music classic attributed to an English/Irish origin, although Ives claimed it dated from colonial America), and "The Erie Canal" (a traditional folk song possibly written by Thomas S. Allen in 1905). The military drafted Ives in 1942 but discharged him a year later for medical problems. In 1944–1945, he starred in *Sing Out Sweet Land,* a Broadway musical salute to American folk and popular music that highlighted folk songs he had popularized on his radio broadcasts. The next year, he made his film debut as a singing cowboy in the film *Smoky* (1946) as well as signing on with Mutual radio. In the postwar era, Burl Ives became a prominent voice in a variety of entertainment pursuits.

CONCLUSION

With messages of love, loss, hope, and failed relationships, country music appealed to many Americans in the early 1940s. By the end of World War II, the phrase *country music* had won out as the preferred description for what had started as folk music and/or hillbilly, and it covered a wide gamut of styles: traditional country, the string band sound, bluegrass, Western, honky-tonk, and Western Swing. Fans came from all parts of the United States; Southern California joined eastern Pennsylvania, Chicago, and Nashville as hot spots for these different genres.

Roy Acuff of Nashville's *Grand Ole Opry* led the mountaineer and string band sound and dominated country music during the war. Bill Monroe, along with Lester Flatt and Earl Scruggs, increasingly defined bluegrass by the end of 1945. Western music flourished thanks to Tex Ritter, Gene Autry, Roy Rogers, and all the other singing cowboys. Honky-tonk received a strong send-off during the war by Ernest Tubb, Ted Daffan, and Floyd Tillman and peaked in the postwar years. Bob Wills and His Texas Playboys, along with Spade Cooley, saw to it that Western Swing, which involved a mixture of country songs and jazz arrangements, became the most commercially popular form of country music. Finally, Woody Guthrie, initially a rural folk singer, became a political activist and contributed significantly to the emergence of a new form: urban protest music.

Much American music has, over the years, focused on wars and America's involvement in them, and World War II proved no exception. The shared experiences coming from that lengthy conflict, and country music's responses to those experiences, exposed a new generation of listeners to the genre. The success of films, radio shows, recordings, and road tours during the war enabled country music to gain a foothold in the entertainment world and to be a commercial success. And what greater stamp of approval could be given than the fact that Bing Crosby, a veritable pop music icon, became one of the most popular interpreters of country music?

8

Classical Music

BACKGROUND

Before World War II, most Americans who listened to classical music believed that compositions of any worth came from Europe. They tended to prefer the well-known, standard classics by the likes of Brahms, Beethoven, and Bach and resisted innovation or experimentation by any newcomers. Thus conductors, when offering American pieces at all, usually only played short, familiar sections from longer works, a practice that hindered native creations from finding their way into concert halls and making it difficult for mainstream audiences to become familiar with the nation's composers.

Despite such struggles to have their music appreciated during the 1930s, U.S. composers took encouragement from two conditions: first, the emerging mass media—radio, recordings, and sound films—along with the Federal Music Project (1935–1943), a New Deal program, had created opportunities for them to reach a much broader listening public; second, under President Franklin D. Roosevelt's leadership, a number of the federal government's projects stressed the cultural welfare of the nation as a whole, and these efforts spoke not to a select or elite group, but to a mass audience. The challenge for composers became one of writing accessible compositions that could be easily appreciated by many.

Acknowledging the possibility of indifference or ignorance on the part of some Americans toward their works, composers such as Aaron Copland, Roy

Harris, Virgil Thomson, William Grant Still, and Morton Gould built on the idea of popular appeal and strove to establish a uniquely American sound during the mid-1930s. They employed recognizable melodies and regional themes that came from the nation's history and folkways. Thanks to this approach, they slowly attracted new listeners to serious music, and their works became

---

RUSSIAN COMPOSERS ON SEPARATE COVERS OF *TIME* MAGAZINE

Under the leadership of its founder, Henry R. Luce, *Time* magazine prided itself on its stern anti-Communist editorial stance. But World War II created strange bedfellows, and even the conservative *Time* occasionally had to praise the country's Soviet allies. So it was that Russian composers Dmitri Shostakovich and Sergei Prokofiev, two famous modernists, found themselves the subjects of two cover stories. Shostakovich had his moment with the July 20, 1942, issue, and Prokofiev was featured on November 19, 1945.

The authors of rousing, patriotic works that related to the war, both Shostakovich and Prokofiev experienced considerable popularity in the United States at the time. The covers and accompanying stories appeared in conjunction with the U.S. premieres of two of their wartime symphonies, events that American audiences eagerly endorsed. Given *Time*'s penchant in those days to tweak anything its writers found even slightly red, the reviews, while flattering, also spend considerable time and space belittling Communism, instead of discussing the music.

On July 26, 1942, the NBC Symphony Orchestra, under the baton of the legendary Arturo Toscanini, gave a special broadcast performance of Shostakovich's new *Seventh Symphony*. Written in 1941–1942 and nicknamed "Leningrad," it refers to the then ongoing siege of that city (now renamed St. Petersburg) by German troops from 1941 until 1944. One of the bloodiest battles of the war, the Russians heroically held out against frightening odds. Shostakovich's music carries both the mournfulness of the German invasion and the chaos of war, and many critics find in its harmonies a subtle slap at totalitarianism in general.

Over three years passed before Prokofiev graced a *Time* cover, but he also enjoyed an American following. Perhaps the more musically accomplished of the two composers, and probably best known for *Peter and the Wolf* (1936), Prokofiev wrote throughout the war, completing his *Fifth Symphony* in 1944. It premiered in Moscow in January 1945; the Boston Symphony Orchestra, under the baton of Sergei Koussevitsky, performed it in the United States in November of that year, thus spurring the cover story.

Again, the *Time* reviewer writes more about the state of music under Communism than he does about the *Fifth Symphony* but nevertheless endorses it as an important piece of twentieth-century composing. Lighter, more melodic, and more accessible than Shostakovich's *Seventh Symphony*, Prokofiev's work possesses an optimism unusual for music written during the war.

---

somewhat fashionable. In time, a significant portion of American classical music moved toward conveying an independent and even nationalistic mode of expression.

SIGNIFICANT COMPOSERS DURING THE WORLD WAR II ERA

As the threat of war enveloped Europe during the later 1930s, the likelihood of American involvement took on an air of inevitability, although concert halls across the nation reflected little of these current events. Composers from potentially hostile countries, such as Italians Giuseppe Verdi and Giacomo Puccini, and Germans like Richard Wagner and Richard Strauss, still remained audience favorites and frequently appeared on symphony orchestra programs. In fairness, however, music lovers also increasingly displayed enthusiasm for the works of Sergei Prokofiev and Dimitri Shostakovich, two modern Russian composers. When Russia came into the war on the side of the Allies, their popularity soared, and the two continued to display their talents even under adverse wartime conditions in their homeland.

Even with the continuing interest offered foreign-born composers, the Great Depression of the 1930s had influenced several aspiring American composers to attempt to reach out more to domestic audiences. Coincidentally, the attack on Pearl Harbor in December 1941 brought a surge of patriotism and caused some music lovers to look more seriously at compositions written by American-born artists. In 1939–1940, or immediately before America's active involvement in World War II, only 8 percent of the classical works performed by major orchestras in the United States claimed U.S. authorship. With the country's entry into the war, the figure climbed to more than 11 percent in 1942–1943 and dropped only slightly to 10 percent in 1943–1944. Hardly overwhelming figures, but they nonetheless show some improvement.[1]

Opera and ballet, two musical forms in which American accomplishments had historically been minimal, constituted part of this change and displayed some growth and promise. Operas, especially those with an English text, became more tolerable to audiences, and ballet gained ground primarily because of professional dancers such as Martha Graham and Agnes de Mille. In the first half of the 1940s, Aaron Copland, who is considered among the most important American composers of the twentieth century, added his own touch to the growing popularity of ballet with musical works that incorporated elements of dance.

Aaron Copland

Three works established Copland as America's foremost contemporary composer of ballet: *Billy the Kid* (1938), *Rodeo* (1942), and *Appalachian Spring*

Martha Graham, another leader in the rise of modern American dance, choreographed the ballet sequences for Aaron Copland's *Appalachian Spring* (1944). She appears here with her husband, Erick Hawkins. Courtesy of Photofest.

(1944). Both *Billy the Kid* and *Rodeo* capture the spirit of prairie life in the American West, including in their format some variations on American tunes that clearly define the composer's national predilections. *Appalachian Spring* also deals with pioneers, not in the West, but in Pennsylvania. After their premieres, these three works quickly and regularly appeared on concert hall playbills across the country, taking their place alongside well-established European compositions.

Born in New York's Brooklyn in 1900, Copland, like so many other aspiring artists, went to Paris at the height of the expatriate movement. Just 21, he enrolled in a school for composers at the Palace at Fontainebleau, where he connected with Nadia Boulanger, a well-known composition teacher who taught and guided him for three years. Upon returning to the United States in 1924, his works contained a mixture of modern classical music motifs with hints of jazz influences that resulted in difficult rhythms. Slowly and steadily, however, Copland gained recognition as an upcoming composer and by 1937 had a string of promising pieces behind him.

During the Great Depression, Copland moved away from his European lessons and set his sights on writing truly American music. This effort, along with a desire to attract a wider audience, caused him to incorporate into his compositions a number of indigenous folk melodies, particularly those identified with the American West. Borrowing from many sources, he developed harmonies and themes that resulted in a unique Copland sound. His deceptively simple compositions, associated with images of the mythic American West, especially the ballet and movie scores he created during the World War II era, accomplished his intention of speaking to a large cross section of the American population.

For example, *Billy the Kid* uses the legend of the colorful, gun-toting outlaw to show the conflict between civilized society and the free-spirited individual. It establishes a Western atmosphere through the use of six traditional cowboy numbers: "Goodbye, Old Paint," "Dying Cowboy," "Git Along Little Dogie," "Trouble for the Range Cook," "Great Granddad," and "Old Chisholm Trail." All date back to the nineteenth century, and the last two had been recorded in the early 1930s by none other than Gene Autry. *Billy the Kid* had its premiere with the Chicago Ballet Caravan on October 16, 1938, with choreography by William Loring. In 1940, an orchestral arrangement debuted in New York with the National Broadcasting System (NBC) Symphony Orchestra, William Steinberg conducting.

Rodeo, like *Billy the Kid,* receives its inspiration from the spacious landscape of the American prairie and draws on cowboy tunes to capture life on the Western range. The story again deals with an outsider, this time a cowgirl who longs to become a ranch hand. The four dance episodes, choreographed by the upcoming Agnes de Mille for the Ballet Russe de Monte Carlo, a European dance company that moved to the United States during World War II, opened at New York's Metropolitan Opera House on October 16, 1942. An unqualified success for both Copland and de Mille, she went on to assure her future when she choreographed Richard Rodgers' and Oscar Hammerstein II's smash musical *Oklahoma!* in 1943. (See chapter 6, "Music on Stage and Screen," for more on Rodgers and Hammerstein and *Oklahoma!*)

Taking advantage of *Rodeo*'s popularity, Copland pulled music from the work and constructed an orchestral suite of four movements suitable for performances in concert halls. The New York Philharmonic, conducted by Alexander

Smallens, played the suite in its entirety in July of 1943. The well-known main theme of "Hoe-Down" comes from an old folk song called "Bonyparte," or "Bonaparte's Retreat," a tune frequently heard at square dances. Fiddler William Hamilton Stepp performed it for a recording made by folklorist Alan Lomax in 1937 under the aspices of the Archive of American Folk Song at the Library of Congress. Years later, the beef industry resurrected "Hoe-Down" for a popular television commercial.

Copland's third blend of dance and music, *Appalachian Spring,* proved an immediate success at the time of its October 1944 introduction at the Library of Congress. It takes place in the early 1800s, revolving around a celebration for two young newlyweds at their newly built farmhouse on the western Pennsylvania frontier. This piece, choreographed by Martha Graham and utilizing her own dance company, features square dance rhythms, revivalist hymns, and country fiddle tunes. The last movement quotes a well-known Shaker song, "Simple Gifts" (1848; words and music by Elder Joseph Brackett). An orchestral suite taken from *Appalachian Spring* received the 1945 Pulitzer Prize in Music.

Active on many fronts, Copland composed a number of other successful works during the first half of the 1940s. After the United States entered World War II, little good news came back from the front lines during the first two years of the conflict. Andre Kostelanetz, a popular conductor for the Columbia Broadcasting System (CBS radio), recognized a need to inspire and comfort an uncertain public and, in 1942, commissioned a series of new orchestral creations with patriotic themes based on famous figures from American history. Kostelanetz asked Copland to submit a piece for this series, and after some deliberation, the two agreed on President Abraham Lincoln as the subject. At first somewhat overwhelmed by the assignment, Copland eventually decided on using a narrator and Lincoln's own words accompanied by an orchestra. The result, *Lincoln Portrait,* incorporates material from speeches and letters of the 16th president as well as snippets from folk songs such as "Camptown Races" (1850; words and music by Stephen Foster and reputed to be one of Lincoln's favorite tunes) and "Springfield Mountain" (one of the first original American ballads and associated with the colonial era).

Lincoln Portrait premiered on May 14, 1942, with the Cincinnati Symphony Orchestra. Kostelanetz served as the quest conductor, and actor William Adams narrated. A radio broadcast from the Hollywood Bowl with Carl Sandburg in Adams's place aired shortly thereafter, and *Lincoln Portrait* quickly became a popular piece. Over the decades, it has continued to be played and frequently serves as a standard for patriotic holidays such as the Fourth of July, Memorial Day, and Presidents' Day.

Kostelanetz, however, was not alone in responding to World War II. Eugene Goosens, resident conductor for the Cincinnati Symphony Orchestra, had requested a musical tribute honoring those engaged in the conflict; he presumably expected something that focused on soldiers, airmen, or sailors. Instead, Copland, in 1942, gave him *Fanfare for the Common Man;* it applauds the wartime citizens at home who did not perform deeds of valor on the battlefield but who shared in the labors, sorrows, and hopes of all those fighting for victory. As with *Lincoln Portrait,* this traditional score with contemporary sound, first performed by the Cincinnati Symphony on March 12, 1943, pleased audiences and since has been played by many and varied ensembles. *Lincoln Portrait* and *Fanfare for the Common Man* represent a turn in Copland's works toward addressing political conditions, patriotism, and concern for social welfare, and both pieces remain among his most-performed compositions.

A short number, *Letter from Home* (1944), written two years after *Lincoln Portrait* and *Fanfare for the Common Man,* came at a time when the country sensed the eventual end of World War II. It conveys the emotions that might be felt by an American GI receiving and reading a letter from home and stands as perhaps the most sentimental music ever composed by Copland. Living in Mexico at the time, his mother had died, his father was ill, and he had two close relatives fighting in the war. Commissioned by the popular dance band leader Paul Whiteman, and first performed by his Radio Hall of Fame Orchestra, *Letter from Home* reflects not only general wartime conditions, but Copland's own homesickness.

In addition to successful ballet and orchestral compositions during this era, Copland also penned several film scores. This medium allowed his music to reach an even larger audience. The first, *The City,* commissioned by the American City Planning Institute and underwritten by the Carnegie Corporation, presents a plea for town planning, and the music perfectly matches the film footage. It played daily at the 1939 New York World's Fair and gave Copland the credentials necessary to write for commercial cinema.

Three Hollywood productions followed shortly thereafter: *Of Mice and Men* (1939), a film version of John Steinbeck's novel of the same name; *Our Town* (1940), a soundtrack to accompany a movie version of Thornton Wilder's 1938 play; and *The North Star* (1943), a picture about the lives of Soviet peasants during the war. Ira Gershwin contributed lyrics for that effort. Copland received Academy Award nominations for both Original Score and best Scoring for *Of Mice and Men,* although the first went to Herbert Stothart for *The Wizard of Oz* (1939), and the second went to Richard Hageman, Frank Harling, John Leipold, and Leo Shuken for *Stagecoach* (1939). He also received a nomination for Original Score and Scoring for *Our Town,* but these awards went to Leigh Harline, Paul J. Smith, and Ned Washington for *Pinocchio* (1940) and Alfred Newman for *Tin Pan Alley* (1940). An Academy Award eluded Copland yet again in 1943, when Alfred Newman's score for *The Song of Bernadette* won over *North Star.*

Undeterred, Copland created *Music for the Movies,* a concert suite of five movements for small orchestra, in 1942. Although altered, much of this composition had earlier appeared in his work for the aforementioned motion pictures *The City, Our Town,* and *Of Mice and Men.* Copland also wrote for other films, including *The Cummington Story* (1945), a production of the U.S. Office of War Information (OWI) about war refugees beginning new lives in a small Connecticut town. He continued to contribute music for the movies following World War II, and the scores consistently met his high standards and received favorable public reception.

For the 1939–1945 period, Aaron Copland wrote simple, plain-spoken music with a richness and depth influenced by many kinds of material. Through his ballets, orchestral music, movie scores, patriotic numbers, and conducting, he captured the attention of many ordinary citizens. A leader among native composers, a significant number of his musical works stand today as icons of American culture.[2]

Roy Harris

Like Copland, Roy Harris traveled to France and studied with Nadia Boulanger in 1926. He similarly incorporated folk music, folk-inspired elements, and cowboy and honky-tonk motifs in his compositions as he strove to produce pieces with mass audience appeal. He finally received recognition as an important American composer with his *Third Symphony,* a 1939 piece based on folk- and hymn-like melodies. Commissioned by Boston Symphony conductor Serge Koussevitzky, it has endured as Harris's most popular composition.

Harris added his *Fourth Symphony* for chorus and orchestra in 1940. Called the *Folksong Symphony* and based on old American songs, its name further signifies his interest in creating a true American musical expression. Just as importantly, its distinct patriotic theme came when many feared the inevitability of U.S. involvement in the ongoing European conflict. This symphony opens with the song "The Girl I Left behind Me" and closes with "When Johnny Comes Marching Home Again," two Civil War tunes. "Bury Me Not on the Lone Prairie" and "He's Gone Away," two other traditional numbers, express the nostalgia of loneliness, certainly a sentiment being anticipated by many Americans at the time. A well-received composition, the *Fourth Symphony* earned Harris an award from the National Committee for Music Appreciation (1940) and a citation from the U.S. Treasury Department for distinguished and patriotic services to the country (1941).

Harris frequently utilized popular dance rhythms, swing music, and jazz, but throughout World War II, his works featured national themes. For example, his *Sixth Symphony,* subtitled "Gettysburg" and based on President

Abraham Lincoln's Gettysburg Address, was dedicated to the U.S. armed forces and performed for the first time in Boston on April 14, 1944, the 79th anniversary of Lincoln's 1865 assassination.

During the course of his career, Harris taught at a number of colleges and universities and continued to write, but he never again achieved the success he experienced with the *Third Symphony.* Nevertheless, during the early 1940s, Harris earned several honors: first place in a national poll of American composers conducted by CBS radio (1940), an Award of Merit from the National Association of Composers and Conductors (1940), election to the National Institute of Arts and Letters (1944), and honorary degrees from several colleges and universities.

Virgil Thomson

A composer and music critic for the New York *Herald Tribune* from 1940 to 1954, Thomson lived primarily in Paris between 1925 and 1940. There he studied with Nadia Boulanger, just as did a number of his counterparts. While abroad, Thomson wrote several pieces that showed an interest in American folk material, popular music, gospel songs, hymns, blues, cowboy tunes, and dance forms such as the tango and waltz, the same areas of interest that Aaron Copland and Roy Harris exhibited.

Thomson even penned scores for two memorable Hollywood documentaries: *The Plow That Broke the Plains* (1936) and *The River* (1938), both directed by Pare Lorentz. The first, sponsored by the U.S. Resettlement Administration (RA; it became the Farm Security Administration in 1937), utilizes cowboy songs and contains titles such as "Cattle," "Git Along, Little Dogies," and "I Ride an Old Paint," while *The River* incorporates music ranging from "There'll Be a Hot Time in the Old Town Tonight" (1896; music by Theodore M. Metz, lyrics by Joseph Hayden) to the traditional *Doxology.* These orchestral adaptations of native tunes from the midwestern plains and the southwestern desert, along with Baptist hymnbook harmonies and pop tunes, perhaps brought Thomson his widest appeal as a composer.

He also wrote the score for *Louisiana Story* (1948), a film about the development of the oil industry and its effect on Louisiana's bayou country; like its two cinematic predecessors, it relies on folk music. This trio of documentaries served for many years as models for any Hollywood composer wishing to write music for Westerns and other motion pictures based on geographical sections of the country.

Thomson returned to full-time residency in the United States in 1940; during the World War II era, he remained best known for his work as a music critic. In 1945, he provided a score for an OWI documentary titled *Tuesday in November.* For this look at how the United States could hold a free and fair presidential election while at war, he incorporated hymns and waltzes into his arrangements.

William Grant Still

Known within the classical music world as the "Dean of African American Composers," William Grant Still, prior to World War II, composed, played in orchestras, and wrote arrangements for a number of individuals performing popular music. His patrons included W. C. Handy, Paul Whiteman, Sophie Tucker, and Artie Shaw. While working with bandleader Shaw, Still created the arrangement for the group's immensely popular rendition of "Frenesi" (1940; music by Alberto Dominguez, lyrics by Sidney K. Russell and Ray Charles). It turned out to be the #2 hit song for the year.

Still also arranged and produced programs for the Mutual and CBS radio networks and provided scores and orchestrations (usually uncredited) for dozens of forgettable B-Hollywood films such as *Beware Spooks!* (1939), a comedy starring Joe E. Brown, *The Secret Seven* (1940), a crime movie with Bruce Bennett, a Buster Keaton short called *She's Oil Mine* (1941), and a film noir mystery titled *The Missing Juror* (1944).

For his more serious work, Still only earned critical attention when he started incorporating elements of ethnic and popular musical styles into his classical works and, in 1931, presented what is perhaps his best-known composition, *Symphony No. 1,* subtitled the "Afro-American Symphony." Premiered by the Rochester Orchestra, it gained prominence as the first symphony written by a black American composer that played for diverse, mainstream American audiences.

By the late 1930s, Still had penned the ballet *Lenox Avenue* (1937) and two operas, *Troubled Island* (1938) and *A Bayou Legend* (1941), followed by a suite, *Pages from Negro History,* in 1943. Because of *Lenox Avenue,* a committee assigned the responsibility of selecting music for the 1939–1940 New York World's Fair commissioned Still to write a theme song to be aired in the fair's Perisphere, the huge white sphere that greeted visitors at the exhibition's entrance. The result, *Rising Tide,* a three-minute piece also known by the titles *Song of a City* and *Victory Tide,* played continuously, or approximately fifty or sixty thousand times, during the two years of the fair. Another honor occurred for Still when his *Festive Overture* (1944) won the Jubilee Prize given by the Cincinnati Symphony Orchestra for the best overture to celebrate its jubilee season that year.

Always struggling to be recognized as a composer of merit, Still wrote politically and racially conscious pieces throughout his life such as *And They*

Lynched Him on a Tree (1940) and *In Memoriam: The Colored Soldiers Who Died for Democracy* (1944). This last piece, commissioned by the League of Composers (founded in 1923 to promote the highest quality of new music and to champion American composers), premiered on January 5, 1944, with the New York Philharmonic Orchestra, under the baton of Arthur Rodzinski. The title carries an ironic aspect since American blacks fought in the armed forces for freedom abroad, while being denied those same freedoms at home.

Morton Gould

Frequently overshadowed by his contemporaries Aaron Copland, Roy Harris, and Virgil Thomson, Morton Gould nonetheless gained a niche as an important American composer in both the classical and popular realms, often mixing the two. Like Copland, Gould's work at times featured well-known American themes of a patriotic or folk origin. *Foster Gallery* (1939), based on popular Stephen Foster numbers, serves as an example. Three compositions in the 1940s also utilized populist idioms: *Spirituals* (1941), *Latin American Symphonette* (1941), and *Cowboy Rhapsody* (1942).

Gould gained national prominence through his work of conducting and arranging music programs for network radio during the 1940s, including CBS's *The Chrysler Hour* and Mutual's *The Cresta Blanca Carnival of Music*. These shows, and others, often carried a mix of classical, popular, and jazz numbers. He earned perhaps his greatest renown for an orchestral work, *American Salute* (1943), written for a patriotic World War II radio broadcast and based on the folk song "When Johnny Comes Marching Home." An eclectic composer, Gould wrote orchestrations for motion pictures, including a documentary titled *Ring of Steel* (1942) and a Jane Powell musical called *Delightfully Dangerous* (1945); he also contributed music for a ballet suite called *Interplay* (1945).

Howard Hansen, Walter Piston, and Roger Sessions

These three men made important contributions to American classical music, but mainly outside the realm of composing. Although Howard Hanson would later create several enduring works, his primary legacy came as an educator, conductor, and promoter of other composers. Appointed head of the Eastman School of Music at the University of Rochester in 1924 at the young age of 28, he remained in that position for 40 years; it has been estimated that during that time, he presented some 1,500 works by 700 composers. In terms of his own writing, Hansen's seven symphonies constitute his most notable compositions, a cycle that began in 1922 and lasted until 1977. His *Symphony*

The "King of Swing," clarinetist Benny Goodman, occasionally crossed the aisle and played with classical musicians. He is seen here in 1940 with John Barbirolli, conductor of the New York Philharmonic Orchestra prior to a performance. Library of Congress, Prints & Photographs Division.

No. 4, Opus 34, written in 1943 and first performed by the Boston Symphony Orchestra in December of that year, received the 1944 Pulitzer Prize in Music, the second year for this prestigious award.

Both Walter Piston and Roger Sessions displayed remarkable craftsmanship in their writing during the World War II era, but neither can be classified as well known or popular. Piston occasionally used the rhythms of jazz and American country dance music in his 1940s works, while Sessions steadfastly avoided any hint of American images or idioms. Piston, residing in Paris from 1924 until 1926, became yet another American student of Nadia Boulanger. He returned to the United States and joined the faculty at Harvard, where, for the next 34 years, he provided solid classical music foundations for many talented individuals, including Leonard Bernstein. He also wrote a widely used textbook on harmony. Teaching did not stop him from composing music, pieces that the Boston Symphony Orchestra frequently performed.

For his part, Sessions taught at a number of American institutions; his longest tenure came at Princeton from 1935 to 1945, and again from 1953 to 1965. The University of California at Berkeley carried Sessions on its roster from 1945 to 1951, and Juilliard did likewise from 1967 to 1983. No orchestras, however, performed his compositions with any regularity. Basically, Sessions remained an outsider who had no interest in creating a unique American sound. His music continues to be largely unknown to the American public, but his successful students and others who have studied his works hold him in high regard.[3]

CLASSICAL MUSIC ON THE RADIO

Since it offered a wide variety of programming, radio emerged as the primary national medium during the 1930s. Early on, conductor Andre Kostelanetz grasped radio's growing power and assembled a 65-piece orchestra, the largest to broadcast at the time, for a network show called *Chesterfield Time* on NBC. He took classical compositions and arranged them as easy-listening numbers, with the result that the program attracted an audience that normally would not have tuned in to such reputedly serious music. Because of his skill in creating light, listenable fare, Kostelanetz became a popular radio star; a 1943 poll of U.S. and Canadian audiences commended him for his support of both serious and popular music.

The honors heaped on Kostelanetz occurred at a time when elitist critics engaged in a debate about the appropriateness of exposing the masses to any kind of popularization of serious music. Nonetheless, the Federal Music Project, in an attempt to reach the largest possible audiences, presented classical fare, oftentimes in popular or commercial settings.

In a similar vein, both NBC and CBS, the two principal national radio networks, elected in the 1930s to take the bold step of establishing in-house orchestras for two weekly shows, *The NBC Symphony Orchestra* (1937–1954) and *The Columbia Symphony Orchestra* (1929–1930; then heard irregularly until renamed *Everybody's Music,* 1936–1938). NBC and CBS did not limit their classical music programming just to these in-house orchestras; they also offered airtime to other major aggregations in hopes of increasing both the number of radio listeners and people appreciative of this musical format.[4]

The networks derived several benefits from these decisions. NBC and CBS, as promoters and supporters in various facets of the music business, especially recordings, profited since more airplay of all forms of music meant higher record sales. Specific to classical music, the networks believed that broadcasting it heightened their prestige, especially with listeners who already appreciated this kind of music. Additionally, it exposed new listeners to previously unheard musical pleasures, or so the networks hoped. As an added bonus, many sponsors also thought it helped polish their image to be associated with this area of programming. Despite these considerations, throughout the heyday of radio (roughly 1930–1950), airtime for serious music remained minimal when compared to that given popular music.

Of the two networks, NBC devoted more hours and investment to classical programming and experienced more success both with its own orchestra's show and its other serious music ventures. One reason for NBC's prominence can be attributed to conductor Arturo Toscanini. The NBC Symphony Orchestra brought the world-famous maestro out of retirement in 1937 to be the leader for most of its broadcasts from Studio 8-H in Rockefeller Center. A dispute erupted between NBC and Toscanini in 1941 that caused him to temporarily withdraw his services, and Leopold Stokowski took the NBC Orchestra baton at that time. Stokowski, however, convinced Toscanini to lead the group in concerts to benefit war bond drives. Pacified, Toscanini shared the directorship with him for the 1942–1943 season. When Stokowski

A quartet of pictures showing various expressions on famed conductor Arturo Toscanini's face. He led the NBC Symphony from 1937 until 1954. Library of Congress, Prints & Photographs Division.

departed in 1944, Toscanini returned as the primary conductor, until his retirement in 1954.

The New York Philharmonic Orchestra, founded in 1842, the oldest active symphonic orchestra in the United States and one of the oldest in the world, became CBS's counter to NBC's programming success. From 1927 until 1963, the network ran *The New York Philharmonic Orchestra* as a regularly scheduled offering. The orchestra had been under the conductorship of Arturo Toscanini in the early 1930s, a time when it achieved a distinct sound by championing the new music of the day. Toscanini retired in 1936, but then he returned to active conducting with NBC in 1937, as noted. He did, however, return to CBS and the New York Philharmonic for a guest appearance in 1942.

Leonard Bernstein, working as assistant conductor for the New York Philharmonic, made his 1943 radio debut on CBS. Critics proclaimed Bernstein's efforts a success, and he instantly gained fame because of this nationwide broadcast. In 1944, Bernstein traveled widely, holding the baton for 89 concerts with orchestras all over the United States. On completion of this stint, he briefly returned to the New York Philharmonic and, in 1945, obtained the directorship of the New York City Symphony. He then proceeded to write the scores for several successful Broadway shows (*Fancy Free* and *On the Town*) and established a reputation as a composer firmly entrenched in both popular and serious music. (See chapter 6, "Music on Stage and Screen," for more on Leonard Bernstein.)

The networks had other classically oriented programming during the 1940s. *The Voice of Firestone,* one of the longest-running and most successful weekly musical shows on radio (NBC, 1928–1954; ABC, 1954–1957), built its programs around classical and semiclassical music, with an emphasis on singers. During the 1940s, the show featured primarily operatic artists but included some pop and film vocalists. *The Voice of Firestone* reached its peak in the late 1930s, when ratings indicated a regular audience of between 7 and 8 million people. Howard Barlow, a man with a long history of conducting both choral groups and orchestras, accepted the conductorship in 1943, and under his leadership, the program maintained a respectable following throughout the 1940s.

Critics rated the Philadelphia Symphony Orchestra, just as they did its New York counterpart, as one of the top ensembles in the country. Much of its success came under the directorships of Leopold Stokowski and, later, Eugene Ormandy. In recognition of its renown, both CBS and NBC ran shows under the orchestra's name in the late 1930s and early 1940s. An appearance in the Disney animated film *Fantasia* (1940) enhanced an already considerable reputation across the United States. In 1945, the Philadelphia Orchestra added radio concerts geared toward children called the *Philadelphia Symphony Orchestra Children's Concerts* (CBS, 1945–1948, 1953–1957).

The Metropolitan Opera (NBC, 1931–1958; CBS, 1958–1960; consortium, 1960 to present), holds several radio records. It has the honor of being the longest-running show of classical music on radio. The program established a commercial relationship with Texaco in 1940, an association that lasted until 2005, making it one of the most enduring corporate sponsorships in radio history. Finally, Milton Cross served as host from 1931 until his death in 1975, another unique feature of this program. Given *The Metropolitan Opera*'s longevity, virtually all operatic artists of some merit have sung on the show at one time or another. Lawrence Tibbet, boasting a tenure of 27 years with the organization, familiarly referred to as *The Met* (1923–1950), stood as perhaps the most-favored and best-known operatic performer during the World War II era. Other singers, such as Lily Pons, Helen Traubel, and Ezio Pinza, also made frequent appearances during this period.

AN EFFECT OF WAR ON CLASSICAL MUSIC

The Berkshire Symphonic Festival, a committee formed in 1934 and committed to bringing outdoor summer concerts to the Berkshire Mountains in Massachusetts, invited conductor Sergei Koussevitzky and the Boston Symphony Orchestra to perform on August 13, 1936. The success of the event warranted a return performance the following year, making Koussevitzky and his Boston musicians the mainstays of the annual festival. The concerts were performed at Tanglewood, a 210-acre estate near Lenox, Massachusetts, donated by the Tappan family for summer music programs. Koussevitzky expanded these offerings in 1940 by adding a summer school for young musicians called the Berkshire Music Center.

The December 7, 1941, attack on Pearl Harbor changed many facets of American life, including musical performances. With gasoline rationing in effect, and blackouts limiting nighttime travel, getting to and from Tanglewood posed a hardship on those wishing to attend the concerts. In addition, military conscription whittled away at the ranks in symphony orchestras. Faced with these problems, on May 26, 1942, the Berkshire Symphonic Festival announced that the annual appearance of the Boston Symphony Orchestra at Tanglewood had been halted for the duration of the war.

This move created a musical silence in the Berkshires that lasted for four years. But the committee's actions were echoed elsewhere as well. Manpower shortages, rationing, extended work schedules—they coalesced into difficulties for musicians and their audiences that could only be remedied with the return of peace. With the surrenders of Germany and Japan, the war drew to an official close in September of 1945. Jubilant trustees of the Boston Symphony Orchestra and the Berkshire Summer Festival proclaimed that the summer concert series would resume at Tanglewood in 1946. With peace, the music returned at its prewar scale, and so it has continued into the present.

The Telephone Hour (NBC, 1940–1958; also known as *The Bell Telephone Hour*) initially offered concerts of light classical music played by a 57-piece symphony orchestra. A Great Artists Series, added in 1942, provided a succession of vocal and instrumental artists from opera and the concert stage. In addition to representative classical performers, the versatile and famous Nelson Eddy of film fame could also be heard on the Great Artists Series.

The airing of *The Boston Symphony Orchestra* alternated across three networks in sporadic segments, starting with the NBC network in 1926 and then from 1932 until 1956 between NBC and the American Broadcasting Company (ABC), the latter an outgrowth of NBC's old Blue network. For the years 1943–1946, the program could be heard on the transitional Blue/ABC network. During this time, the orchestra, under the directorship of Serge Koussevitzky, gained considerable recognition. It had performed its first summer concert in the Berkshire Mountains in Massachusetts in 1936, establishing a permanent summer residence at Tanglewood in 1937. Three years later, Koussevitzky founded the Berkshire Music Center (now known as the Tanglewood Music Center), a place for composers and conductors to gather and teach, plus the young musicians in attendance had an opportunity to learn and play music together. For example, the 1940–1941 season saw Aaron Copland teaching composition and Leonard Bernstein enrolled in Koussevitzky's conducting class.

Long before NBC had created its own orchestra, it offered a groundbreaking educational program for children, *The Music Appreciation Hour* (1928–1942). During its 14 years of broadcasting on Fridays, first at 11:00 A.M. and later at 2:00 P.M., the program served as an integral part of the school day across the country. Estimates indicate that millions of schoolchildren listened to and learned about orchestral music from the host, Dr. Walter Damrosch. In 1942, NBC asked Damrosch to cut his program to a half hour to increase its coverage of war news, but he declined and instead retired. His departure brought to an end a unique opportunity for radio to educate and expand an interest in and appreciation of classical music.

The war, however, had brought cutbacks in much musical programming, usually in the form of limited money and reduced personnel. Several shows endured the interruptions of war, while others aired for the last time. Examples of programs that closed down include the following: *The Cincinnati Conservatory Symphony* (CBS, 1935–1941), *The Curtis Institute Musicale* (CBS, 1933–1941), *The Eastman School of Music Symphony* (NBC, 1932–1942), *The Ford Sunday Evening Hour* (CBS, 1934–1942), *The Indianapolis Symphony Orchestra* (Mutual, 1937–1938; CBS, 1938–1943), *The Radio City Music Hall of the Air* (NBC, 1932–1942), *The Rochester Civic Orchestra* (NBC, 1929–1942), and *The Rochester Philharmonic Orchestra* (NBC, 1929–1930, 1935–1937, 1939–1942).

In an attempt to keep new music before radio audiences during these difficult times, NBC Blue instructed bandleader Paul Whiteman, in his network role as musical director, to establish a Creative Music Fund. Its purpose involved commissioning short pieces (five to six minutes) by current American composers for a new radio show that presented contemporary music. The program aired from September 5 to November 14, 1944, and in that short time spotlighted many composers from both the classical and popular music fields, including Aaron Copland, Leonard Bernstein, Ferde Grofe, Roy Harris, Igor Stravinksy, and Duke Ellington.

CONTRIBUTIONS TO THE WAR EFFORT

Like other performers from all forms of music, many classical music artists participated actively in patriotic activities during World War II. Marc Blitzstein, the composer of the controversial political musical *The Cradle Will Rock* (1937), joined the U.S. Army and served as the music director of the government-run American broadcasting station in London. While in Great Britain, he wrote *Freedom Morning,* a symphonic poem for orchestra, which opened in London at the Royal Albert Hall in September 1943. Soon afterward, the Army Air Force commissioned him to compose a large-scale choral piece. Out of that came *Symphony: The Airborne,* a score for soloists, male voice choir, and orchestra. In 1946, Leonard Bernstein led its premiere in New York. An award-winning recording followed shortly thereafter, but because the general public wished to put the war behind them, the piece experienced a lukewarm reception and never gained a strong reputation.

Once the United States entered the war, a display of patriotism and working for the war effort became a part of everyday life for all Americans. In 1942, the Office of War Information put together a film called *The World at War.* Gail Kubik, a staff composer and musical program advisor for NBC radio, wrote the score. In the classical music arena, Toscanini revived *Hymn of the Nations* (1944; originally written in the early 1860s by Italian opera composer Giuseppe Verdi) for inclusion in an OWI documentary about the role of Italian Americans in aiding the Allies during World War II. Originally, Verdi had utilized the national anthems of several European nations, and Toscanini added arrangements of those of the United States and the Soviet Union. Actor Burgess Meredith served as narrator, tenor Jan Peerce as the primary soloist, and the Westminster Choir and the NBC Symphony Orchestra joined Toscanini for this patriotic endeavor. Similarly, many other musicians participated in OWI productions, including composers Virgil Thomson and Morton Gould, while Roy Harris served as director of music for the agency.

Nelson Eddy, a classically-trained baritone who sang in operas, on the concert stage, radio, and most famously in Hollywood operettas, made his first war-related appearance with Leopold Stokowski on October 19, 1939. He sang in a concert to benefit Polish war relief. Eddy later became an air raid warden, appeared frequently at the Hollywood Canteen, and, in 1943, gave concerts for military personnel in South America, Africa, Egypt, and Persia (now Iran). Throughout the war, he also broadcast for Armed Forces Radio, a service for American troops everywhere, as did many other classical and popular music artists.

During the war years, composer and conductor Ferde Grofé, in addition to many professional music endeavors, frequently held the baton for military bands and appeared at USO shows. In 1939, New York's Julliard School of Music appointed him to its teaching staff. When in New York, he served as the maestro for a wide variety of radio shows such as NBC's *Paul Whiteman Presents* (summer 1943) and *A Song Is Born* (1944). Grofe also traveled to Hollywood to collaborate on several films; his credits include *Strike Up the Band* (1940), *Red Hot Riding Hood* (1943), and *Thousands Cheer* (1943). Phillip Morris cigarettes had already heightened his reputation across the United States by using "On the Trail" from his famous *Grand Canyon Suite* (1931) in radio advertisements. Hollywood capitalized on the recognition of "On the Trail" in *The Homeless Flea* (1940), a cartoon feature. An original score by Grofe for the film *Minstrel Man* (1945) received an Oscar nomination for Best Music and Scoring of a musical picture that year, but Morris Stoloff and Carmen Dragon's work on for *Cover Girl* (1945) won.

V-Discs, a recording project and a popular venue for getting a wide variety of music to American troops stationed overseas, offered classical recordings, along with occasional critical evaluations. The discs included material provided by such esteemed artists as Aaron Copland, Leonard Bernstein, Andre Kostelanetz, and Arturo Toscanini and the NBC Symphony Orchestra. Other ensembles, such as the Philadelphia Symphony Orchestra and the Voice of Firestone Orchestra, also participated in this widely praised war effort. (See chapter 4, "Recordings and the Music Business," for more on V-Discs.)

CONCLUSION

American classical music developed and expanded in several ways between 1939 and 1945. During this turbulent time, a group of American composers, a number of them previously trained in Paris by Nadia Boulanger, searched for a true American voice in classical music, one that would go beyond musical elitists and speak to a broader listening audience. In this effort, artists such as Aaron Copland, Roy Harris, William Grant Still, Morton Gould, and Virgil Thomson successfully included American images and themes in their compositions and gained varying degrees of popularity.

Additionally, some composers attempted to reach out to both the musically educated and uneducated through lectures, articles, and books. For example, Walter Piston authored a number of textbooks during the 1930s and 1940s. Virgil Thomson likewise wrote *The State of Music* in 1939. Aaron Copland, in *What to Listen for in Music* (1939), even included a chapter on scoring for films.

The movies drew Aaron Copland and Virgil Thomson to California, where they demonstrated their craftsmanship. Although they continued to focus primarily on compositions for the concert hall, both of these men contributed scores for Hollywood productions. Thomson, the first to write for films, offered encouragement to Copland, and in a twist, the latter's work became the more influential in this area. Together, they have been credited with raising the standards of the soundtracks accompanying movies and showed that quality music can enhance a motion picture.

An especially significant event in the classical music world occurred in 1937, when a single corporation, the National Broadcasting Company, created the NBC Symphony Orchestra and committed significant resources to fine orchestral programming. This venture established a new and unique relationship between a commercial entity and classical music, and it allowed the network to make a statement about the importance of balance between public service and profit, high culture and entertainment. Classical music never attained the level of acceptance that popular music enjoyed, but it played an important part in providing audiences exposure to serious culture during World War II.

A Musical Timeline for the Period 1939–1945

1939 The Glenn Miller Orchestra leads the big bands with 5 of the Top-10 *Billboard* hits for the year: #2, "Over the Rainbow"; #6, "Moon Love"; #7, "Wishing (Will Make It So)"; #8, "Stairway to the Stars"; and #9, "The Man with the Mandolin."

1939 Because of segregation rules then in effect, the Daughters of the American Revolution deny contralto Marian Anderson the use of Washington's Constitution Hall; she therefore sings, with the blessing of President and Mrs. Roosevelt, at the Lincoln Memorial instead. Estimates place the integrated crowd at 75,000 people.

1939 The Coon Creek Girls, an old-time country string band, perform for the King and Queen of England during the monarchs' visit to the United States, and do so at the express invitation of Eleanor Roosevelt, the nation's First Lady.

1939 Jukeboxes become one of the most popular means of supplying music. Since they utilize phonograph records for their selections, suppliers buy thousands of singles for the ubiquitous machines, causing them to influence what tunes will be hits as much as ordinary record purchases by consumers.

1940 The boogie-woogie craze reaches new heights when "Beat Me, Daddy, Eight to the Bar," in a recording by the popular Andrews Sisters, makes radio's popular *Your Hit Parade*.

1940 "In the Mood," released in late 1939, tops most lists for 1940, although Tommy Dorsey's rendition of "I'll Never Smile Again," featuring his young vocalist Frank Sinatra, proves a tough challenger. The Dorsey/ Sinatra success signals a shift in musical tastes: singers would become dominant in the 1940s, replacing the bands as public favorites.

1940 As the war worsens in Europe, many composers and conductors flee to the United States, among them Bela Bartok, Paul Hindemith, Fritz Kreisler, Darius Milhaud, Ignace Jan Paderewski, Arnold Schoenberg, Igor Stravinsky, Bruno Walter, and Kurt Weill.

1940 Films featuring singing cowboys begin to appeal to broad audiences, and Gene Autry and Roy Rogers lead the way in popularity. Cheaply made variations on the traditional Western, they eschew elaborate choreography and lavish settings, and the cowboys simply sit around the campfire, strum their guitars, and sing country songs both old and new.

1941 Among the hit songs of the year, "Deep in the Heart of Texas" emerges as a Western-flavored favorite, while "Chattanooga Choo Choo," as performed by Glenn Miller, becomes the #2 song for the year, a strong indicator that the big bands still have plenty of life in them.

1941 Tenor Jan Peerce makes his debut with the Metropolitan Opera Company in *La Traviata* after years in radio and with various symphonies; New York born, his success encourages many music lovers to hope for a new level of acceptance for American classical performers.

1941 Composer Kurt Weill and lyricist Ira Gershwin collaborate on a new Broadway musical, *Lady in the Dark;* it features a book by the renowned Moss Hart. A rather cerebral play, it deals with the unlikely topic of psychoanalysis, but the classic "My Ship" comes from the score.

1941 Both a 1941 Western called *Sierra Sue* and a 1942 swing-oriented picture titled *Strictly in the Groove* feature the same cowboy number, "Be Honest with Me." The tune consequently receives an Academy Award nomination for Best Song, the first country composition to be so honored.

1941 At the end of the year, the bombing of Pearl Harbor brings a wave of pro-war and patriotic songs. Often led by country and Western singers, this outpouring stands in sharp contrast to the absence of music dealing with war in any way prior to the attack.

1942 With the United State now an active participant in the war, musicals on Broadway and from Hollywood begin to lose some of their escapism. Shows like *Banjo Eyes* and *This Is the Army,* along with movies like *Call Out the Marines, The Fleet's In, Star Spangled Rhythm,* and *Yankee Doodle Dandy,* make appeals to patriotism, feature numbers of characters in uniform, and openly acknowledge the impacts the conflict is having on the home front.

1942 In like manner, music publishers seek heart-tugging lyrics such as "A Boy in Khaki—A Girl in Lace," humor directed at the enemy in pieces like "Der Fuehrer's Face," appeals to patriotism from compositions similar to "Praise the Lord and Pass the Ammunition," and anything else that might stir listeners in their attitudes toward the war, including the likes of "Good-Bye, Mama, I'm Off to Yokohoma," "It's Taps for the Japs," "Let's Bring New Glory to Old Glory," and "Remember Pearl Harbor." "There's a Star-Spangled Banner Waving Somewhere" becomes one of the biggest sellers; a recording by Elton Britt sells over 1 million copies, the first country song to do so.

1942 As the military draft takes its toll on musicians, a few of the big bands go out of existence, others re-emerge as service bands, and a number of all-girl orchestras appear, ready to fill some of the gaps at nightclubs and dance halls. Most of the "girl bands" survive only for the duration of the war, and their male counterparts quickly replace them in the postwar era.

1942 The movie *Holiday Inn* features a tune titled "White Christmas" by composer Irving Berlin. It immediately becomes a #1 hit, a position it would continue to hold into 1943. Bing Crosby's rendition, from the motion-picture soundtrack, sells in the millions, and many other artists hasten to record it, but never with his success.

1943 On the classical side, composer Aaron Copland unveils *Fanfare for the Common Man,* a stirring ode to those serving the country, a well-known short piece that frequently opens concert performances. His contemporary Robert Russell Bennett receives a commission from the *Saturday Evening Post* to write a composition based on the Four Freedoms (of speech, of worship, from want, from fear). President Roosevelt had enumerated these in a 1941 broadcast, and artist Norman Rockwell famously illustrated them in a series of four paintings done for the magazine. It becomes a much-played item in the repertoires of numerous orchestras during the war years.

1943 Popular radio variety shows provide lots of music in their formats, keeping the airwaves bright and breezy. *The Chamber Music Society of Lower Basin Street* mixes irreverent satire with good jazz; throughout the war, crooner Bing Crosby hosts the immensely popular *Kraft Music Hall,* a long-standing Thursday night tradition on NBC; rival CBS counters with its well-established *Kate Smith Hour;* and Broadway celebrities entertain real servicemen at New York's Stage Door Canteen, while movie stars do likewise at the Hollywood Canteen.

1943 The pairing of composer Richard Rodgers with lyricist Lorenz Hart, a team usually called Rodgers and Hart, comes to a final end with Hart's death in 1943. But earlier in the year, a new force in American musical theater has already arisen: Richard Rodgers and Oscar Hammerstein II, or, as Broadway comes to know them, Rodgers and Hammerstein. The premiere of their first collaboration, *Oklahoma!* occurs in March, and they would follow that classic show with a remarkable string of other hit musicals in the years to come.

1943 Leonard Bernstein, a young, relatively unknown composer and conductor, takes the podium of the prestigious New York Philharmonic to substitute for the ailing Bruno Walter. Only 25 years old, Bernstein performs admirably and becomes, overnight, an important figure in serious music circles.

1944 With the Allies on the offensive on all fronts, European and Pacific, people sense that it is only a matter of time before World War II will come to a close. The music business, however, continues in high gear, still rousing public spirits with various calls to patriotism. As a hit song has it, "Ac-Cen-Tchu-Ate the Positive." But sadness and loneliness also remain as themes, as in "Goodnight, Wherever You Are" and "Have Yourself a Merry Little Christmas."

1944 Aaron Copland, at the peak of his form, premieres *Appalachian Spring* at the Library of Congress in October. A mix of American themes, including the infectious Shaker tune "Simple Gifts," it proves immediately popular. In addition, choreographer Martha Graham and her troupe perform an original ballet in accompaniment to the music, introducing much of the attending public to modern dance. In 1945, this composition wins the Pulitzer Prize for music.

1944 October also witnesses hordes of screaming teenage fans storming the Paramount Theatre in New York City to get a glimpse of their latest idol, singer Frank Sinatra. In a newly-established ritual to be repeated for other music celebrities, it takes over 400 police officers to restore a semblance of order before the crooner can perform.

1944 An officer in the U.S. Army Air Force, and leader of a large service band, Captain Glenn Miller disappears over the English Channel while aboard a plane heading for Europe. Searchers never find any trace of him or his aircraft, and the music world mourns his loss.

1945 In the area of country music, two significant recording events occur in Nashville, Tennessee. In March, Red Foley cuts several sides at radio station WSM's Studio B, becoming the first performer, country or otherwise, to officially record in Nashville. In January of 1946, Foley will replace Roy Acuff as the star of NBC's *Prince Albert Show,* a part of the famous *Grand Ole Opry.* Meanwhile, Ernest Tubb cuts two songs for the Decca label in September; many date that as the real beginning of commercial recording in Nashville.

1945 With victory in the air, music takes on an upbeat note, with tunes like "Dream," "Give Me the Simple Life," "I Was Here When You Left Me (I'll Be Here When You Get Back)," "I'll Be Walkin' with My Honey (Soon, Soon, Soon)," "I'm Gonna Love That Guy [Gal] (Like He's [She's] Never Been Loved Before)," "It's Been a Long, Long Time," and "My Guy's Come Back."

1945 Rodgers and Hammerstein open their second big hit (after *Oklahoma!*) on Broadway with *Carousel* and make their only joint foray into movies with *State Fair.* In keeping with the improving mood of the country, *Carousel* boasts "June Is Bustin' Out All Over," while *State Fair* offers "It Might As Well Be Spring." Everywhere, the ideas of rebirth, new hopes, and new promise get expressed more and more in musical terms.

1945 Germany surrenders in May; Japan follows suit in September. Popular music welcomes new voices and new stars such as June Christy, Nat "King" Cole, Perry Como, Doris Day, Billy Eckstine, Vaughn Monroe, and Mel Torme. In jazz, change becomes the byword, with bebop leading the way. Dizzy Gillespie, Thelonious Monk, and Charlie Parker abandon traditional swing patterns, and controversial new tonal and instrumental arrangements begin to take hold in the heady atmosphere of peace.

Appendix A: Broadway and Hollywood Musicals by Title, 1939–1945

What follows is a reasonably complete listing of American stage musicals from 1939 through 1945; its film counterpart deliberately omits many minor pictures, especially those in which the music plays an incidental role in the overall production. Even as approximations, these titles suggest both the wide variety of musicals being produced during the period as well as their popularity.

Totals: stage musicals = 87 productions; movie musicals = 283 releases; combined = 370 musicals

1939

Broadway Musicals [13]

Du Barry Was a Lady (1943 movie)
George White's Scandals
The Man Who Came to Dinner
One for the Money
Set to Music
Sing for Your Supper
Stars in Your Eyes
The Straw Hat Revue
The Streets of Paris
Swingin' the Dream
Too Many Girls
Very Warm for May
Yokel Boy (1942 movie)

Hollywood Musicals [22]

Babes in Arms
Balalaika
Broadway Serenade
Dancing Co-Ed
Destry Rides Again
East Side of Heaven
The Great Victor Herbert
Hawaiian Nights

Let Freedom Ring
Man About Town
The Marx Brothers at the Circus
Naughty but Nice
On Your Toes
Rose of Washington Square
Second Fiddle
Some Like It Hot
The Star Maker
St. Louis Blues
The Story of Vernon and Irene Castle
Swanee River
That's Right—You're Wrong
The Wizard of Oz

1940

Broadway Musicals [13]

All in Fun
Boys and Girls Together
Cabin in the Sky (1943 movie)
Earl Carroll's Vanities
Higher and Higher
Hold On to Your Hats
It Happens on Ice
Keep Off the Grass
Louisiana Purchase (1941 movie)
Panama Hattie (1942 movie)
Tis of Thee
Two for the Show
Walk with Music

Hollywood Musicals [33]

Andy Hardy Meets Debutante
Argentine Nights
Bitter Sweet
The Boys from Syracuse
Broadway Melody of 1940
Dance, Girl, Dance
Dancing on a Dime
Down Argentine Way
Fantasia
Grand Ole Opry
Gulliver's Travels
Hit Parade of 1941
If I Had My Way
Lillian Russell
Little Nellie Kelly
The Marx Brothers Go West
Music in My Heart
New Moon
A Night at Earl Carroll's
One Night in the Tropics
The Philadelphia Story
Pinocchio
Rhythm on the River
The Road to Singapore
Second Chorus
Spring Parade
Strike Up the Band
Take Me Back to Oklahoma
Tin Pan Alley
Too Many Girls
Two Girls on Broadway
You'll Find Out
Young People

1941

Broadway Musicals [10]

Best Foot Forward (1943 movie)
Crazy with the Heat
High Kickers
Lady in the Dark (1944 movie)
Let's Face It (1943 movie)
Meet the People (opened December 25, 1940; 1944 movie)
Night of Love
Pal Joey (opened December 25, 1940)
Sons o' Fun
Sunny River

Hollywood Musicals [37]

Babes on Broadway
The Big Store
Birth of the Blues

Blues in the Night
Buck Privates
The Chocolate Soldier
Dumbo
Four Jacks and a Jill
Go West, Young Lady
The Great American Broadcast
In the Navy
Keep'em Flying
Kiss the Boys Goodbye
Lady Be Good
The Lady Eve
Las Vegas Nights
Louisiana Purchase (1940 play)
Moon Over Miami
Navy Blues
No, No, Nanette
Pot O' Gold
Ridin' on a Rainbow
Rise and Shine
Road to Zanzibar
Rookies on Parade
San Antonio Rose
Sis Hopkins
Smilin' Through
Sun Valley Serenade
Sunny
That Night in Rio
They Met in Argentina
Time Out for Rhythm
Week-End in Havana
You'll Never Get Rich
You're the One
Ziegfeld Girl

1942

Broadway Musicals [12]

Banjo Eyes (opened December 25, 1941)
Beat the Band
By Jupiter
Count Me In
The Lady Comes Across
New Faces of 1943
Of V We Sing
Priorities of 1942
Rosalinda
Star and Garter
This Is the Army (1943 movie)
You'll See Stars

Hollywood Musicals [44]

Behind the Eight Ball
Born to Sing
Cairo
Call Out the Marines
Casablanca
The Fleet's In
Footlight Serenade
For Me and My Gal
Give Out, Sisters
Hellzapoppin'
Hi, Neighbor
Holiday Inn
I Married an Angel
Iceland
Mayor of 44th Street
My Favorite Blonde
My Favorite Spy
My Gal Sal
Orchestra Wives
Panama Hattie (1940 play)
Pardon My Sarong
Playmates
Priorities on Parade
Private Buckaroo
Rhythm Parade
Ride 'em Cowboy
Rio Rita
Road to Morocco
Seven Days' Leave
Ship Aho
Sleepy Time Gal
Song of the Islands
Springtime in the Rockies
Star Spangled Rhythm
Strictly in the Groove
Sweater Girl

Swing It Soldier
Syncopation
What's Cookin'?
When Johnny Comes Marching Home
Yankee Doodle Dandy
Yokel Boy (1939 play)
You Were Never Lovelier
Youth on Parade

1943

Broadway Musicals [13]

Artists and Models
Bright Lights of 1944
Carmen Jones
A Connecticut Yankee
Early to Bed
Hairpin Harmony
My Dear Public
Oklahoma!
One Touch of Venus
Something for the Boys (1944 movie)
What's Up?
Winged Victory (1944 movie)
Ziegfeld Follies of 1943

Hollywood Musicals [54]

Always a Bridesmaid
Best Foot Forward (1941 play)
Cabin in the Sky (1940 play)
Campus Rhythm
Coney Island
Crazy House
The Desert Song
Dixie
Du Barry Was a Lady (1939 play)
Follow the Band
Gals, Incorporated
The Gang's All Here
Girl Crazy
Happy-Go-Lucky
The Hard Way
The Heat's On
Hello, Frisco, Hello
Hers to Hold
He's My Guy
Hi Ya, Sailor
Higher and Higher
Hit the Ice
Hit Parade of 1943
How's About It?
I Dood It
It Ain't Hay
Larceny with Music
Let's Face It (1941 play)
Mister Big
Moonlight in Vermont
Phantom of the Opera
The Powers Girl
Presenting Lily Mars
Reveille with Beverly
Riding High
Salute for Three
Shantytown
Silver Skates
The Sky's the Limit
Sleepy Lagoon
Something to Shout About
Stage Door Canteen
Stormy Weather
Sweet Rosie O'Grady
Swing Fever
Swingtime Johnny
Thank Your Lucky Stars
This Is the Army (1942 play)
Thousands Cheer
Top Man
True to Life
What's Buzzin', Cousin?
Wintertime
Youth on Parade

1944

Broadway Musicals [10]

Allah Be Praised
Bloomer Girl
Dream with Music
Follow the Girls

Helen Goes to Troy
Jackpot
Mexican Hayride
Sadie Thompson
The Seven Lively Arts
Song of Norway

Hollywood Musicals [55]

And the Angels Sing
Around the World
Atlantic City
Babes on Swing Street
Bathing Beauty
Belle of the Yukon
Broadway Rhythm
Can't Help Singing
Carolina Blues
Cover Girl
Cowboy Canteen
Ever Since Venus
Follow the Boys
Four Jills in a Jeep
Going My Way
Greenwich Village
Here Come the Waves
Hey Rookie
Hollywood Canteen
Irish Eyes Are Smiling
Jamboree
Knickerbocker Holiday
Lady in the Dark (1941 play)
Lady, Let's Dance
Laura
Lost in a Harem
Louisiana Hayride
Meet Me in St. Louis
Meet Miss Bobby Socks
Meet the People (1941 play)
The Merry Monahans
Minstrel Man
Moonlight and Cactus
Music for Millions
Pardon My Rhythm
Pin Up Girl
Rainbow Island
Rosie the Riveter
Sensations of 1945
Seven Days Ashore
Shine On, Harvest Moon
Show Business
Since You Went Away
Sing, Neighbor, Sing
Something for the Boys (1943 play)
Song of the Open Road
Stars on Parade
Step Lively
Sweet and Low-down
This Is the Life
The Three Caballeros
Two Girls and a Sailor
Up in Arms
Winged Victory (1943 play)
You Can't Ration Love

1945

Broadway Musicals [16]

Are You With It?
Carib Song
Carousel
The Day Before Spring
The Firebrand of Florence
The Girl from Nantucket
A Lady Says Yes
Laffing Room Only (opened December 23, 1944)
Marinka
Memphis Bound
Mr. Strauss Goes to Boston
On the Town (opened December 28, 1944)
Polonaise
The Red Mill
Sing Out, Sweet Land
Up in Central Park

Hollywood Musicals [38]

Anchors Aweigh
Bells of St. Mary's
Bring on the Girls
Delightfully Dangerous

Diamond Horseshoe
The Dolly Sisters
Duffy's Tavern
Earl Carroll's Vanities
Easy to Look At
Flaming Bullets
George White's Scandals of 1945
Here Come the Co-eds
In Society
Incendiary Blonde
Lake Placid Serenade
Man from Oklahoma
Masquerade in Mexico
Nob Hill
On Stage Everybody
Out of This World
Pan-Americana
Patrick the Great
Radio Stars on Parade
Rhapsody in Blue
Rhythm Roundup
Rockin' in the Rockies
Sing Your Way Home
A Song to Remember
State Fair
Sunbonnet Sue
That's the Spirit
Three in the Saddle
Thrill of a Romance
Tonight and Every Night
Week-End at the Waldorf
Where Do We Go from Here?
Wonder Man
Yolanda and the Thief

Appendix B: The Songs, Composers, and Lyricists of World War II, 1939–1945

Thousands of songs came out during the war years; this listing serves as but a sampling of the period, with most of the major compositions included, and does not claim to be complete. Within the text, a number of older works receive mention but do not appear here unless they happened to achieve significant popularity in the years 1939–1945. For example, "Always in My Heart" (originally 1932) and "As Time Goes By" (originally 1931) meet these criteria and credits are given here. Other older works, however, such as the "Jimmy Crack Corn" folksong (n.d.) or "Good Night Ladies" (1853), because they had no particular play or impact in the 1940s, are found in the index only.

"Ac-Cen-Tchu-Ate the Positive" (1944; music by Harold Arlen, lyrics by Johnny Mercer).
"All or Nothing at All" (1939; words and music by Jack Lawrence and Arthur Altman).
"All Out Bugle Call" (1942; words and music by Ann Ronell).
"All the Things You Are" (1939; music by Jerome Kern, lyrics by Oscar Hammerstein II).
"All Too Soon" (1940; music by Duke Ellington, lyrics by Carl Sigman).
"Allegiance to the Red, White and Blue" (1942; words and music by Ethel Lee Buxton).
"Along the Navajo Trail" (1945; words and music by Dick Charles, Eddie De Lange, and Larry Marks).
"Always" (1944 [popular revival of a 1925 song]; words and music by Irving Berlin).
"Always in My Heart" (1942 [popular revival of a 1932 song]; music by Ernesto Lecuona, lyrics by Kim Gannon).
"Amapola (Pretty Little Poppy)" (1941 [popular revival of a 1924 song]; music by Joseph M. Lacalle, lyrics by Albert Gamse). *The #1 song for 1941.*

"America, I Love You" (1942; music by Archie Gottler, lyrics by Edgar Leslie).
"America's Call" (1942; words and music by Winnetta Lamson).
"American Patrol" (1942 [adaptation of an 1885 composition by F. W. Meacham]; arrangement by Jerry Gray).
"Amor" (1944; music by Gabriel Ruiz, English lyrics by Sunny Skylar).
"And the Angels Sing" (1939; words and music by Johnny Mercer and Ziggy Elman).
"And There You Are" (1945; music by Sammy Fain, lyrics by Ted Koehler).
"Angels of Mercy" (1942; words and music by Irving Berlin).
"Any Bonds Today?" (1941; words and music by Irving Berlin).
"Apple Honey" (1945; music by Woody Herman).
"Are You Havin' Any Fun?" (1939; music by Sammy Fain, lyrics by Jack Yellin).
"The Army's Made a Man Out of Me" (1942; words and music by Irving Berlin).
"Arthur Murray Taught Me Dancing in a Hurry" (1942; music by Victor Schertzinger, lyrics by Johnny Mercer).
"Artistry in Rhythm" (1943; music by Stan Kenton).
"Artistry Jumps" (1943; music by Stan Kenton).
"As Time Goes By" (1943 [popular revival of a 1931 song]; words and music by Herman Hupfield).
"At Last" (1942; music by Harry Warren, lyrics by Mack Gordon).
"At Mail Call Today" (1945; words and music by Gene Autry and Fred Rose).
"Attention" (1943; music by Bob Carleton, lyrics by Rose M. Gonia).
"Babes on Broadway" (1941; music by Burton Lane, lyrics by Ralph Freed).
"Back in the Saddle Again" (1940; words and music by Gene Autry and Ray Whitley).
"Ballad for Americans" (1940; music by Earl Robinson, lyrics by John Latouche).
"The Ballad of October 16" (1941; words and music by Millard Lampell).
"The Ballad of Pretty Boy Floyd" (1939; words and music by Woody Guthrie).
"Be a Hero, My Boy" (1943; music by Henry Kane, lyrics by Mark Minkus).
"Be Careful! It's My Heart" (1942; words and music by Irving Berlin).
"Be Honest with Me" (1941; words and music by Fred Rose and Gene Autry).
"Beat Me, Daddy, Eight to the Bar" (1940; music by Don Raye, lyrics by Hughie Prince and Eleanor Sheehy).
"Because of You" (1940; music by Dudley Wilkinson, lyrics by Arthur Hammerstein).
"Beer Barrel Polka" (1939; music by Jaramir Vejvoda, lyrics by Lew Brown and Wladimir A. Timm). *The #1 song for 1939.*
"Begin the Beguine" (1935; words and music by Cole Porter). *Artie Shaw's 1938 recording of this song made it so popular that it endured throughout the war.*
"Bell Bottom Trousers" (1945 [possibly taken from a traditional chantey]; contemporary words and music by Moe Jaffe).
"Besame Mucho" (1944 [popular revival of a 1941 song]; music by Consuelo Velazquez, English lyrics by Sunny Skylar).
"Better Not Roll Those Blue, Blue Eyes (at Somebody Else)" (1942; music by Al Goodhart, lyrics by Kay Twomey).

"Bewitched (Bothered and Bewildered)" (1941; music by Richard Rodgers, lyrics by Lorenz Hart).
"(There's a) Big Parade in the Sky" (1942; words and music by Cecil Taylor).
"The Bigger the Army and Navy, the Better the Lovin'" (1942; words and music by Jack Yellin).
"Bijou" (1945; music by Ralph Burns).
Black, Brown, and Beige (1943; music and libretto by Duke Ellington).
"Blitzkrieg Baby (You Can't Bomb Me)" (1941; words and music by Fred Fisher).
"Blue Eyes Crying in the Rain" (1945; words and music by Fred Rose).
"Blue Flame" (1941; music by Joe Bishop).
"Blueberry Hill" (1940; music by Vincent Rose, lyrics by Al Lewis and Larry Stock).
"Blues in the Night" (1941; music by Harold Arlen, lyrics by Johnny Mercer).
"Body and Soul" (1939 [popular revival of a 1930 song]; music by John Green, lyrics by Edward Heyman, Robert Sour, and Frank Eyton).
"The Bombardier Song" (1942; music by Richard Rodgers, lyrics by Lorenz Hart).
"Boogie Woogie" (1943 [popular revival of a 1938 song, which in turn came from a 1930 composition]; original music by Pinetop Smith; 1938 and 1943 arrangements by Dean Kincaide).
"Boogie Woogie Bugle Boy (of Company B)" (1941; music by Hughie Prince, lyrics by Don Raye).
"Born to Lose" (1943; words and music by Frankie Brown).
"Bounce Me, Brother, with a Solid Four" (1941; music by Hughie Prince, lyrics by Don Raye).
"A Boy in Khaki—A Girl in Lace" (1942; music by Allie Wrubel, lyrics by Charles Newman).
"The Boy Next Door" (1944; music by Hugh Martin, lyrics by Ralph Blane).
"Brazil" (1943 [popular revival of a 1939 song]; music by Ary Barroso, lyrics by Bob Russell).
"The Breeze and I" (1940 [adapted from Ernesto Lecuona's "Andalucia"]; music by Tony Camerata, lyrics by Al Stillman).
"C for Conscription" (1941; words and music by Millard Lampell and Pete Seeger).
"C-Jam Blues" (1942; music by Duke Ellington).
"Cabin in the Sky" (1940; music by Vernon Duke, lyrics by John Latouche).
"Caldonia" (1945; words and music by Fleecie Moore).
"Candy" (1944; music by Alex Kramer and Joan Whitney, lyrics by Mack David).
"Can't You Read Between the Lines?" (1945; music by Jule Styne, lyrics by Sammy Cahn).
"Captain Custard" (1940; music by Victor Schertzinger, lyrics by Johnny Burke).
"Care of Uncle Sam" (1942; words and music by Denver Darling, Vaughn Horton, and Harry Duncan).
"Carried Away" (1945; music by Leonard Bernstein, lyrics by Betty Comden and Adolph Green).
"Cattle Call" (1943; words and music by Tex Owens).
"Celery Stalks at Midnight" (1940; words and music by George Harris and Will Bradley).

"Chattanooga Choo Choo" (1941; music by Harry Warren, lyrics by Mack Gordon). *The #2 song for 1941.*

"Cherokee Maiden" (1942; words and music by Cindy Walker).

"Chica Chica Boom Chic" (1941; music by Harry Warren, lyrics by Mack Gordon).

"Chickery Chick" (1945; music by Sidney Lippman, lyrics by Sylvia Dee).

"Chin Up, Cheerio, Carry On" (1941; music by Burton Lane, lyrics by E. Y. Harburg).

"Chloe" (1945 [parody adaptation of a 1927 tune]; music by Gus Kahn, lyrics by Charles N. Daniels).

"Close as Pages in a Book" (1944; music by Sigmund Romberg, lyrics by Dorothy Fields).

"Close to You" (1943; words and music by Al Hoffman, Carl G. Lampe, and Jerry Livingston).

"Cocktails for Two" (1944 [parody adaptation of a 1934 tune]; music by Sam Coslow, lyrics by Arthur Johnston).

"Comin' in on a Wing and a Prayer" (1942; music by Jimmy McHugh, lyrics by Harold Adamson).

"Cotton Tail" (1940; music by Duke Ellington).

"Counting the Days" (1945; words and music by Alex Kramer and Hy Zaret).

"Cow Cow Boogie" (1943; music by Gene De Paul and Benny Carter, lyrics by Don Raye).

"Cowards over Pearl Harbor" (1941; words and music by Fred Rose).

"Cowboy Serenade" or "My Last Cigarette" (1942; words and music by Rich Hall).

"Daddy" (1941; words and music by Bobby Troup).

"Dance with a Dolly (with a Hole in Her Stockin')" (1944 [adapted from the folk tune "Buffalo Girls"]; music by Terry Shand, lyrics by Jimmy Eaton and Mickey Leader).

"Dawn of a New Day" (1939 [adapted from posthumous notes of George Gershwin]; music and lyrics by Ira Gershwin and Kay Swift). *Official song of the 1939–1940 New York World's Fair.*

"Day by Day" (1945; music by Paul Weston and Axel Stordahl, lyrics by Sammy Cahn).

"Day In–Day Out" (1939; music by Rube Bloom, lyrics by Johnny Mercer).

"Daybreak" (1942 [from Ferde Grofe's *Mississippi Suite*]; music adapted by Ferde Grofe, lyrics by Harold Adamson).

"Dear God, Watch Over Joe" (1944; words and music by Jenny Lou Carson).

"Dear Mom" (1941; words and music by Maury Coleman Harris).

"Dear Mrs. Roosevelt" (c. 1940; words and music by Woody Guthrie).

"Dearest Darling" (1945; words and music by Dick Robertson, James Cavanaugh, and Frank Weldon).

"Dearly Beloved" (1942; music by Jerome Kern, lyrics by Johnny Mercer).

"Deep in the Heart of Texas" (1941; music by Don Swander, lyrics by June Hershey).

"Deep Purple" (1934, 1939; music by Peter DeRose, lyrics by Mitchell Parish).

"The Deepest Shelter in Town" (1940; words and music by W. W. Massie).

"Der Fuehrer's Face" (1942; words and music by Oliver Wallace).

"Did You See Daddy Over There?" (1943; music by Bill Shownet, lyrics by Eddie Arnold).

"Dig Down Deep" (1942; words and music by Walter Hirsch, Gerald Marks, and Sano Marco).

"Dig You Later (A Hubba-Hubba-Hubba)" (1945; music by Jimmy McHugh, lyrics by Harold Adamson).

"Ding Dong, the Witch Is Dead" (1939; music by Harold Arlen, lyrics by H. Y. Harburg).

"Do Nothin' 'Till You Hear from Me" (1943; music by Duke Ellington, lyrics by Bob Russell).

"Doctor, Lawyer, Indian Chief" (1945; music by Hoagy Carmichael, lyrics by Paul Francis Webster).

"Dolores" (1941; music by Louis alter, lyrics by Frank Loesser).

"Don't Cry" (1942; words and music by Sunny Skylar).

"Don't Fence Me In" (1944 [popular revival of a 1934 song]; words and music by Cole Porter [with Robert Fletcher]). *The #2 song of 1944.*

"Don't Get Around Much Any More" (1943 [adapted from Duke Ellington's 1942 "Never No Lament"]; music by Duke Ellington, lyrics by Bob Russell).

"Don't Let's Be Beastly to the Germans" (1943; words and music by Noel Coward).

"Don't Sit Under the Apple Tree (With Anyone Else But Me)" (1942 [popular revival of a 1939 song]; music by Sam H. Stept, lyrics by Lew Brown and Charlie Tobias).

"Don't Worry, Mom" (1943; words and music by Harry Duncan and Paul William).

"Down on Ami Ami Oni Oni Isle" (1942; words and music by Mack Gordon and Harry Owens).

"Draftin' Blues" (1940 [popular revival of a 1918 song]; words and music by Maceo Pinkard).

"Dream" (1945; words and music by Johnny Mercer).

"Each Night at Nine" (1944; words and music by Floyd Tillman).

"Eager Beaver" (1943; music by Stan Kenton).

"Easy Street" (1945; words and music by Alan R. Jones).

"Elmer's Tune" (1941; words and music by Elmer Albrecht, Sammy Gallop, and Dick Jurgens).

"Everything but You" (1945; music and lyrics by Duke Ellington, Harry James, and Don George).

"Everything Happens to Me" (1941; music by Matt Dennis, lyrics by Tom Adair).

"Ev'ry Time We Say Goodbye" (1944; words and music by Cole Porter).

"Ev'rything I've Got" (1942; music by Richard Rodgers, lyrics by Lorenz Hart).

"A Fellow on a Furlough" (1943; words and music by Bobby Worth).

"Fightin' Doug MacArthur" (1942; words and music by Buck Ram).

"Fightin' Son-of-a-Gun" (1942; words and music by Van Sciver and Shelby Darnell [pseudonym of Bob Miller]).

"Fireball Mail" (1942; words and music by Floyd Jenkins).

"Flamingo" (1941; music by Ted Grouya, lyrics by Ed Anderson).

"Flying Home" (1939; music by Lionel Hampton and Benny Goodman).

"Follow the Yellow Brick Road" (1939; music by Harold Arlen, lyrics by E. Y. Harburg).

"Fools Rush In (Where Angels Fear to Tread)" (1940; music by Rube Bloom, lyrics by Johnny Mercer).

"For the Flag, for the Home, for the Family" (1942; words and music by George M. Cohan).

"For the Duration" (1943; words and music by Neva Raymor and Charles McCollister).

"Frenesi" (1940; music by Alberto Dominguez, lyrics by Sidney K. Russell and Ray Charles). *The #2 song for 1940.*

"Friendship" (1939; words and music by Cole Porter).

"The General Jumped at Dawn" (1943; words and music by Jimmy Mundy).

"Georgia on My Mind" (1941; music by Hoagy Carmichael, lyrics by Stuart Gorrell).

"Get Your Gun and Come Along (We're Fixin' to Kill a Skunk)" (1942; words and music by Carson Robison).

"The G.I. Jive" (1944; words and music by Johnny Mercer).

"A G.I. Wish" (1945; words and music by Borelli, Niederman, and Sarnoff).

"Girls, Don't Refuse to Kiss a Soldier" (1943; words and music by K. Davis).

"Give Me the Simple Life" (1945; music by Rube Bloom, lyrics by Harry Ruby).

"Gobs of Love" (1942; words and music by Redd Evans).

"God Bless America" (1938 [popular revival of a patriotic song penned in 1917 and performed throughout World War II]; words and music by Irving Berlin).

"Going My Way" (1944; music by Jimmy Van Heusen, lyrics by Johnny Burke).

"Gone with the Draft" (1940; words and music by Earl Dramin, Wesley Price, and Nat King Cole).

"Gone with What Draft?" (1941; music by Benny Goodman).

"Good Morning" (1939; music by Nacio Herb Brown, lyrics by Arthur Freed).

"Goodbye, Dear, I'll Be Back in a Year" (1940; words and music by Mack Kay).

"Good-Bye, Mama (I'm Off to Yokohoma)" (1942; words and music by J. Fred Coots).

"Goodnight, Good Neighbor" (1943; words and music by Arthur Schwartz and Frank Loesser).

"Goodnight, Soldier" (1943; words and music by Harry Johnson).

"Goodnight, Wherever You Are" (1944; words and music by Dick Robertson, Al Hoffman, and Frank Weldon).

"Gotta Be This or That" (1945; words and music by Sunny Skylar).

"Green Eyes" ("Aquellos Ojos Verdes)," (1941; music by Nilo Menendez, lyrics by Adolfo Utrera, E. Rivera, and Eddie Woods).

"Groovin' High" (1945; music by Dizzy Gillespie).

"Guess I'll Hang My Tears Out to Dry" (1945; music by Jule Styne, lyrics by Sammy Cahn).

"The Gypsy" (1945; words and music by Billy Reid).

"Happiness Is Just a Thing Called Joe" (1943; music by Harold Arlen, lyrics by E. Y. Harburg).

"Harlem Nocturne" (1940; music by Earle Hagen).
"Harlem on Parade" (1942; words and music by Ray Evans and Benny Carter).
"Have I Stayed Away Too Long?" (1943; words and music by Frank Loesser).
"Have I Told You Lately That I Love You?" (1946; words and music by Scotty Wiseman).
"Have Yourself a Merry Little Christmas" (1944; music by Hugh Martin, lyrics by Ralph Blane).
"He Loved Me Till the All-Clear Came" (1942; music by Harold Arlen, lyrics by Johnny Mercer).
"He Wears a Pair of Silver Wings" (1941; music by Michael Carr, lyrics by Eric Maschwitz).
"He's Home for a Little While" (1945; music by Ted Shapiro, lyrics by Kermit Goell).
"He's My Guy" (1942; music by Gene DePaul, lyrics by Don Raye).
"He's My Uncle" (1940; music by Lew Pollack, lyrics by Charles Newman).
"He's 1-A in the Army (and He's A-1 in My Heart)" (1941; words and music by Redd Evans).
"Headin' Down the Wrong Highway" (1945; words and music by Ted Daffan).
"High on a Windy Hill" (1941; words and music by Alex Kramer and Joan Whitney).
"Hinky Dinky Parlez Vous (Mademoiselle from Armentieres)" (1942 [popular revival of a 1918 song introduced during World War I]; attributed to Alfred J. Walden or Gitz Rice).
"Hip, Hip, Hooray!" (1942; music by Henry Nemo, lyrics by Milt Ebbins).
"Hirohito's Letter to Hitler" (1945; words and music by Carson Robison).
"Hit the Road to Dreamland" (1942; music by Harold Arlen, lyrics by Johnny Mercer).
"Hitler's Last Letter to Hirohito" (1945; words and music by Carson Robison).
"Hitler's Reply to Mussolini" (1942; words and music by Carson Robison).
"Holiday for Strings" (1943; music by David Rose, lyrics by Sammy Gallop).
"Hooray for Spinach" (1939; music by Harry Warren, lyrics by Johnny Mercer).
"(There'll Be a) Hot Time in the Town of Berlin (When the Yanks Go Marching In)" (1943; words and music by Joe Bushkin and John De Vries).
"Hothouse" (1945; music by Tadd Dameron [based on the chord structure of Cole Porter's 1930 song "What Is This Thing Called Love?"]).
"Hotcha Cornia" (1943; parody adaptation of a traditional 1800 Russian folk melody called "Otshi Tshornye" ["Dark Eyes"]).
"An Hour Never Passes" (1944; words and music by Jimmy Kennedy).
"The House I Live In (That's America to Me)" (1942; music by Earl Robinson, lyrics by Lewis Allan).
"How About You?" (1941; music by Burton Lane, lyrics by Ralph Freed).
"How High the Moon" (1940; music by Morgan Lewis, lyrics by Nancy Hamilton).
"How Little We Know" (1944; music by Hoagy Carmichael, lyrics by Johnny Mercer).
"How Ya Gonna Keep 'em Down on the Farm?" (1942 [popular revival of a 1919 song]; music by Walter Donaldson, lyrics by Sam M. Lewis and Joe Young).
"A Hubba Hubba Hubba (Dig You Later)" (1945; music by Jimmy McHugh, lyrics by Harold Adamson).
"Huckleberry Duck" (1939; music by Raymond Scott, lyrics by Jack Lawrence).

"The Hut-Sut Song (A Swedish Serenade)" (1941 [popular revival of a 1939 song]; words and music by Jack Owens, Leo V. Killion, and Ted McMichael).
"I Cain't Say No" (1943; music by Richard Rodgers, lyrics by Oscar Hammerstein II).
"I Came Here to Talk for Joe" (1942; music by Sam H. Stept, lyrics by Lew Brown and Charles Tobias).
"I Can't Begin to Tell You" (1945; music by James V. Monaco, lyrics by Mack Gordon).
"I Concentrate on You" (1940; words and music by Cole Porter).
"I Could Write a Book" (1941; music by Richard Rodgers, lyrics by Lorenz Hart).
"I Couldn't Sleep a Wink Last Night" (1944; music by Jimmy McHugh, lyrics by Harold Adamson).
"I Didn't Know About You" (1944; music by Duke Ellington, lyrics by Bob Russell).
"I Didn't Know What Time It Was" (1939; music by Richard Rodgers, lyrics by Lorenz Hart).
"I Don't Want to Set the World on Fire" (1941; words and music by Eddie Seiler, Sol Marcus, Bennie Benjamin, and Eddie Durham).
"I Don't Want to Walk without You" (1942; music by Jule Styne, lyrics by Frank Loesser).
"I Fall in Love Too Easily" (1945; music by Jule Styne, lyrics by Sammy Cahn).
"I Feel the Draft Coming On" (1940; words and music by Bill Nettles).
"I Got It Bad (and That Ain't Good)" (1941; music by Duke Ellington, lyrics by Paul Francis Webster).
"I Had the Craziest Dream" (1942; music by Harry Warren, lyrics by Mack Gordon).
"I Hear a Rhapsody" (1940; words and music by Jack Baker, George Fragos, and Dick Gasparre).
"I Know Why" (1941; music by Harry Warren, lyrics by Mack Gordon).
"I Left My Heart at the Stage Door Canteen" (1942; words and music by Irving Berlin).
"I Love Coffee (I Love Tea)" (1943; words and music by Vick Knight).
"I Love You" (1944 [adapted from Edvard Grieg's "Ich Liebe Dich"]; words and music by Robert Wright and George Forrest).
"I Love You" (1944; words and music by Cole Porter).
"I Remember You" (1942; music by Victor Schertzinger, lyrics by Johnny Mercer).
"I Should Care" (1945; music by Paul Weston and Axel Stordahl, lyrics by Sammy Cahn).
"I Think of You" (1941 [adapted from Rachmaninov's *Piano Concerto No. 2*]; music by Don Marcotte and Jack Elliott).
"I Thought About You" (1939; music by James Van Heusen, lyrics by Johnny Mercer).
"I Wanna Be a Western Cowgirl" (1939; words and music by Gene Autry).
"I Wanna Zoot Suit" (1942; music by Ray Gilbert, lyrics by Bob O'Brien).
"I Was Here When You Left Me (I'll Be Here When You Get Back)" (1945; words and music by Sam H. Stept).
"I Wish That I Could Hide Inside This Letter" (1943; music by Nat Simon, lyrics by Charlie Tobias).

"I Won't Be Back in a Year, Little Darling" (1941; words and music by Bradley Kincaid and Buck Nation).

"I Yi Yi Yi Yi (I Like You Very Much)" (1941; music by Harry Warren, lyrics by Mack Gordon).

"Idaho" (1942; words and music by Jesse Stone).

"I'd Know You Anywhere" (1940; music by Jimmy McHugh, lyrics by Johnny Mercer).

"If I Didn't Care" (1939; words and music by Jack Lawrence).

"If I Loved You" (1945; music by Richard Rodgers, lyrics by Oscar Hammerstein II).

"If I Only Had a Brain" (1939; music by Harold Arlen, lyrics by E. Y. Harburg).

"If the Boys Come Home for Christmas, We'll Have a Happy New Year" (1943; music by J. Russel Robinson, lyrics by Arthur Terker and Harry Pyle).

"I'll Be Around" (1943; words and music by Alec Wilder).

"I'll Be Back in a Year, Little Darlin'" (1941; words and music by Ben Shelhamer Jr., Claude Heritier, and Russ Hull).

"I'll Be Home for Christmas" (1943; music by Walter Kent, lyrics by Kim Gannon and Buck Ram).

"I'll Be Seeing You" (1944 [popular revival of a 1938 song]; music by Sammy Fain, lyrics by Irving Kahal).

"I'll Be True While You're Gone" (1941; words and music by Gene Autry and Fred Rose).

"I'll Be Walkin' with My Honey (Soon, Soon, Soon)" (1945; music by Sam Medoff, lyrics by Buddy Kaye).

"I'll Be With You (in Apple Blossom Time)" (1941 [popular revival of a 1920 song]; music by Albert Von Tilzer, lyrics by Neville Fleeson).

"I'll Buy That Dream" (1945; music by Allie Wrubel, lyrics by Herb Magidson).

"I'll Forgive You But I Can't Forget" (1944; words and music by Joe Frank and Pee Wee King).

"I'll Get By (as Long as I Have You)" (1944 [popular revival of a 1928 song]; music by Fred Ahlert, lyrics by Roy Turk).

"I'll Keep the Love Light Burning" (1942; words and music by Harry Tobias, Nick Kenny, and Harold Leavey).

"I'll Never Smile Again" (1940; words and music by Ruth Lowe).

"I'll Pray for You" (1942; music by Arthur Altman, lyrics by Kim Gannon).

"I'll Remember April" (1942; music by Gene DePaul, lyrics by Don Raye and Pat Johnston).

"I'll Walk Alone" (1944; music by Jule Styne, lyrics by Sammy Cahn).

"Imagination" (1940; music by Jimmy Van Heusen, lyrics by Johnny Burke).

"I'm Beginning to See the Light" (1944; words and music by Duke Ellington, Johnny Hodges, Harry James, and Don George).

"I'm Coming Home" (1945; music by Lyn Murray, lyrics by Sylvia Golden).

"I'm Doing It for Defense" (1942; music by Harold Arlen, lyrics by Johnny Mercer).

"I'm Dreaming Tonight of My Blue Eyes" (1943; words and music by Don Marcotte and A. P. Carter). [Also called "I'm Thinking Tonight of My Blue Eyes"].

"I'm Glad I Waited for You" (1945; music by Jule Styne, lyrics by Sammy Cahn).

"I'm Glad There Is You" (1942; music by Jimmy Dorsey, lyrics by Paul Medeira).

"I'm Going to Get Lit Up (When the Lights Go On in London)" (1943; words and music by Hubert Gregg).

"I'm Gonna Love That Guy [Gal] (Like He's [She's] Never Been Loved Before)" (1945; words and music by Frances Ash).

"I'm Gonna Move to the Outskirts of Town" (1941; music by Casey Bill Weldon and Roy Jacobs, lyrics by Andy Razaf).

"I'm Just a Lucky So-and-So" (1945; music by Duke Ellington, lyrics by Mack David).

"I'm Making Believe" (1944; music by James V. Monaco, lyrics by Mack Gordon).

"I'm Old Fashioned" (1942; music by Jerome Kern, lyrics by Johnny Mercer).

"I'm Wastin' My Tears on You" (1944; words and music by Frank Harford and Tex Ritter).

"In a Mellotone" (1940; music by Duke Ellington, lyrics by Milt Gabler).

"In an Eighteenth-Century Drawing Room" (1939; music by Raymond Scott, lyrics by Jack Lawrence).

"In My Arms" (1943; words and music by Frank Loesser and Ted Grouya).

"In the Army Now" (1941; words and music by Big Bill Broonzy).

"In the Mood" (1939; music by Joe Garland, lyrics by Andy Razaf). *Although released in 1939, this composition ranked as the #1 song of 1940.*

"Indian Summer" (1940 [popular revival of a 1919 song]; music by Victor Herbert, lyrics by Al Dubin).

"(My Feet Are Killing Me, Marching in) The Infantry" (1943; words and music by Louis Jordan).

"Is You Is or Is You Ain't My Baby?" (1944; music by Louis Jordan, lyrics by Billy Austin).

"Isn't It Kind of Fun?" (1945; music by Richard Rodgers, lyrics by Oscar Hammerstein II).

"It Could Happen to You" (1944; music by Jimmy Van Heusen, lyrics by Johnny Burke).

"It Makes No Difference Now" (1939; words and music by Floyd Tillman and Jimmie Davis).

"It Might As Well Be Spring" (1945; music by Richard Rodgers, lyrics by Oscar Hammerstein II).

"It Never Entered My Mind" (1940; music by Richard Rodgers, lyrics by Lorenz Hart).

"It's a Grand Night for Singing" (1945; music by Richard Rodgers, lyrics by Oscar Hammerstein II).

"It's a Wonderful World" (1940; words and music by Jan Savitt, Leo Watson, and Harold Adamson).

"It's Always You" (1941; music by Jimmy Van Heusen, lyrics by Johnny Burke).

"It's Been a Long, Long Time" (1945; music by Jule Styne, lyrics by Sammy Cahn).

"It's Been So Long, Darling" (1945; words and music by Ernest Tubb).

"It's Just a Matter of Time" (1942; words and music by Carson Robison).

"It's Me Again" (1939; words and music by Sam Stept, Lew Brown, and Charles Tobias).

"It's So Peaceful in the Country" (1941; words and music by Alec Wilder).

"It's Taps for the Japs" (1942; words and music by James Cox).

"I've Changed My Penthouse for a Pup Tent" (1942; words and music by Bob Crawford).

"I've Got a Gal in Kalamazoo" (1942; music by Harry Warren, lyrics by Mack Gordon).

"I've Heard That Song Before" (1943; music by Jule Styne, lyrics by Sammy Cahn). *The #1 song for 1943.*

"Jack the Bear" (1940; music by Duke Ellington).

"Java Jive" (1941; music by Ben Oakland, lyrics by Milton Drake).

"Jealous Heart" (1944; words and music by Jenny Lou Carson).

"Jerry, My Soldier Boy" (1941; words and music by Cole Porter).

"Jersey Bounce" (1942, 1946; music by Bobby Plater, Tiny Bradshaw, Edward Johnson, and Robert B. Wright, lyrics by Buddy Feyne and Robert B. Wright).

"(I've Got Spurs That) Jingle Jangle Jingle" (1942; music by Joseph J. Lilley, lyrics by Frank Loesser).

"Johnny Doughboy Found a Rose in Ireland" (1942; music by Al Goodhart, lyrics by Kay Twomey).

"Johnny Zero" (1943; music by Vee Lawnhurst, lyrics by Mack David).

"Joltin' Joe DiMaggio" (1941; words and music by Ben Homer and Alan Courtney).

"Jukebox Saturday Night" (1942; music by Paul McGrane, lyrics by Al Stillman).

"(Hep! Hep!) The Jumpin' Jive" (1939; words and music by Cab Calloway, Frank Froeba, and Jack Palmer).

"June Is Bustin' Out All Over" (1945; music by Richard Rodgers, lyrics by Oscar Hammerstein II).

"Just a Blue Serge Suit" (1945; words and music by Irving Berlin).

"Just a Gigolo" (1939 [revival of a 1931 song]; music by Leonello Casucci, English lyrics by Irving Caesar).

"Just a Little Joint with a Jukebox" (1941; music by Hugh Martin, lyrics by Ralph Blane).

"Just a Prayer Away" (1944; music by David Kapp, lyrics by Charles Tobias).

"Just As Though You Were Here" (1942; music by John Brooks, lyrics by Eddie DeLange).

"Just Squeeze Me" (1940; music by Duke Ellington, lyrics by Lee Gaines).

"Keep That Oil A-Rollin'" (1942; words and music by Woody Guthrie).

"Keep 'Em Flying" (1942; music and lyrics by Bill Coleman).

"The King Who Couldn't Dance" (1945; music by Sammy Fain, lyrics by Arthur Freed).

"Kiss the Boys Goodbye" (1941; music by Victor Schertzinger, lyrics by Frank Loesser).

"Knock Me a Kiss" (1942; music by Mike Jackson, lyrics by Andy Razaf).

"Ko-Ko" (1940; music by Duke Ellington).

"Ko Ko" (1945; music by Charlie Parker [based on the chord changes of Ray Noble's 1938 swing classic "Cherokee" and not to be confused with Duke Ellington's 1940 composition bearing the same title]).

"The Lamp Is Low" (1939 [adapted from Maurice Ravel's "Pavane pour une Infante Defunte"]; music by Peter De Rose, lyrics by Mitchell Parish).

"Lamplighter's Serenade" (1942; music by Hoagy Carmichael, lyrics by Paul Francis Webster).

"The Lady in the Tutti Frutti Hat" (1943; music by Harry Warren, lyrics by Leo Robin).

"Last Page of *Mein Kampf*" (1945; words and music by Jack B. Johnstone and Will Livernash).

"The Last Time I Saw Paris" (1940; music by Jerome Kern, lyrics by Oscar Hammerstein II).

"Laura" (1945; music by David Raskin, lyrics by Johnny Mercer).

"Leave the Dishes in the Sink, Ma" (1945; words and music by Spike Jones, Milton Berle, and Gene Doyle).

"Left-Right" (1942; music by Jule Styne, lyrics by Sol Meyer).

"Let It Snow! Let It Snow! Let It Snow!" (1945; music by Jule Styne, lyrics by Sammy Cahn).

"Let Me Off Uptown" (1941; words and music by Earl Bostic, Roy Eldridge, and Redd Evans).

"Let's Bring New Glory to Old Glory" (1942; music by Harry Warren, lyrics by Mack Gordon).

"Let's Get Away from It All" (1941; music by Matt Dennis, lyrics by Tom Adair).

"Let's Get Lost" (1943; music by Jimmy McHugh, lyrics by Frank Loesser).

"Let's Put the Axe to the Axis" (1942; words and music by Paul Mann and Stephan Weiss).

"Let's Say Goodnight with a Dance" (1941; music by Sammy Fain, lyrics by Jack Yellin).

"Let's Take the Long Way Home" (1944; music by Harold Arlen, lyrics by Johnny Mercer).

"Life Was Pie for the Pioneer" (1940; music by Burton Lane, lyrics by E. Y. Harburg).

"Like Someone in Love" (1944; music by Jimmy Van Heusen, lyrics by Johnny Burke).

"Lili Marlene" (1943 [originally a 1915 poem by Hans Liep, set to music in 1937 by Norbert Schultze, lyrics adapted in 1943 by Tommie Connor]; American version by Mack David).

"Little Bo-Peep Has Lost Her Jeep" (1942; words and music by Spike Jones and band members).

"Little Bo Peep Has Lost Her Sheep" (1942; music by Frank DeVol, lyrics by Jerry Bowne).

"Little Brown Jug" (1939; arranged by Bill Finegan, based on a traditional 1869 melody).

"A Little Old Church in England" (1941; words and music by Irving Berlin).

"A Little on the Lonely Side" (1944; words and music by Dick Robertson, James Cavanaugh, and Frank Weldon).

"London Pride" (1941; words and music by Noel Coward).

"Lonely Town" (1945; music by Leonard Bernstein, lyrics by Betty Comden and Adolph Green).

"Long Ago (and Far Away)" (1944; music by Jerome Kern, lyrics by Ira Gershwin).

"Lovely Luana" (1942; words and music by Don Raye and Gene DePaul).

"A Lovely Way to Spend an Evening" (1944; music by Jimmy McHugh, lyrics by Harold Adamson).

"Lover Man (Oh, Where Can You Be?)" (1942; words and music by Jimmy Davis, Ram Ramirez, and Jimmy Sherman).

"Lydia, the Tattooed Lady" (1939; music by Harold Arlen, lyrics by E. Y. Harburg).

"Ma! I Miss Your Apple Pie" (1941; words and music by Carmen Lombardo and John Jacob Loeb).

"Main Stem" (1944; music by Duke Ellington).

"Mairzy Doats" (1944; words and music by Jerry Livingston, Milton Drake, and Al Hoffman).

"Maluna Malolo Mawaena" (1942; words and music by Mack Gordon and Harry Owens).

"Mandy Is Two" (1942; music by Fulton McGrath, lyrics by Johnny Mercer).

"The Man with the Mandolin" (1939; music by Frank Weldon, lyrics by James Cavanaugh and John Redmond).

"(We'll Be Singing Hallelujah) Marching Through Berlin" (1942; words and music by Bob Reed and Harry Miller).

"Maria Elena" (1941 [popular revival of a 1933 tune]; words and music by S. K. Russell, Lorenzo Barcalata, and William H. Heagney).

"Marie" (1940 [popular revival of a 1928 song]; words and music by Irving Berlin).

"Martyrs of the Air" (1942; words and music by K. R. Barnum).

"May I Never Love Again" (1941; words and music by Jack Erickson and Sano Marco).

"Maybe" (1940 [popular revival of a 1926 song]; music by George Gershwin, lyrics by Ira Gershwin).

"The Mem'ry of This Dance" (1942; words and music by Robert Effros and Ben Selvin).

"Memphis in June" (1945; music by Hoagy Carmichael, lyrics by Paul Francis Webster).

"Milkman, Keep Those Bottles Quiet" (1944; words and music by Don Raye and Gene DePaul).

"Minnie from Trinidad" (1941; words and music by Roger Edens).

"Mister Five by Five" (1942; music by Gene DePaul, lyrics by Don Raye).

"Mister Meadowlark" (1940; music by Walter Donaldson, lyrics by Johnny Mercer).

"Mommy, Please Stay Home With Me" (1943; words and music by Eddy Arnold, Wally Fowler, and Graydon J. Hall).

"Moon Love" (1939 [adapted from a theme in Tchaikovsky's *Fifth Symphony*]; music by Andre Kostelanetz, lyrics by Mack Davis and Mack David).

"Moonlight Becomes You" (1942; music by Jimmy Van Heusen, lyrics by Johnny Burke).

"Moonlight Cocktail" (1942; music by Lucky Roberts, lyrics by Kim Gannon). *The #2 song for 1942.*
"Moonlight in Vermont" (1944; music by Karl Suessedorf, lyrics by John Blackburn).
"Moonlight Serenade" (1939; music by Glenn Miller, lyrics by Mitchell Parish).
"The More I See You" (1945; music by Harry Warren, lyrics by Mack Gordon).
"Mother: 'Till I Come Home Again" (1943; music by Keith Crosby Brown, lyrics by Dorothy Bassett Brown).
"Mussolini's Letter to Hitler" (1942; words and music by Carson Robison).
"My Adobe Hacienda" (1941; words and music by Louise Massey and Lee Penny).
"My Devotion" (1942; words and music by Roc Hillman and Johnny Napton).
"My Dream of Tomorrow" (1943; music by Vic Mizzy and Irving Taylor, lyrics by Nat Burton).
"My Dreams Are Getting Better All the Time" (1945; music by Vic Mizzy, lyrics by Mann Curtis).
"My Guy's Come Back" (1945; music by Mel Powell, lyrics by Ray McKinley).
"My Heart Tells Me" (1944; music by Harry Warren, lyrics by Mack Gordon).
"My Prayer" (1940 [adapted from Georges Boulanger's "Avant de Mourir"]; words and music by Jimmy Kennedy).
"My Shining Hour" (1943; music by Harold Arlen, lyrics by Johnny Mercer).
"My Ship" (1941; music by Kurt Weill, lyrics by Ira Gershwin).
"My Sister and I" (1941; words and music by Joan Whitney, Hy Zaret, and Alex Kramer).
"My Wife's a W.A.A.C." (1943; music by Jule Styne, lyrics by Kim Gannon).
"Nancy (with the Laughing Face)" (1945; music by Jimmy Van Heusen, lyrics by Phil Silvers).
"The Nearness of You" (1940; music by Hoagy Carmichael, lyrics by Ned Washington).
"Never a Day Goes By" (1943; words and music by Walter Donaldson, Peter De Rose, and Mitchell Parish).
"Never No Lament" (1940; music by Duke Ellington [retitled "Don't Get Around Much Anymore" in 1943, with lyrics added by Bob Russell]).
New World A-Comin' (1943; music by Duke Ellington).
"New York, New York" (1945; music by Leonard Bernstein, lyrics by Betty Comden and Adolph Green).
"A Night in Tunisia" (1942; music by Dizzy Gillespie).
"Night Train to Memphis" (1942; words and music by Owen Bradley, Harry Beasley Smith, and Marvin Hughes).
"The Night We Called It a Day" (1942; music by Matt Dennis, lyrics by Tom Adair).
"A Nightingale Sang in Berkeley Square" (1940; music by Manning Sherwin, lyrics by Eric Maschwitz and Jack Strachey).
"1942 Turkey in the Straw" (1942; words and music by Carson Robison).
"No Letter Today" (1943; words and music by Frankie Brown).
"No Love, No Nothin'" (1943; music by Harry Warren, lyrics by Leo Robin).

"No Name Jive" (1940; music by Larry Wagner).
"Nobody's Heart" (1942; music by Richard Rodgers, lyrics by Lorenz Hart).
"Northwest Passage" (1945; music by Woody Herman, Chubby Jackson, and Ralph Burns).
"Nothing Can Replace a Man" (1944; words and music by Jerry Seelen and Lester Lee).
"Now's the Time" (1945; music by Charlie Parker).
"Obey Your Air Raid Warden" (1942; words and music by Les Bruness and John Morris).
"Off We Go (into the Wild Blue Yonder)" (1939; words and music by Robert Crawford). *The Army Air Corps song.*
"Oh! How I Hate to Get Up in the Morning" (1943 [popular revival of a 1918 song]; words and music by Irving Berlin).
"Oh Johnny, Oh Johnny, Oh!" (1940 [popular revival of a 1917 song]; music by Abe Olman, lyrics by Ed Rose).
"Oh! Look at Me Now" (1941; music by Joe Bushkin, lyrics by John DeVries).
"Oh, What a Beautiful Mornin'" (1943; music by Richard Rodgers, lyrics by Oscar Hammerstein II).
"Oh! What It Seemed to Be" (1945; words and music by Bennie Benjamin, George Weiss, and Frankie Carle).
"Oklahoma!" (1943; music by Richard Rodgers, lyrics by Oscar Hammerstein II).
"Oklahoma Hills" (1945; words and music by Woody Guthrie and Jack Guthrie).
"Old Glory" (1942; music by Harold Arlen, lyrics by Johnny Mercer).
"The Old Music Master" (1943; music by Hoagy Carmichael, lyrics by Johnny Mercer).
"Old Shep" (1941 [popular revival of a 1933 song]; words and music by Red Foley).
"On Behalf of the Visiting Firemen" (1940; music by Walter Donaldson, lyrics by Johnny Mercer).
"On Leave for Love" (1942; music and lyrics by Ann Ronell).
"On That Old Production Line" (1943; words and music by Harold Rome).
"On the Atchison, Topeka, and Santa Fe" (1945; music by Harry Warren, lyrics by Johnny Mercer).
"On the Swing Shift" (1942; music by Harold Arlen, lyrics by Johnny Mercer).
"One for My Baby (and One More for the Road)" (1943; music by Harold Arlen, lyrics by Johnny Mercer).
"One Letter Home" (1941; words and music by W. "Jazz" Gillum).
"One Little WAC" (1944; music by Eddie Dunstedter, lyrics by Frank Loesser).
"One Meat Ball" (1944 [a popular revision of an 1868 song called "The Lone Fish Ball"]; music by Lou Singer, lyrics by Hy Zaret).
"Only Forever" (1940; music by James V. Monaco, lyrics by Johnny Burke).
"Opus Number One" (1943; words and music by Sy Oliver).
"Ornithology" (1945; music by Charlie Parker and Benny Harris [based on the chord structure of the 1940 tune "How High the Moon"]).

"Our Love" (1939 [adapted from Tchaikovsky's *Romeo and Juliet*]; music by Larry Clinton, lyrics by Larry Clinton, Buddy Bernier, and Bob Emmerich).

"Out of This World" (1945; music by Harold Arlen, lyrics by Johnny Mercer).

"Over the Rainbow" (1939; music by Harold Arlen, lyrics by E. Y. Harburg). *The #2 song for 1939.*

"Paper Doll" (1943 [popular revival of a 1915 song]; words and music by Johnny S. Black). *The #2 song for 1943.*

"Pearl Harbor Blues" (1942; words and music by Joe "Doctor" Clayton).

"Peggy the Pin-Up Girl" (c. 1943; words and music by Ray Evans and John Jacob Loeb).

"Pennsylvania 6–5000" (1940; music by Jerry Gray, lyrics by Carl Sigman).

"People Will Say We're in Love" (1943; music by Richard Rodgers, lyrics by Oscar Hammerstein II).

"Perdido" (1942; words and music by Ervin Drake and Hans Lengsfelder).

"Perfidia" (1940; music by Alberto Dominguez, lyrics by Milton Leeds).

Perfume Suite (1944; music by Duke Ellington and Billy Strayhorn).

"Personality" (1945; music by Jimmy Van Heusen, lyrics by Johnny Burke).

"Pistol Packin' Mama" (1943; words and music by Al Dexter).

"Plain Talk" (1942; words and music by Carson Robison).

"Playmates" (1940; words and music by Saxie Dowell).

"Please Think of Me" (1942; words and music by Russ Morgan, Ted Murray, and Benny Davis).

"Plow Under" (1941; words and music by Lee Hays and Pete Seeger).

"Poinciana" (1943; music by Nat Simon, lyrics by Buddy Bernier).

"Polka Dots and Moonbeams" (1940; music by Jimmy Van Heusen, lyrics by Johnny Burke).

"Praise the Lord and Pass the Ammunition" (1942; words and music by Frank Loesser).

"Precious Jewel" (1943; words and music by Roy Acuff).

"The Prodigal Son" (1944; words and music by Floyd Jenkins).

"Put Another Chair at the Table" (1944; words and music by Richard Nelson and Cecil Gant).

"Put Your Dreams Away" (1942; words and music by Ruth Lowe, Stephan Weiss, and Paul Mann).

"Racing with the Moon" (1941; music by Johnny Watson, lyrics by Vaughn Monroe and Pauline Pope).

"Ration Blues" (1943; words and music by Louis Jordan, Collenane Clark, and Antonio Casey).

"Reconversion Blues" (1945; words and music by Steve Graham and Fleecie Moore).

"Remember Pearl Harbor" (1941; words and music by Frank Luther).

"Remember Pearl Harbor" (1942; music by Sammy Kaye and Don Reid, lyrics by Don Reid).

"Rhumboogie" (1940; music by Don Raye and Vic Schoen, lyrics by Hughie Prince).

"Ridin' Herd on a Cloud" (1943; words and music by Perry Botkin, Bernie Schwartz, and Jon Bushallow Jr.).

"The Road to Victory" (1943; words and music by Frank Loesser).

"Rocky Mountain Lullaby" (1942; words and music by Roy Rogers).

"Rodger Young" (1945; words and music by Frank Loesser).

"Roll On Columbia" (1941 [music adapted from Leadbellly's 1936 "Goodnight, Irene"]; lyrics by Woody Guthrie).

"Rose Ann of Charing Cross" (1942; music by Mabel Wayne, lyrics by Kermit Goell).

"Rosie the Riveter" (1944; words and music by Redd Evans and John Jacob Loeb).

"Round and Round Hitler's Grave" (1941 [music adapted by Woody Guthrie from the traditional "Old Joe Clark"]; lyrics by Woody Guthrie, Millard Lampell, and Pete Seeger).

"'Round Midnight" (1944; music by Thelonious Monk and Cootie Williams, lyrics by Bernie Hanighen).

"Rum and Coca-Cola" (1945 [adapted from Lionel Belasco's 1906 "L'Année Passée"]; music by Paul Baron and Jeri Sullavan, lyrics by Morey Amsterdam). *The #1 song for 1945.*

"Sailboat in the Sky" (1941; words and music by Steve Graham).

"Sailors of the Sky" (1943; words and music by Cole Porter).

"Sally, Don't You Grieve" (1944; words and music by Woody Guthrie).

"Salt Peanuts" (1944; music by Dizzy Gillespie and Kenny Clarke).

"Saludos Amigos" (1942; words and music by Ned Washington and Charles Wolcott).

"San Antonio Rose" or "Rose of San Antone" (1940 [popular revival of a 1938 song; sometimes retitled "New San Antonio Rose"]; words and music by Bob Wills).

"San Fernando Valley" (1944; words and music by Gordon Jenkins).

"Sand in My Shoes" (1941; music by Victor Schertzinger, lyrics by Frank Loesser).

"Saturday Night Is the Loneliest Night of the Week" (1944; music by Jule Styne, lyrics by Sammy Cahn).

"Savin' Myself for Bill" (1942; words and music by Vick Knight).

"Say a Prayer for the Boys Over There" (1943; music by Jimmy McHugh, lyrics by Herb Magidson).

"Scatterbrain" (1939; music by Frankie Masters, Kahn Keene, and Carl Bean, lyrics by Johnny Burke).

"Scrub Me, Mama, with a Boogie Beat" (1940; words and music by Don Raye).

"Seamen Three" (c. 1942; words and music by Woody Guthrie).

"Searching for a Soldier's Grave" (1945; words and music by Jim Anglin and Roy Acuff).

"Seems Like Old Times" (1945; words and music by Carmen Lombardo and John Jacob Loeb).

"Sentimental Journey" (1944; music by Ben Homer and Les Brown, lyrics by Bud Green). *Although released in 1944, this composition ranked as the #2 song of 1945.*

"Serenade in Blue" (1942; music by Harry Warren, lyrics by Mack Gordon).

"720 in the Books" (1940; words and music by Jan Savitt, Leo Watson, and Harold Adamson).

"Shame on You" (1945; words and music by Spade Cooley).

"Sharp As a Tack" (1942; music by Harold Arlen, lyrics by Johnny Mercer).

"She'll Always Remember" (1942; words and music by Eddie Pola and Johnny Marks).

"Shhh! It's a Military Secret" (1942; words and music by Alan Courtney, Earl Allvine, and Walter Bishop).

"Shine On, Victory Moon" (1944; words and music by Joseph George Gilbert).

"Shoo-Shoo, Baby" (1943; words and music by Phil Moore).

"Siam" (1942; words and music by Del Porter).

"Silver Dew on the Bluegrass Tonight" (1943; words and music by Ed Burt).

"Silver Wings in the Moonlight" (1943; words and music by Hughie Charles, Leo Towers, and Sonny Miller).

"Since He Traded His Zoot Suit for a Uniform" (1942; words and music by Carmen Lombardo and Pat Innisfree).

"Since You Went Away" (1944; music by Ted Grouya and Lou Forbes, lyrics by Kermit Goell).

"Sing and Fight for America!" (1943; music by Henry Kane, lyrics by Mark Minkus).

"Sing Me a Song of the Islands" (1943; words and music by Mack Gordon and Harry Owens).

"Sioux City Sue" (1945; music by Dick Thomas, lyrics by Ray Freedman).

"Six Lessons from Madame LaZonga" (1940; music by James V. Monaco, lyrics by Charles Newman).

"Sky Anchors" (1942; words and music by Fred Waring).

"Skylark" (1942; music by Hoagy Carmichael, lyrics by Johnny Mercer).

"Sleepy Lagoon" (1942 [popular revival of a 1930 song]; music by Eric Coates, lyrics by Jack Lawrence).

"A Slip of the Lip (Can Sink a Ship)" (1942; words and music by Luther Henderson and Mercer Ellington).

"Slipped Disc" (1945; music by Benny Goodman).

"The Smiths and Jones (the Kellys and Cohens)" (1943; words and music by Kay Twomey, Al Goodhart, and Irwin S. Joseph).

"Smoke on the Water" (1943; words and music by Zeke Clements and Earl Nunn).

"Snowfall" (1941; music by Claude Thornhill).

"So Long, It's Been Good to Know Yuh" (1940 [also known as "Dusty Old Dust"]; words and music by Woody Guthrie [rewritten in 1942 as a World War II song]).

"So Long Pal" (1944; words and music by Al Dexter).

"So Long, Sarah Jane" (1943; music by Sammy Fain, lyrics by Lew Brown and Ralph Freed).

"So Long 'Til Victory" (1943; words and music by Sam W. Braverman, Audrey Bradshaw, Loreen Bradshaw, and Sammy Watkins).

"So Tired" (1943; words and music by Russ Morgan and Jack Stuart).

"So You're the One" (1941; words and music by Alex Kramer, Joan Whitney, and Hy Zaret).
"A Soldier Dreams of You Tonight" (1942; music by Cliff Friend, lyrics by Al Dubin).
"Soldier's Last Letter" (1944; words and music by Ernest Tubb and Redd Stewart).
"Some Peaceful Evening (in Some Peaceful Town)" (1944; words and music by Dewey Bergman, Carley Mills, and Ann Roberts).
"Somebody Else Is Taking My Place" (1942 [popular revival of a 1937 song]; words and music by Russ Morgan, Dick Howard, and Bob Ellsworth).
"Somebody's Thinking of You Tonight" (1942; music by Teddy Powell and Ira Schuster, lyrics by Marty Symes).
"Someday, Somewhere (We'll Meet Again)" (1944; words and music by Joan Brooks, Jack Segal, and Dick Miles).
"Something to Remember You By" (1942 [popular revival of a 1930 song]; music by Howard Schwartz, lyrics by Howard Dietz).
"Somewhere in France with You" (1939; words and music by Michael Carr).
"Somewhere, Sometime (I'll Come Back to You)" (1942; music by George Duning, lyrics by Bill Hampton).
"The Son-of-a-Gun Who Picks on Uncle Sam" (1942; music by Burton Lane, lyrics by E. Y. Harburg).
"Song of Freedom" (1942; words and music by Irving Berlin).
"The Song of the Seebees" (1942; music by Peter De Rose, lyrics by Sam M. Lewis).
"Song of the Volga Boatmen" (1941; traditional Russian folk melody, adapted and arranged by Bill Finegan).
"South of the Border (Down Mexico Way)" (1939; words and music by Jimmy Kennedy and Michael Carr).
"Speak Low" (1943; music by Kurt Weill, lyrics by Ogden Nash).
"Spring Will Be a Little Late This Year" (1944; words and music by Frank Loesser).
"St. Louis Blues March" (1943 [arrangement based on 1914's "St. Louis Blues"]; words and music by W. C. Handy).
"Stairway to the Stars" (1935, 1939; music by Matty Malneck and Frank Signorelli, lyrics by Mitchell Parish).
"Stalin Wasn't Stallin' (A Modern Spiritual)" (1943; words and music by Willie Johnson).
"Stand Behind the Boys" (1943; music by Bob Carleton, lyrics by Helen Taylor Caton).
"A Star on the Service Flag for Me" (1942; words and music by Ralph Walker).
"Stars and Stripes on Iwo Jima Isle" (1945; words and music by Bob Wills and Clifton "Cactus Jack" Johnson).
"Stick to Your Knittin', Kitten" (1944; words and music by Vic Mizzy).
"Stop the War (the Cats Are Killin' Themselves)" (1941; words and music by Wingy Manone).
"The Story of Jitterbug Joe" (1942; words and music by Carson Robison).
"Straighten Up and Fly Right" (1944; music by Nat Cole, lyrics by Irving Mills).
"The Strange Death of John Doe" (1941; words and music by Millard Lampell).

"Strange Fruit" (1939; words and music by Lewis Allan [pseudonym of Abel Meeropol]).

"Strictly Instrumental" (1942; words and music by Bennie Benjamin, Sol Marcus, and Eddie Seiler).

"A String of Pearls" (1941; music by Jerry Gray, lyrics by Eddie De Lange).

"The Strip Polka" (1942; words and music by Johnny Mercer).

"The Sun Will Soon Be Setting on the Land of the Rising Sun" (1941; words and music by Sam Lerner).

"Sunday, Monday, or Always" (1943; music by Jimmy Van Heusen, lyrics by Johnny Burke).

"Sunrise Serenade" (1939; music by Frankie Carle, lyrics by Jack Lawrence).

"The Surrey with the Fringe on Top" (1943; music by Richard Rodgers, lyrics by Oscar Hammerstein II).

"Sweet Dreams, Sweetheart" (1944; music by M. K. Jerome, lyrics by Ted Koehler).

"Sweet Potato Piper" (1940; music by James V. Monaco, lyrics by Johnny Burke).

"Swinging on a Star" (1944; music by Jimmy Van Heusen, lyrics by Johnny Burke). *The #1 song for 1944.*

"Take Me Back to Tulsa" (1941; words and music by Bob Wills and Tommy Duncan).

"Take the 'A' Train" (1941; words and music by Billy Strayhorn).

"Taking a Chance on Love" (1940; music by Vernon Duke, lyrics by John Latouche).

"Talking Union" (1941; words and music by the Almanac Singers: Pete Seeger, Lee Hays, and Millard Lampell).

"Tangerine" (1942; music by Victor Schertzinger, lyrics by Johnny Mercer).

"Tara's Theme" (1939; music by Max Steiner).

"Tears on My Pillow" (1941; words and music by Fred Rose and Gene Autry).

"Ten Little Soldiers (on a Ten-Day Leave)" (1942; music by Abner Silver, lyrics by Sue and Kay Werner).

"Thank God for America" (1942; words and music by Madalyn Phillips).

"Thanks for a Lousy Evening" (1944; music by Philip Charig, lyrics by Dan Shapiro and Milton Pascal).

"Thanks, Mr. Roosevelt" (1941; words and music by Tommie Connor).

"That Old Black Magic" (1942; music by Harold Arlen, lyrics by Johnny Mercer).

"That Soldier of Mine" (1942; music by Matt Dennis, lyrics by Paul Herrick).

"That's What I Like About the South" (1944; words and music by Andy Razaf).

"That's What the Well-Dressed Man in Harlem Will Wear" (1942; words and music by Irving Berlin).

"That's What You Jolly Well Got" (1943; music by Arthur Schwartz, lyrics by Frank Loesser).

"There Are No Wings on a Foxhole" (1944; words and music by Irving Berlin).

"There Are Such Things" (1942; music by George W. Meyer, lyrics by Abel Baer and Stanley Adams).

"There Goes That Song Again" (1941; words and music by Allie Wrubel).

"There, I've Said It Again" (1945; words and music by Redd Evans and David Mann).

"There Must Be a Way" (1945; words and music by Sammy Gallop and David Saxon).
"There Will Never Be Another You" (1942; music by Harry Warren, lyrics by Mack Gordon).
"There Won't Be a Shortage of Love" (1941; words and music by Carmen Lombardo and John Jacob Loeb).
"There'll Always Be an England" (1939; words and music by Ross Parker and Hughie Charles).
"There'll Be Some Changes Made" (1941; words and music by Billy Higgins and W. Benton Overstreet).
"(We're Gonna Make Sure) There'll Never Be Another War!" (1942; words and music by Nelson Cogane, Ira Schuster, and Joseph Meyer).
"There's a Boy Coming Home on Leave" (1940; words and music by Jimmy Kennedy).
"There's a Cowboy Ridin' Thru The Sky" (1942; music by Michael Carr, lyrics by Michael Carr and Jack Popplewell).
"There's a Gold Star Hanging in the Window (Where a Blue Star Used to Be)" (1943; words and music by Floyd Wilkins, Ray Marcell, and Russ Hall).
"There's a Gold Star in Her Window" (1944; words and music by Tex Ritter and Frank Harford).
"There's a New Flag On Iwo Jima" (1945; music by Jimmy McHugh, lyrics by Harold Adamson).
"There's a New Moon over My Shoulder" (1943; words and music by Jimmie Davis, Lee Blastic, and E. Whelan).
"There's a Ship Rolling Home" (1943; words and music by Jimmy Kennedy).
"There's a Star Spangled Banner Waving Somewhere" (1942; words and music by Paul Roberts and Shelby Darnell [pseudonym of Bob Miller]).
"There's Nobody Home on the Range" (1944; music by Jacques Press, lyrics by Eddie Cherkose).
"These Foolish Things (Remind Me of You)" (1945; words and music by Harry Link, Holt Marvell, and Jack Strachey).
"They Can't Black-Out the Moon" (1939; words and music by Art Strauss, Bob Dale, and Sonny Miller).
"They Just Chopped Down the Old Apple Tree" (1943; music by Jimmy McHugh, lyrics by Harold Adamson).
"They Started Somethin' (but We're Gonna End It!)" (1942; words and music by Robert Sour, Don McCray, and Ernest Gold).
"They Took the Stars out of Heaven" (1944; words and music by Floyd Tillman).
"They're Either Too Young or Too Old" (1943; music by Arthur Schwartz, lyrics by Frank Loesser).
"Things Ain't What They Used to Be" (1942; music by Duke Ellington).
"This Is My Country" (1940; music by Al Jacobs, lyrics by Don Raye).
"This Is the Army, Mr. Jones" (1942; words and music by Irving Berlin).
"This Is Worth Fighting For" (1942; music by Sam H. Stept, lyrics by Eddie DeLange).
"This Land Is Your Land" (1940; words and music by Woody Guthrie).

"This Love of Mine" (1941; music by Sol Parker and Harry Sanicola, lyrics by Frank Sinatra).

"This Time the Dream's on Me" (1941; music by Harold Arlen, lyrics by Johnny Mercer).

"Three Little Fishes" (1939; words and music by Saxie Dowell).

"Three Little Sisters" (1942; words and music by Irving Taylor and Vic Mizzy).

"Tico-Tico" (1944; music by Zequinha Abreu, lyrics by Ervin Drake and Aloysio Oliviera).

"(Lights Out) 'Til Reveille" (1941; music by Stanley Cowan, lyrics by Bobby Worth).

"Till the End of Time" (1945 [adapted from Chopin's *Polonaise*]; music by Buddy Kaye and Ted Mossman).

"Till the Lights of London Shine Again" (1940; music by Edward Pola, lyrics by Thomas Connor).

"Till Then" (1944; words and music by Eddie Seiler, Sol Marcus, and Guy Wood).

"Tippin' In" (1945; music by Bobby Smith).

"Today Will Be Yesterday Tomorrow" (1944; music by Philip Charig, lyrics by Dan Shapiro and Milton Pascal).

"Tomorrow (When You Are Gone)" (1943; words and music by Margaret Kennedy and Erich Wolfgang Korngold).

"Tomorrow Never Comes" (1945; words and music by Ernest Tubb and Johnny Bond).

"Tonight We Love" (1941 [adapted from Tchaikovsky's *Piano Concerto in B-Flat*]; music by Ray Austin and Freddy Martin, lyrics by Bobby Worth).

"Too Late (Too Late Too Late Too Late)" (1941; words and music by Jimmy Wakely, Todd Cerney, and Nancy Montgomery).

"Too-Ra-Loo-Ra-Rai" (1944 [popular revival of a 1914 song]; words and music by J. R. Shannon).

"Trav'lin' Light" (1943; music by Jimmy Mundy and Trummy Young, lyrics by Johnny Mercer).

"The Trolley Song" (1944; music by Hugh Martin, lyrics by Ralph Blane).

"Truck Driver's Blues" (1940; words and music by Ted Daffan).

"Try Me One More Time" (1941; words and music by Ernest Tubb).

"Tumbling Tumbleweeds" (1944 [popular revival of a 1934 song originally called "Tumbling Leaves"]; words and music by Bob Nolan).

"Tuxedo Junction" (1940; music by Erskine Hawkins, Julian Dash, and William Johnson, lyrics by Buddy Feyne).

"$21 a Day—Once a Month" (1941; music by Felix Bernard, lyrics by Raymond Klages).

"Twilight Time" (1945; words and music by Buck Ram, Al Nevins, Morty Nevins, and Artie Dunn).

"Undecided" (1939; music by Charlie Shavers, lyrics by Sid Robin).

"The Union Maid" (1940; words and music by Woody Guthrie).

"The Very Thought of You" (1944 [popular revival of a 1934 song]; words and music by Ray Noble).

"Vict'ry Polka" (1943; music by Jule Styne, lyrics by Sammy Cahn).

"Vingo Jingo" (1942; music and lyrics by Don Raye and Gene DePaul).

"Violets for Your Furs" (1941; music by Matt Dennis, lyrics by Tom Adair).
"Wabash Cannonball" (1940; words and music by A. P. Carter).
"Wait for Me, Mary" (1943; music by Nat Simon and Charles Tobias, lyrics by Harry Tobias).
"Wait Till the Girls Get in the Army, Boys" (1942; words and music by Al Goodhart and Kay Twomey).
"Wait Till You See Her" (1942; music by Richard Rodgers, lyrics by Lorenz Hart).
"The Waiter and the Porter and the Upstairs Maid" (1941; words and music by Johnny Mercer).
"Waitin' for the Train to Come In" (1945; words and music by Sunny Skylar and Martin Block).
"Walkin' by the River" (1941; words and music by Una Mae Carlisle and Robert Sour).
"Walkin' with My Honey (Soon, Soon, Soon)" (1945; words and music by Sunny Skylar and Martin Block).
"Walking the Floor over You" (1941; words and music by Ernest Tubb).
"Waltzing Matilda" (1941 [traditional Australian folk tune]; words and music adapted by Marie Cowan, A. B. Paterson, and Orrie Lee).
"Wartime Blues" (1940; words and music by W. "Jazz" Gillum).
"The Warsaw Concerto" (1941; music by Richard Addinsell).
"Way Back in 1939 A.D." (1939; music by Hoagy Carmichael, lyrics by Johnny Mercer).
"We Did It Before and We Can Do It Again" (1941; words and music by Cliff Friend and Charles Tobias).
"We Must All Stick Together" (1939; words and music by Ralph Butler and Raymond Wallace).
"We Mustn't Say Goodbye" (1943; music by James V. Monaco, lyrics by Al Dubin).
"We Three (My Echo, My Shadow, and Me)" (1940; words and music by Sammy Mysels, Dick Robertson, and Nelson Cogane).
"Welcome Home" (1944; words and music by Tommie Tucker, Paul Cunningham, and Leonard Whitcup).
"Well, Did You Evah!" (1939; words and music by Cole Porter).
"We'll Be Together Again" (1945; music by Carl Fischer, lyrics by Frankie Laine).
"We'll Go Back to Faithful Dobbin (Just to Help the U.S.A.)" (1942; words and music by Mabel Leavene, Betty Sue Patrick, and Gene Fray).
"We'll Knock the Japs Right into the Laps of the Nazis" (1941; words and music by Ned Washington and Lew Pollock).
"We'll Meet Again" (1942 [popular revival of a 1939 song]; music by Ross Parker, lyrics by Hughie Charles).
"We'll Swing It Through" (1942; music by Lee Wainer, lyrics by John Lund).
"We're Gonna Hang Out Our Washing on the Siegfried Line" (1939; words and music by Jimmy Kennedy and Michael Carr).
"We're Gonna Have to Slap the Dirty Little Jap (and Uncle Sam's the Guy Who Can Do It)" (1942; words and music by Bob Miller).
"We're Off to See the Wizard" (1939; music by Harold Arlen, lyrics by E. Y. Harburg).

"We've Got to Do a Job on the Japs, Baby" (1942; words and music by Edgar Leslie, Abel Baer, and George W. Meyer).

"What a Diff'rence a Day Made" (1944; words and music by Stanley Adams and Maria Grever).

"What Am I Here For?" (1942; music by Duke Ellington, lyrics by Frank Paul Lovecchio [also known as Frankie Laine]).

"What Are You Doing the Rest of Your Life?" (1944; music by Burton Lane, lyrics by Ted Koehler).

"What Do You Do in the Infantry?" (1943; words and music by Frank Loesser).

"Whatcha Know Joe?" (1943; words and music by James Young).

"What's New?" (1939; words and music by Bob Haggart and Joe Burke).

"What's Your Number?" (1940; music by Buck Clayton).

"When Johnny Comes Marching Home" (1942 [updated revision of an 1863 Civil War song, "Johnny, Fill Up the Bowl"]; new words and arrangement by Harold Dickinson, Bill Conway, and Bill Finegan).

"When My Blue Moon Turns to Gold Again" (1941; words and music by Wiley Walker and Gene Sullivan).

"When That Man Is Dead and Gone" (1941; words and music by Irving Berlin).

"When the Boys Come Home" (1944; music by Harold Arlen, lyrics by E. Y. Harburg).

"When the Lights Go On Again (All Over the World)" (1943; words and music by Eddie Seiler, Sol Marcus, and Bennie Benjamin).

"When the Swallows Come Back to Capistrano" (1940; words and music by Leon Rene).

"When They Sound the Last 'All Clear'" (1941; words and music by Hugh Charles and Louis Elton).

"When You Put on That Old Blue Suit Again" (1944; words and music by Robert Sour, Floria West, and Gordon Andrews).

"When You Wish Upon a Star" (1940; music by Leigh Harline, lyrics by Ned Washington).

"While We're Young" (1943; music by Alec Wilder and Marty Palitz, lyrics by Bill Engvick).

"White Christmas" (1942; words and music by Irving Berlin). *The #1 song for 1942.*

"(There'll Be Blue Birds Over) The White Cliffs of Dover" (1941; music by Walter Kent, lyrics by Nat Burton).

"White Cross On Okinawa" (1945; words and music by Bob Wills, Clifton "Cactus Jack" Johnson, and Cliff Sundin).

"Who Can I Turn To?" (1942; music by Alec Wilder, lyrics by Bill Engvick).

"Who Do You Think We Are?" (1943; music by Henry Kane, lyrics by Mark Minkus).

"Why Don't You Do Right?" (1943 [popular revival of a 1939 song]; words and music by Joe McCoy).

"Wild Root" (1945; music by Woody Herman and Neal Hefti).

"Will You Still Be Mine?" (1941; music by Matt Dennis, lyrics by Tom Adair).

"Win the War Blues" (1944; words and music by Sonny Boy Williamson).

"Wings to Victory" (1941; music by Rob Lehigh, lyrics by Dick Kirschbaum).
"Wish You Were Waiting for Me" (1944; words and music by Bob Russell and David Saxon).
"Wishing (Will Make It So)" (1939; words and music by Buddy Desylva).
"Wonder When My Baby's Coming Home" (1942; music by Arthur Kent, lyrics by Kermit Goell).
"Woodchopper's Ball" (1939; music by Woody Herman and Joe Bishop).
"The Woodpecker Song" (1940; music by Eldo di Lazzaro, lyrics by C. Bruno [English version by Harold Adamson]).
"The World Is Waiting for the Sunrise" (1943 [popular revival of a 1919 song]; music by Ernest Seitz, lyrics by Gene Lockhart).
"The World Will Sing Again" (1942; words and music by Harry Ralton and Ned Miller).
"Worried Mind" (1941; words and music by Ted Daffan and Jimmie Davis).
"Yankee Doodle Ain't Doodlin' Now" (1942; words and music by Pearl Fein).
"Yes Indeed!" (1941; music by Sy Oliver).
"You Always Hurt the One You Love" (1944 [parody adaptation]; words and music by Allan Roberts and Doris Fisher).
"You Are My Sunshine" (1940; words and music by Jimmie Davis and Charles Mitchell).
"You Belong to My Heart" (1941; music by Dora Luz and Augustin Lara, English lyrics by Ray Gilbert).
"You Buy 'em, We'll Fly 'em" (1943; words and music by Wilfred H. Baetz).
"You Can't Put Catsup on the Moon" (1940; music by Sammy Fain, lyrics by Irving Kahal).
"You Can't Say No to a Soldier" (1942; music by Harry Warren, lyrics by Mack Gordon).
"You Can't Win This War through Love" (1942; music by Henry Kane, lyrics by Mark Minkus).
"You Don't Know What Love Is" (1941; music by Gene De Paul, lyrics by Don Raye).
"You Made Me Love You (I Didn't Want to Do It)" (1941 [popular revival of a 1913 song]; music by James V. Monaco, lyrics by Joe McCarthy).
"You Send Me" (1943; music by Jimmy McHugh, lyrics by Harold Adamson).
"You Stepped Out of a Dream" (1941; music by Nacio Herb Brown, lyrics by Gus Kahn).
"You Two-Timed Me One Time Too Often" (1945; words and music by Jenny Lou Carson).
"You Were Never Lovelier" (1942; music by Jerome Kern, lyrics by Johnny Mercer).
"You Won't Be Satisfied (Until You Break My Heart)" (1945; words and music by Freddy James and Larry Stock).
"You'd Be So Nice to Come Home To" (1943; words and music by Cole Porter).
"You'll Never Know" (1943; music by Harry Warren, lyrics by Mack Gordon).
"You'll Never Walk Alone" (1945; music by Richard Rodgers, lyrics by Oscar Hammerstein II).

"You're a Sap, Mr. Jap" (1941; words and music by James Cavanaugh, John Redmond, and Nat Simon).

"You're Easy to Dance With" (1942; words and music by Irving Berlin).

"You're My Little Pin-Up Girl" (1944; music by James V. Monaco, lyrics by Mack Gordon).

"You're Nobody 'Til Somebody Loves You" (1944; words and music by Russ Morgan, Larry Stock, and James Cavanaugh).

"You're Perf" (1944; music by Philip Charig, lyrics by Dan Shapiro and Milton Pascal).

"You're So Sweet to Remember" (1945; music by David Rose, lyrics by Leo Robin).

"Yours (Quiereme Mucho)" (1941 [popular revival of a 1931 song]; music by Gonzalo Roig, lyrics by Augustin Rodriguez, English adaptation by Jack Sherr).

"You've Changed" (1941; music by Carl Fischer, lyrics by Bill Carey).

Notes

CHAPTER 1

1. A general history of the Almanac Singers can be found in R. Serge Denisoff, *Great Day Coming: Folk Music and the American Left* (Baltimore: Penguin Books, 1971), 70–98.

2. A remarkably thorough listing and discussion of hundreds of songs relating to World War II serve as the foundation of John Bush Jones's *The Songs That Fought the War: Popular Music and the Home Front, 1939–1945* (Waltham, MA: Brandeis University Press, 2006).

3. Further details on the tensions in the music industry as a result of efforts on the part of agencies like the NWMC and the MWC to find the ideal war song can be found in Kathleen E. R. Smith's *God Bless America: Tin Pan Alley Goes to War* (Lexington: University Press of Kentucky, 2003), esp. 81–83 and 114–44.

4. Technically not a war song at all, but one that touched the hearts of military personnel and civilians alike, "White Christmas" became one of the most popular tunes in the history of American music. See chapter 2, "Popular Hits and Standards," for further discussion of this composition, along with a host of other non–war-related music.

5. Philip Furia, *Skylark: The Life and Times of Johnny Mercer* (New York: St. Martin's Press, 2003), 105–67.

6. Smith, *God Bless America*, 87–88, 137, 167.

7. Jones, *The Songs that Fought the War*, 74–83.

CHAPTER 2

1. Specific information on many of the war-related and mainstream songs of the 1939–1945 era can be found in John Bush Jones, *The Songs That Fought the War: Popular Music and the Home Front, 1939–1945* (Waltham, MA: Brandeis University Press, 2006), and Kathleen E. R. Smith, *God Bless America: Tin Pan Alley Goes to War* (Lexington: University Press of Kentucky, 2003). In addition, Roger D. Kinkle, *The Complete Encyclopedia of Popular Music and Jazz, 1900–1950,* 4 vols. (Westport, CT: Arlington House, 1974), and Roger Lax and Frederick Smith, *The Great Song Thesaurus,* 2nd ed. (New York: Oxford University Press, 1989), provide comprehensive listings that include most of the songs mentioned in this text.

2. Joel Whitburn's *A Century of Pop Music* (Menomonee Falls, WI: Record Research, 1999) provides data, taken from *Billboard* magazine listings, on how most of the songs in this chapter fared during the war years.

3. The content of movie soundtracks, usually including both songwriters and composers, along with performers, can be accessed through the Internet Movie Database (http://imdb.com/), using either title or names in the search instructions.

4. A useful biography of Mercer is Philip Furia, *Skylark: The Life and Times of Johnny Mercer* (New York: St. Martin's Press, 2003).

5. Jody Rosen, *"White Christmas": The Story of an American Song* (New York: Charles Scribner's Sons, 2002), provides a fact-filled history about Berlin's composition.

CHAPTER 3

1. A good stating point for general information about the swing phenomenon is Scott Yanow's *Swing: Great Musicians, Influential Groups* (San Francisco: Miller Freeman, 2000). George T. Simon's *The Big Bands* (New York: Macmillan, 1967) contains countless anecdotes about the era, whereas Leo Walker's well-named *Big Band Almanac,* rev. ed. (New York: Da Capo Press, 1989) provides brief details on most of the orchestras that played swing.

2. Two useful Web sites for information on band vocalists are http://www.parabrisas.com/index.php and http://www.nfo.net/cal/tr5.html.

3. Sherrie Tucker's *Swing Shift: "All-Girl" Bands of the 1940s* (Durham, NC: Duke University Press, 2000) provides a wealth of details about the many women's orchestras that played during the war years. Additional information can be found at http://cornslaw.net/allgirlorchestra/index.html.

4. See Ted Gioia, *The History of Jazz* (New York: Oxford University Press, 1997), 277–92; Gary Giddens, *Visions of Jazz: The First Century* (New York: Oxford University Press, 1998), 59–65, 130–37; and Richard Hadlock, "The New Orleans Revival," in *The Oxford Companion to Jazz,* ed. Bill Kirchner (New York: Oxford University Press, 2000), 305–15, for more on the revival of traditional jazz.

5. A good overview of Ellington's life and work is given in Derek Jewell's *Duke: A Portrait of Duke Ellington* (New York: W. W. Norton, 1977).

6. Scott Yanow, in *Bebop* (San Francisco: Miller Freeman, 2000), supplies a wealth of information about this style.

7. Piero Scaruffi provides a good overview of rhythm 'n' blues in "A Brief History of Rhythm and Blues," http://www.scaruffi.com/history/rb.html.

CHAPTER 4

1. One of the best sources for a history of the business side of American music is Russell Sanjek's, *Pennies from Heaven: The American Popular Music Business in the Twentieth Century* (New York: Da Capo Press, 1996).

2. Ibid., 159–211, 253–74.

3. Ibid., 215–30.

4. Two useful electronic sites for jukebox history are http://www.tomszone.com and http://www.nationaljukebox.com.

5. See Chuck Miller, "Victory Music: The Story of the V-Disc Record Label," http://members.aol.com/boardwalk7/vdisc/vdisc.html, and Richard Sears, *V-Discs: A History and a Discography* (Westport, CT: Greenwood Press, 1980).

CHAPTER 5

1. Christopher H. Sterling and John M. Kitross, in *Stay Tuned: A Concise History of American Broadcasting* (Belmont, CA: Wadsworth, 1990), provide extensive statistics on media growth in the United States.

2. Detailed lists of conductors and soloists, along with brief broadcasting histories, can be found alphabetically in John Dunning, *On the Air: The Encyclopedia of Old-Time Radio* (New York: Oxford University Press, 1998).

3. Playlists for many of Waring's wartime shows can be found at the following Web site: http://www.libraries.psu.edu/waring/songlists.htm.

4. Space does not permit a complete listing of band and radio shows. Much more thorough coverage of this subject can be found in Jim Cox, *Music Radio: The Great Performers and Programs of the 1920s through Early 1960s* (Jefferson, NC: McFarland, 2005), 16–51, 206–27.

5. Richard K. Hayes, *Kate Smith: A Biography, with a Discography, Filmography, and List of Stage Appearances* (Jefferson, NC: McFarland, 1995).

CHAPTER 6

1. These figures, obtainable through a variety of reference sources, were primarily compiled from Roger D. Kinkle, *The Complete Encyclopedia of Popular Music and Jazz, 1900–1950,* 4 vols. (Westport, CT: Arlington House, 1974), and Richard Lewine and Alfred Simon, *Songs of the American Theater* (New York: Dodd, Mead, 1973).

2. Considerably more detail on the Crosby-Hope Road Pictures can be found in Gary Giddins, *Bing Crosby, A Pocketful of Dreams: The Early Years, 1903–1940* (Boston: Little, Brown, 2001), esp. 563–92.

3. For more on Berlin's long and brilliant career, see Robert Kimball and Linda Emmet, eds., *The Complete Lyrics of Irving Berlin* (New York: Alfred A. Knopf, 2001).

4. A frame-by-frame analysis of *Casablanca* can be found in Richard J. Anobile, ed., *Michael Curtiz's Casablanca* (New York: Flare Books, 1974).

5. Two overviews of the movies of the 1940s, including musicals, are Allen L. Woll, *The Hollywood Musical Goes to War* (Chicago: Nelson-Hall, 1983), and Colin Shindler, *Hollywood Goes to War: Films and American Society, 1939–1952* (Boston: Routledge Kegan Paul, 1979).

CHAPTER 7

1. A good overview of the history of country music and its many formats that includes statistics from other sources and discussion of barn dance shows is found in Jeffrey J. Lange, *Smile When You Call Me a Hillbilly: Country Music's Struggle for Respectability, 1939–1954* (Athens: University of Georgia Press, 2004), 19–110, 130–33; and Bill C. Malone, *Country Music, U.S.A.* (Austin: University of Texas Press, 1968), 41, 68–94, 171–81, 194, 279–300, 305–34.

2. A comprehensive account of country music songs relating to World War II and their level of popularity is found in Charles K. Wolfe and James E. Akenson, *Country Music Goes to War* (Lexington: University Press of Kentucky, 2005), 33–99; a detailed listing of songs, songwriters and lyricists, performers, and copyright dates, along with discographies and biographies for various musical styles, can be found at http://www.lpdiscography.com and http://www.allmusic.com.

3. Paul D. Casdorph, *Let the Good Times Roll: Life at Home in America during World War II* (New York: Verso, 1995), 152.

4. "Bull Market in Corn," *Time*, October 4, 1943, http://www.time.com/time/printout/0,8816,932168,00.html.

5. Quoted in Peggy Langrall, "Appalachian Folk Music: From Foothills to Footnotes," *Music Educators Journal* 72 (March 1986): 39.

6. Adam Komorowski, booklet accompanying *Take Me Back to Tulsa: Bob Wills & His Texas Playboys*, 4 CDs, Proper Records P1225-P1228, 2006.

7. Woody Guthrie, "This Land Is Your Land," http://www.memory.loc.gov/cocoon/ihas/loc.natlib.ihas.200000022/default.html.

CHAPTER 8

1. Charles C. Alexander, *Nationalism in American Thought, 1930–1945* (Chicago: Rand McNally, 1973), 208–11.

2. An overview of the accomplishments of the most significant American classical music composers during the 1930s and the World War II era can be found in John Warthen Struble, *The History of American Classical Music: MacDowell through Minimalism* (New York: Facts on File, 1995), 152–65, 180–255.

3. Joseph Horowitz, *Classical Music in America: A History of Its Rise and Fall* (New York: W. W. Norton, 2005), 433–48, provides a good history of American classical music that includes information about the composers discussed in this chapter.

4. An excellent compilation that supplies full descriptive details and statistical data about radio programming is John Dunning, *On the Air: The Encyclopedia of Old-Time Radio* (New York: Oxford University Press, 1998), 174–80, 535, 546, 623–24, 705, as well as many other places in this wide-ranging work.

Selected Bibliography

PRINT SOURCES

Alexander, Charles C. *Nationalism in American Thought, 1930–1945.* Chicago: Rand McNally, 1973.

Allen, Bob, ed. *The Blackwell Guide to Recorded Country Music.* Oxford, UK: Blackwell, 1994.

Ancelet, Barry Jean, Jay D. Edwards, and Glen Pitre. *Cajun Country.* Jackson: University Press of Mississippi, 1991.

Anobile, Richard J., ed. *Michael Curtiz's Casablanca.* New York: Flare Books, 1974.

Awmiller, Craig. *This House on Fire: The Story of the Blues.* New York: Franklin Watts, 1996.

Barfield, Ray. *Listening to Radio, 1920–1950.* Westport, CT: Praeger, 1996.

Barnouw, Erik. *A History of Broadcasting in the United States.* Vol. 1, *A Tower in Babel.* New York: Oxford University Press, 1966.

———. *A History of Broadcasting in the United States.* Vol. 2, *The Golden Web.* New York: Oxford University Press, 1968.

Bastin, Bruce. *Red River Blues: The Blues Tradition in the Southeast.* Urbana: University of Illinois Press, 1986.

Bergreen, Lawrence. *As Thousands Cheer: The Life of Irving Berlin.* New York: Viking-Penguin, 1990.

Big Bands Database Plus. http://nfo.net/index.html.

Biracree, Tom. *The Country Music Almanac.* New York: Prentice Hall, 1993.

Block, Geoffrey. *Enchanted Evenings: The Broadway Musical from Show Boat to Sondheim.* New York: Oxford University Press, 1997.

Bloom, Ken. *The American Songbook: The Singers, the Songwriters, and the Songs.* New York: Black Dog and Leventhal, 2005.

Bogdanov, Vladimir, Chris Woodstra, and Stephen Thomas Erlewine, eds. *All-Music Guide to Country.* San Francisco, CA: Backbeat Books, 2003.

Bordman, Gerald. *Jerome Kern: His Life and Music.* New York: Oxford University Press, 1980.

Boyd, Jean A. "Western Swing: Working-Class Southwestern Jazz of the 1930s and 1940s." In *Perspectives on American Music, 1900–1950,* edited by Michael Saffle, 193–214. New York: Garland, 2000.

———. *"We're the Light Crust Doughboys from Burris Mill": An Oral History.* Austin: University of Texas Press, 2003.

"Cajun Music." http://www.cajunculture.com.

Casdorph, Paul D. *Let the Good Times Roll: Life at Home in America during World War II.* New York: Verso, 1995.

Chanin, Michael. *Repeated Takes: A Short History of Recording and Its Effects on Music.* New York: Verso, 1995.

Chipman, John H. *Index to Top-Hit Tunes, 1900–1950.* Boston: Bruce Humphries, 1962.

Clarke, Donald. *The Rise and Fall of Popular Music.* New York: St. Martin's Press, 1995.

Cohen, Norm. *Folk Music: A Regional Exploration.* Westport, CT: Greenwood Press, 2005.

Cohen, Stan. *V for Victory: America's Home Front during World War II.* Missoula, MT: Pictorial Histories, 1991.

Composers and Lyricists Database. http://www.nfo.net/cal/tr1.html.

The Comprehensive Country Music Encyclopedia. New York: Random House, 1994.

Cooke, Alistar. *The American Home Front, 1941–1942.* Boston: Atlantic Monthly Press, 2006.

Cornslaw Industries. "Phil Spitalny's All Girl Orchestra." http://cornslaw.net/allgirlorchestra/index.html.

Cox, Jim. *Music Radio: The Great Performers and Programs of the 1920s through Early 1960s.* Jefferson, NC: McFarland, 2005.

Crawford, Richard. *America's Musical Life.* New York: W. W. Norton, 2001.

Crowther, Bruce, and Mike Pinfold. *Singing Jazz: The Singers and Their Styles.* San Francisco: Miller Freeman Books, 1997.

Csida, Joseph, and June Bundy Csida. *American Entertainment: A Unique History of Popular Show Business.* New York: Watson-Guptill, 1978.

Dahl, Linda. *Stormy Weather: The Music and Lives of a Century of Jazzwomen.* New York: Pantheon Books, 1984.

Dale, Rodney. *The World of Jazz.* New York: Elsevier-Dutton, 1980.

Dance, Stanley. *The World of Duke Ellington.* New York: Charles Scribner's Sons, 1970.

———. *The World of Count Basie.* New York: Charles Scribner's Sons, 1980.

Davis, Francis. *The History of the Blues.* New York: Hyperion, 1995.

Davis, Ronald L. *A History of Music in American Life.* Vol. 3, *The Modern Era, 1920–Present.* Malabar, FL: Robert Krieger, 1981.

Dawidoff, Nicholas. *In the Country of Country: People and Places in American Music.* New York: Pantheon Books, 1997.

DeLong, Thomas A. *The Mighty Music Box: The Golden Age of Musical Radio.* Los Angeles: Amber Crest Books, 1980.

Denisoff, R. Serge. *Great Day Coming: Folk Music and the American Left.* Baltimore: Penguin Books, 1971.

Denisoff, R. Serge, and Richard A. Peterson, eds. *The Sounds of Social Change.* New York: Rand McNally, 1972.

Dick, Bernard F. *The Star-Spangled Screen: The American World War II Film.* Lexington: University Press of Kentucky, 1985.

Doherty, Thomas. *Projections of War: Hollywood, American Culture, and World War II.* New York: Columbia University Press, 1993.

Doss, Erika, ed. *Looking at LIFE Magazine.* Washington, DC: Smithsonian Institution Press, 2001.

Dryer, Sherman H. *Radio in Wartime.* New York: Greenberg, 1942.

Dunkleberger, A. C. *King of Country Music: The Life Story of Roy Acuff.* Nashville, TN: Williams, 1971.

Dunning, John. *Tune in Yesterday: The Ultimate Encyclopedia of Old-Time Radio, 1925–1976.* Englewood Cliffs, NJ: Prentice Hall, 1976.

———. *On the Air: The Encyclopedia of Old-Time Radio.* New York: Oxford University Press, 1998.

Eells, George. *The Life That Late He Led: A Biography of Cole Porter.* New York: G. P. Putnam's Sons, 1967.

Epstein, Daniel Mark. *Nat King Cole.* New York: Farrar, Straus and Giroux, 1999.

Ewen, David. *A Journey to Greatness: The Life and Music of George Gershwin.* New York: Henry Holt, 1956.

———. *Panorama of American Popular Music.* Englewood Cliffs, NJ: Prentice Hall, 1957.

———. *The Life and Death of Tin Pan Alley: The Golden Age of American Popular Music.* New York: Funk and Wagnalls, 1964.

———. *Great Men of American Popular Song.* Englewood Cliffs, NJ: Prentice Hall, 1970.

———. *All the Years of American Popular Music.* Englewood Cliffs, NJ: Prentice Hall, 1977.

Feather, Leonard. *The New Edition of the Encyclopedia of Jazz.* New York: Bonanza Books, 1962.

Feather, Leonard, and Ira Gitler. *The Biographical Encyclopedia of Jazz.* New York: Oxford University Press, 1999.

Ferris, William, and Mary L. Hart, eds. *Folk Music and Modern Sound.* Jackson: University Press of Mississippi, 1982.

Forte, Allen. *Listening to Classic American Popular Songs.* New Haven, CT: Yale University Press, 2001.

Freedland, Michael. *Jerome Kern.* London: Robson Books, 1978.

Friedwald, Will. *Jazz Singing: America's Great Voices.* New York: Da Capo Press, 1996.

———. *Stardust Melodies: A Biography of Twelve of America's Most Popular Songs.* New York: Pantheon Books, 2002.

Furia, Philip. *The Poets of Tin Pan Alley: A History of America's Great Lyricists.* New York: Oxford University Press, 1990.

———. *Skylark: The Life and Times of Johnny Mercer.* New York: St. Martin's Press, 2003.
Fyne, Robert. *The Hollywood Propaganda of World War II.* Lanham, MD: Scarecrow Press, 1997.
Garraty, John A., and Mark C. Carnes, eds. *American National Biography.* 24 vols. New York: Oxford University Press, 1999.
Giddins, Gary. *Visions of Jazz: The First Century.* New York: Oxford University Press, 1998.
———. *Bing Crosby, A Pocketful of Dreams: The Early Years, 1903–1940.* Boston: Little, Brown, 2001.
Ginell, Cary. *The Decca Hillbilly Discography, 1927–1945.* Westport, CT: Greenwood Press, 1989.
Gioia, Ted. *The History of Jazz.* New York: Oxford University Press, 1997.
Gleason, Ralph J., ed. *Jam Session: An Anthology of Jazz.* New York: G. P. Putnam's Sons, 1958.
Godfrey, Donald C., and Frederic A. Leigh, eds. *Historical Dictionary of American Radio.* Westport, CT: Greenwood Press, 1998.
Goodman, Jack, ed. *While You Were Gone: A Report on Wartime Life in the United States.* New York: Simon and Schuster, 1946.
Gottfried, Martin. *Broadway Musicals.* New York: Harry N. Abrams, 1979.
Gottlieb, William P. *The Golden Age of Jazz.* New York: Simon and Schuster, 1979.
Gourse, Leslie. *Louis' Children: American Jazz Singers.* New York: Quill, 1984.
Green, Benny. *Let's Face the Music: The Golden Age of Popular Song.* London: Pavilion Books, 1989.
Green, Douglas B. *Singing in the Saddle: The History of the Singing Cowboy.* Nashville, TN: Vanderbilt University Press, 2002.
Green, Stanley. *Encyclopaedia of the Musical Film.* New York: Oxford University Press, 1981.
———. *Broadway Musicals: Show by Show.* 4th ed. Milwaukee, WI: Hal Leonard, 1994.
Haas, Robert Bartlett, ed. *William Grant Still and the Fusion of Cultures in American Music.* Flagstaff, AZ: Master-Player Library, 1972.
Hajduk, John C. "Tin Pan Alley on the March: Popular Music, World War II, and the Quest for a Great War Song." *Popular Music and Society,* December 2003, 497–512.
Hamm, Charles. *Yesterdays: Popular Song in America.* New York: W. W. Norton, 1979.
Harris, Mark Jonathan, Franklin D. Mitchell, and Steven J. Schechter. *The Homefront: America during World War II.* New York: G. P. Putnam's Sons, 1984.
Harris, Rex. *Jazz.* New York: Penguin Books, 1952.
Hart, Dorothy. *Thou Swell, Thou Witty: The Life and Lyrics of Lorenz Hart.* New York: Harper and Row, 1976.
Hayes, Richard K. *Kate Smith: A Biography, with a Discography, Filmography, and List of Stage Appearances.* Jefferson, NC: McFarland, 1995.
Heide, Robert, and John Gilman. *Home Front America: Popular Culture of the World War II Era.* San Francisco: Chronicle Books, 1995.
Henderson, Amy, and Dwight Blocker Bowers. *Red, Hot and Blue: A Smithsonian Salute to the American Musical.* Washington, DC: Smithsonian Institution Press, 1996.

Hentoff, Nat, and Albert McCarthy, eds. *Jazz*. New York: Grove Press, 1959.

Hentoff, Nat, and Nat Shapiro, eds. *The Jazz Makers*. New York: Grove Press, 1957.

Higham, Charles, and Joel Greenberg. *Hollywood in the Forties*. New York: A. S. Barnes, 1968.

Horowitz, Joseph. *Classical Music in America: A History of Its Rise and Fall*. New York: W. W. Norton, 2005.

Hyland, William G. *The Song Is Ended: Songwriters and American Music, 1900–1950*. New York: Oxford University Press, 1995.

———. *Richard Rodgers*. New Haven, CT: Yale University Press, 1998.

Inge, Thomas M. *Handbook of American Popular Culture*. 3 vols. Westport, CT: Greenwood Press, 1981.

———, ed. *Concise Histories of American Popular Culture*. Westport, CT: Greenwood Press, 1982.

Internet Movie Database. http://imdb.com/.

Jablonski, Edward. *Gershwin*. New York: Doubleday, 1987.

Jablonski, Edward, and Lawrence D. Stewart. *The Gershwin Years*. Garden City, NY: Doubleday, 1958.

Jasen, David A. *Tin Pan Alley: The Composers, the Songs, the Performers and Their Times*. New York: Donald I. Fine, 1988.

Jeffries, John W. *Wartime America: The World War II Home Front*. Chicago: Ivan R. Dee, 1996.

Jewell, Derek. *Duke: A Portrait of Duke Ellington*. New York: W. W. Norton, 1977.

Jones, John Bush. *The Songs That Fought the War: Popular Music and the Home Front, 1939–1945*. Waltham, MA: Brandeis University Press, 2006.

Jones, Max, and John Chilton. *Louis: The Louis Armstrong Story*. Boston: Little, Brown, 1971.

Karolyi, Otto. *Modern American Music: From Charles Ives to the Minimalists*. Cranbury, NJ: Fairleigh Dickinson University Press, 1996.

Keepnews, Orrin, and Bill Grauer Jr. *A Pictorial History of Jazz*. New York: Crown, 1955.

Kennedy, Michael. *The Concise Oxford Dictionary of Music*. New York: Oxford University Press, 1980.

Kenney, William Howland. *Recorded Music in American Life: The Phonograph and Popular Memory, 1890–1945*. New York: Oxford University Press, 1999.

Kenrick, John. Musicals 101. http://www.musicals101.com/.

Kimball, Robert, and Linda Emmet, eds. *The Complete Lyrics of Irving Berlin*. New York: Alfred A. Knopf, 2001.

Kingsbury, Paul, and Alan Axelrod, eds. *Country: The Music and the Musicians*. New York: Abbeville Press, 1988.

Kinkle, Roger D. *The Complete Encyclopedia of Popular Music and Jazz, 1900–1950*. 4 vols. Westport, CT: Arlington House, 1974.

Kirby, Edward M., and Jack W. Harris. *Star-Spangled Radio*. Chicago: Ziff-Davis, 1948.

Kirchner, Bill, ed. *The Oxford Companion to Jazz*. New York: Oxford University Press, 2000.

Koppes, Clayton R., and Gregory D. Black. *Hollywood Goes to War: How Politics, Profits, and Propaganda Shaped World War II Movies*. New York: Free Press, 1987.

Krivine, John. *Jukebox Saturday Night*. London: New English Library, 1977.

Lange, Jeffrey J. *Smile When You Call Me a Hillbilly: Country Music's Struggle for Respectability, 1939–1954*. Athens: University of Georgia Press, 2004.

Langrell, Peggy. "Appalachian Folk Music: From Foothills to Footlights." *Music Educators Journal* 72 (March 1986); 37–39.

Lax, Roger, and Frederick Smith. *The Great Song Thesaurus*. 2nd ed. New York: Oxford University Press, 1989.

Lesy, Michael. *Long Time Coming: A Photographic Portrait of America, 1935–1943*. New York: W. W. Norton, 2002.

Lewine, Richard, and Alfred Simon. *Songs of the American Theater*. New York: Dodd, Mead, 1973.

Lingeman, Richard. *Don't You Know There's a War On? The American Home Front, 1941–1945*. New York: Thunder's Mouth Press, 1970.

Lornell, Kip. "Black Gospel Music." In *Encyclopedia of Southern Culture*, edited by W. Ferris and C. Reagan. Chapel Hill: University of North Carolina Press, 1989. http://www.arts.state.ms.us/crossroads/music/gospel/mu2_text.html.

Lynch, Vincent, and Bill Henkin. *Jukebox: The Golden Age*. Berkeley, CA: Lancaster-Miller, 1981.

Lynes, Russell. *The Lively Audience: A Social History of the Visual and Performing Arts in America, 1890–1950*. New York: Harper and Row, 1985.

MacDonald, J. Fred. *Don't Touch That Dial! Radio Programming in American Life, 1920–1960*. Chicago: Nelson-Hall, 1979.

Magee, Jeffrey. *The Uncrowned King of Swing: Fletcher Henderson and Big Band Jazz*. New York: Oxford University Press, 2005.

Malone, Bill C. *Country Music, U.S.A.* Austin: University of Texas Press, 1968.

Malone, Bill C., and Judith McCulloh, eds. *Stars of Country Music: Uncle Dave Macon to Johnny Rodriguez*. Urbana: University of Illinois Press, 1975.

Maltby, Richard. *Passing Parade: A History of Popular Culture in the Twentieth Century*. New York: Oxford University Press, 1989.

Manvell, Roger. *Films and the Second World War*. New York: Dell, 1974.

Marx, Samuel, and Jan Clayton. *Rodgers and Hart: Bewitched, Bothered, and Bewildered*. New York: G. P. Putnam's Sons, 1976.

Mattfeld, Julius. *Variety Music Cavalcade*. Englewood Cliffs, NJ: Prentice Hall, 1962.

Mauldin, Bill. *Up Front*. New York: Henry Holt, 1945.

McBrien, William. *Cole Porter: A Biography*. New York: Alfred A. Knopf, 1998.

McClellan, Lawrence, Jr. *The Later Swing Era, 1942 to 1955*. Westport, CT: Greenwood Press, 2004.

McCutcheon, Marc. *The Writer's Guide to Everyday Life from Prohibition through World War II*. Cincinnati, OH: Writer's Digest Books, 1995.

McLaughlin, Robert L., and Sally E. Perry. *We'll Always Have the Movies: American Cinema during World War II*. Lexington: University Press of Kentucky, 2006.

Meeker, David. *Jazz in the Movies*. New York: Da Capo Press, 1981.

Millard, Andre. *America on Record: A History of Recorded Sound.* New York: Cambridge University Press, 1995.

Millard, Bob. *Country Music: 70 Years of America's Favorite Music.* New York: HarperCollins, 1993.

Miller, Chuck. "Victory Music: The Story of the V-Disc Record Label." http://members.aol.com/boardwalk7/vdisc/vdisc.html.

Moon, Krystyn. "There's No Yellow in the Red, White, and Blue: The Creation of Anti-Japanese Music during World War II." *Pacific Historical Review* 72 (August 2003): 333–52.

Morath, Max. *The NPR Curious Listener's Guide to Popular Standards.* New York: Berkley, 2002.

Mordden, Ethan. *Better Foot Forward: The History of American Musical Theatre.* New York: Grossman, 1976.

Morella, Joe, Edward Z. Epstein, and John Griggs. *The Films of World War II.* Secaucus, NJ: Citadel Press, 1973.

Morgan, Robert P. *Twentieth-Century Music: A History of Musical Styles in Modern Europe and America.* New York: W. W. Norton, 1991.

Morthland, John. *The Best of Country Music.* Garden City, NY: Doubleday, 1984.

Morton, Brian. "Swing Time for Hitler." *Nation* 277 (2003): 33–38.

Muller, Jurgen. *Movies of the 40s.* Cologne, Germany: Taschen, 2005.

———. *Movies of the 30s.* Cologne, Germany: Taschen, 2006.

Murray, Albert. *Stomping the Blues.* New York: Da Capo Press, 1976.

National Jukebox. "Jukebox History." http://www.nationaljukebox.com.

Nye, Russel. *The Unembarrassed Muse: The Popular Arts in America.* New York: Dial Press, 1970.

O'Brien, Kenneth Paul, and Lynn Hudson Parsons, eds. *The Home-Front War: World War II and American Society.* Westport, CT: Greenwood Press, 1995.

Oermann, Robert K. *America's Music: The Roots of Country.* Atlanta, GA: Turner, 1996.

———. *A Century of Country: An Illustrated History of Country Music.* New York: TV Books, 1999.

Oliphant, Dave. *The Early Swing Era: 1930 to 1941.* Westport, CT: Greenwood Press, 2002.

Oliver, Paul, ed. *The Blackwell Guide to Recorded Blues.* Cambridge, MA: Basil Blackwell, 1991.

Panati, Charles. *Extraordinary Origins of Everyday Things.* New York: Harper and Row, 1987.

———. *Panati's Parade of Fads, Follies, and Manias.* New York: HarperCollins, 1991.

Peatman, John Gray. "Radio and Popular Music." In *Radio Research 1942–1943,* edited by Paul F. Lazarsfeld and Frank N. Stanton, 335–93. New York: Duell, Sloan and Pearce, 1944.

Penn State University Libraries. "Fred Waring." http://www.libraries.psu.edu/waring/songlists.htm.

Peterson, Richard A. *Creating Country Music: Fabricating the Authentic.* Chicago: University of Chicago Press, 1997.

Peyser, Joan. *The Memory of All That: The Life of George Gershwin.* New York: Simon and Schuster, 1993.

Placksin, Sally. *American Women in Jazz: 1900 to the Present.* New York: Wideview Books, 1982.

Prendergast, Roy M. *Film Music: A Neglected Art.* New York: W. W. Norton, 1977.

Read, Oliver, and Walter L. Welch. *From Tin Foil to Stereo: Evolution of the Phonograph.* Indianapolis, IN: Howard W. Sams, 1959.

Rogers, Donald I. *Since You Went Away.* New Rochelle, NY: Arlington House, 1973.

Rosen, Jody. *"White Christmas": The Story of an American Song.* New York: Charles Scribner's Sons, 2002.

Rosenberg, Deena. *Fascinating Rhythm: The Collaboration of George and Ira Gershwin.* New York: Penguin Books, 1991.

Rosenberg, Neil V. *Bluegrass: A History.* Urbana, IL: University of Illinois Press, 1985.

Sadie, Stanley, ed. *The New Grove Dictionary of Music and Musicians.* 29 vols. New York: Macmillan, 2001.

Saffle, Michael, ed. *Perspectives on American Music, 1900–1950.* New York: Garland, 2000.

Sanjek, Russell. *Pennies from Heaven: The American Popular Music Business in the Twentieth Century.* New York: Da Capo Press, 1996.

Santelli, Robert, and Emily Davidson, eds. *Hard Travelin': The Life and Legacy of Woody Guthrie.* Hanover, NH: Wesleyan University Press, 1999.

Santelli, Robert, Holly George-Warren, and Jim Brown, eds. *American Roots Music.* New York: Harry N. Abrams, 2001.

Scanlan, Tom. *The Joy of Jazz: The Swing Era, 1935–1947.* Golden, CO: Fulcrum, 1996.

Scaruffi, Piero. "A Brief History of Rhythm 'n' Blues." http://www.scaruffi.com/history/rb.html.

Schicke, C. A. *Revolution in Sound: A Biography of the Recording Industry.* Boston: Little, Brown, 1974.

Schoenberg, Loren. *The NPR Curious Listener's Guide to Jazz.* New York: Berkley, 2002.

Schuller, Gunther. *The Swing Era: The Development of Jazz, 1930–1945.* New York: Oxford University Press, 1989.

Sears, Richard S. *V-Discs: A History and a Discography.* Westport, CT: Greenwood Press, 1980.

Settel, Irving. *A Pictorial History of Radio.* New York: Grosset and Dunlap, 1967.

Sheppard, W. Anthony. "An Exotic Enemy: Anti-Japanese Musical Propaganda in World War II Hollywood." *Journal of the American Musicological Society* 54 (2001): 303–57.

Shestack, Melvin. *The Country Music Encyclopedia.* New York: Thomas Y. Crowell, 1974.

Shindler, Colin. *Hollywood Goes to War: Films and American Society, 1939–1952.* Boston: Routledge Kegan Paul, 1979.

Sickels, Robert. *American Popular Culture through History: The 1940s.* Westport, CT: Greenwood Press, 2004.

Simon, George T. *The Big Bands.* New York: Macmillan, 1967.

———. *Glenn Miller and His Orchestra.* New York: Thomas Y. Crowell, 1974.

Sklar, Robert. *Movie-Made America: A Cultural History of American Movies.* New York: Random House, 1975.

Smith, Kathleen E. R. *God Bless America: Tin Pan Alley Goes to War.* Lexington: University Press of Kentucky, 2003.

Snider, Lee. *80 Years of American Song Hits, 1892–1972.* New York: Chappell, 1973.

Solid!. "Big Band Vocalists." http://www.parabrisas.com/index.php.

Stearns, Marshall. *The Story of Jazz.* New York: Oxford University Press, 1958.

Stehman, Dan. *Roy Harris: A Bio-Bibliography.* Westport, CT: Greenwood Press, 1991.

Sterling, Christopher H., and John M. Kitross. *Stay Tuned: A Concise History of American Broadcasting.* Belmont, CA: Wadsworth, 1990.

Struble, John Warthen. *The History of American Classical Music: MacDowell through Minimalism.* New York: Facts on File, 1995.

Sudhalter, Richard M. *Stardust Melody: The Life and Music of Hoagy Carmichael.* New York: Oxford University Press, 2002.

Suskin, Steven. *Show Tunes: The Songs, Shows, and Careers of Broadway's Major Composers.* 3rd ed. New York: Oxford University Press, 2000.

Tawa, Nicholas E. *Serenading the Reluctant Eagle: American Musical Life, 1925–1945.* New York: Schirmer Books, 1984.

Thomas, Tony. *The Films of the Forties.* Secaucus, NJ: Citadel Press, 1975.

Tichi, Cecelia. *High Lonesome: The American Culture of Country Music.* Chapel Hill: University of North Carolina Press, 1994.

Time-Life Books. *This Fabulous Century.* Vol. 4, *1930–1940.* New York: Time-Life Books, 1969.

Time-Life Books. *This Fabulous Century.* Vol. 5, *1940–1950.* New York: Time-Life Books, 1969.

Toll, Robert C. *The Entertainment Machine: American Show Business in the Twentieth Century.* New York: Oxford University Press, 1982.

TomsZone. "The inComplete Jukebox." http://www.tomszone.com.

Tribe, Ivan. *Country: A Regional Exploration.* Westport, CT: Greenwood Press, 2006.

Tucker, Mark, ed. *The Duke Ellington Reader.* New York: Oxford University Press, 1993.

Tucker, Sherrie. *Swing Shift: "All-Girl" Bands of the 1940s.* Durham, NC: Duke University Press, 2000.

Tudor, Dean, and Nancy Tudor. *Grass Roots Music.* Littleton, CO: Libraries Unlimited, 1979.

Tyler, Don. *Hit Parade: An Encyclopedia of the Top Songs of the Jazz, Depression, Swing, and Sing Eras.* New York: William Morrow, 1985.

Ulanov, Barry. *A History of Jazz in America.* New York: Da Capo Press, 1952.

Variety Books. *The Variety History of Show Business.* New York: Harry N. Abrams, 1993.

Vocalists Database. http://www.nfo.net/index.html.

Walker, Leo. *The Wonderful Era of the Great Dance Bands.* Berkeley, CA: Howell-North Books, 1964.

———. *The Big Band Almanac.* Rev. ed. New York: Da Capo Press, 1989.

Ward, Geoffrey C., and Ken Burns. *Jazz: A History of America's Music.* New York: Alfred A. Knopf, 2000.

Whisnant, David E. "Forgotten Soldier Boy: War and the Politics of Country Music." Duke University. http://dukenews.duke.edu/2003/01/country0103._print.htm.

Whitburn, Joel. *Pop Memories, 1890–1954: The History of American Popular Music.* Menomonee Falls, WI: Record Research, 1986.

———. *A Century of Pop Music.* Menomonee Falls, WI: Record Research, 1999.

Whitcomb, Ian. *After the Ball: Pop Music from Rag to Rock.* Baltimore: Penguin Books, 1972.

White, Mark. *"You Must Remember This...": Popular Songwriters 1900–1980.* New York: Charles Scribner's Sons, 1985.

Wilder, Alec. *American Popular Song: The Great Innovators, 1900–1950.* New York: Oxford University Press, 1972.

Williams, John R. *This Was "Your Hit Parade."* Camden, ME: Courier-Gazette, 1973.

Williams, Martin T., ed. *The Art of Jazz.* New York: Oxford University Press, 1959.

———. *The Jazz Tradition.* New York: Oxford University Press, 1983.

Willis, Barry R. *America's Music: Bluegrass.* Franktown, CO: Pine Valley Music, 1989.

Wills, Rosetta. *The King of Western Swing: Bob Wills Remembered.* New York: Watson-Guptill, 1998.

Winer, Deborah Grace. *On the Sunny Side of the Street: The Life and Lyrics of Dorothy Fields.* New York: Schirmer Books, 1997.

Winkler, Allan M. *Home Front U.S.A.: America during World War II.* Wheeling, IL: Harlan Davidson, 1986.

Wolfe, Charles K., and James E. Akenson, eds. *Country Music Goes to War.* Lexington: University Press of Kentucky, 2005.

Woll, Allen L. *The Hollywood Musical Goes to War.* Chicago: Nelson-Hall, 1983.

WoodyGuthrie.org. http://www.woodyguthrie.org/index.htm.

"World War II: The Home Front." http://www.teacheroz.com.

Wurts, Richard. *The New York World's Fair, 1939/1940.* New York: Dover Publications, 1977.

Wrynn, V. Dennis. *Coke Goes to War.* Missoula, MT: Pictorial Histories, 1996.

Yanow, Scott. *Bebop.* San Francisco: Miller Freeman, 2000.

———. *Swing: Great Musicians, Influential Groups.* San Francisco: Miller Freeman, 2000.

Yellin, Emily. *Our Mothers' War: American Women at Home and at the Front during World War II.* New York: Free Press, 2004.

Young, William H., and Nancy K. Young. *American Music through History: The Great Depression.* Westport, CT: Greenwood Press, 2005.

Zinsser, William. *Easy to Remember: The Great American Songwriters and Their Songs.* Jaffrey, NH: David R. Godine, 2000.

AUDIO SOURCES

40's Hits: Country. CD. Curb Records D2–77346. 1990.

American Musical Theater. 6 LPs. Smithsonian Collection of Recordings. R 036. 1989.

American Popular Song. 7 LPs. Smithsonian Collection of Recordings. R 031. 1984.

American War Songs, 1933–1947: Hitler and Hell. CD. Trikont 0280. 1971.

An Anthology of Big Band Swing, 1930–1955. 2 CDs. Decca GRD 2-629. 1993.

As Time Goes By: World War II Songs. 3 CDs. Dynamic Entertainment DYN 3508. 2004.

Big Band Jazz. 4 CDs. Smithsonian Collection of Recordings. RD 030. 1983.

Classic Songs from World War II. 2 CDs. *Kiss the Boys Goodbye,* BMG 66702, and *Always in My Heart,* BMG 66703. 1995.

Commodore Records. *The Commodore Story.* 2 CDs. Commodore CMD-2-400. 1997.

Copland, Aaron. *Copland Conducts Copland: Appalachian Spring, Rodeo, Others.* CD. CBS Records Masterworks MK 42430. 1988.

The Country Hits of the 40s. ASV Living Era CD AJA 5418. 2002.

Forty #1 Hits of the Forties. 2 CDs. Collector's Choice Music CCM 307. 2002.

G.I. Favorites: The Tunes of World War II. 2 CDs. Sounds of Yesteryear DSOY685. 2005.

G.I. Jukebox. CD. St. Clair Entertainment VNL14512. 2005.

Great Vocalists of the Big Band Era. 6 LPs. Columbia Special Products, CBS Records. 1978.

The Great War Songs. 3 CDs. REDX Entertainment RXBOX31063. 2006.

The Jazz Singers. 5 CDs. Smithsonian Collection of Recordings. RD 113. 1998.

Jones, Spike. *(Not) Your Standard Spike Jones Collection.* 3 CDs. Collectors' Choice Music CCM-329-2. 2005.

Mercer, Johnny. *The Johnny Mercer Songbook. Vol. 1, Blues in the Night; Vol. 2, Trav'lin' Light; Vol. 3, Too Marvelous for Words.* 3CDs. Verve 314555 268–2; 314555 402–2; 314557 140–2. 1997–1998.

The Road to Nashville: A History of Country Music, 1926–1953. 3 CDs. Sanctuary Records IGOTCD 2559. 2004.

Rock 'n' Roll Roots: The Country Influence. CD. Smith and Co. SCCD 1103. 2005.

Rock 'n' Roll Roots: The R&B Influence. CD. Smith and Co. SCCD 1105. 2005.

Singers and Soloists of the Swing Bands. 4 LPs. Smithsonian Collection of Recordings. R 035. 1987.

Star Spangled Rhythm: Voices of Broadway and Hollywood. 4 CDs. Smithsonian Collection of Recordings. RD 111. 1997.

Swing That Music! The Big Bands, the Soloists, and the Singers. 4 CDs. Smithsonian Collection of Recordings. RD 102. 1993.

V-E Day: Musical Memories. CD. ASV Living Era AJA5163. 1995.

The Victory Collection: The Smithsonian Remembers When America Went to War. 3 CDs. Smithsonian Collection of Recordings. RD 106-1, -2, -3. DMC3-1243. 1995.

The War Years. 4 CDs. Intersound CDC 1046-1049. 2003.

Wills, Bob. *Take Me Back to Tulsa: Bob Wills and His Texas Playboys.* 4 CDs. Proper Records Box 32. 2001.

The Words and Music of World War II. 2 CDs. Columbia/Legacy C2K 48516. 2001.

The World of Swing. CD. Columbia/Legacy CK 66080. 2000.

Index

About the Authors

WILLIAM H. YOUNG is a freelance writer and independent scholar. He retired in 2000 after 36 years from Lynchburg College where he taught American Studies and popular culture. Young has published books and articles on various aspects of popular culture, including three Greenwood volumes co-written with his wife, Nancy K. Young.

NANCY K. YOUNG is a researcher and independent scholar. She retired in 2005 after 26 years from a career in management consulting. With her husband, William H. Young, she has co-written three recent Greenwood titles, *The 1930s*, *The 1950s*, and *Music of the Great Depression*.